THE LITERARY MAFIA

THE
LITERARY
MAFIA

Jews, Publishing, and
Postwar American Literature

Josh Lambert

Yale
UNIVERSITY PRESS
NEW HAVEN AND LONDON

Published with assistance from the Kingsley Trust Association Publication Fund established by the Scroll and Key Society of Yale College, and from the Mary Cady Tew Memorial Fund.

Excerpts from the letters of Lionel Trilling, copyright © 1952–1963 by Lionel Trilling, are used by permission of The Wylie Agency LLC. Quotations from unpublished writing by Alfred A. Knopf and Blanche Knopf are used by permission of Alice L. Knopf. The excerpt from "Note in Lieu of a Suicide" by Donald Finkel, from *Simeon* (Atheneum © 1964), is reprinted with permission of the Estate of Donald Finkel. Permission to quote from the unpublished work of Ann Birstein is granted by the Estate of Ann Birstein and Cathrael Kazin, Executor.

Yale University Press books may be purchased in quantity for educational, business, or promotional use. For information, please e-mail sales.press@yale.edu (U.S. office) or sales@yaleup.co.uk (U.K. office).

Set in Alternate Gothic and the Yale typeface by Integrated Publishing Solutions, Grand Rapids, Michigan.
Printed in the United States of America.

Library of Congress Control Number: 2021948507
ISBN 978-0-300-25142-5 (hardcover : alk. paper)

A catalogue record for this book is available from the British Library.

This paper meets the requirements of ANSI/NISO Z39.48-1992 (Permanence of Paper).

10 9 8 7 6 5 4 3 2 1

To my parents and my children

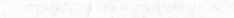

Perhaps some smart-ass fellow should write a book called *The Literary Mafia*.

—ROBERT DEMARIA SR. to Ann Birstein, November 30, 1976

CONTENTS

THE LITERARY MAFIA

INTRODUCTION

The Idea of a Literary Mafia

By the middle of the 1960s, the beat novelist Jack Kerouac, whose *On the Road* (1957) had made him a national celebrity, was disaffected, increasingly isolated from his friends, and drinking heavily. He knew whom to blame for his problems. A posthumous profile in *Esquire* explained that in the years leading up to his death in 1969, "he would rant for hours about the Jewish literary mafia that he believed had placed a moratorium on publication of his work."[1]

A Jewish literary mafia? Really? Could that be anything but the paranoid, anti-Semitic fantasy of a washed-out, resentful alcoholic? Surprisingly, other writers as different from Kerouac and from each other as Mario Puzo and Katherine Anne Porter expressed similar concerns, though they focused less on the literary mafia's persecution of their own work and more on its deleterious effects on U.S. literary culture in general. In a 1968 article, Puzo half jokingly suggested that "two literary Mafia gangs" — a Jewish one and a southern one — were controlling "those juicy Guggenheim and Ford grants," ensuring that "independent, working writers" had no chance to receive them.[2] Porter meanwhile seems not to have been joking whatsoever when she complained to an interviewer for *Harper's*, in the fall of 1965, that writers like her, from "the South and the West and other faraway places," who "are in the direct, legitimate line" (of what exactly, she did not say) because they have English as their "mother tongue," were

—

1

being threatened by a different group of literary professionals, a "crowd with headquarters in New York," "a stylish sort of mob" or "clique," speaking "a curious kind of argot, more or less originating in New York, a deadly mixture of academic, guttersnipe, gangster, fake-Yiddish, and dull old wornout dirty words." Porter particularly disdained that group for its clannishness, for the way that its members boost one another; the writers she favors appear, by contrast, "one at a time — never in a group, never with a school, never the fashionable pet of a little cartel."[3] With these remarks, Porter echoed an academic essayist, Marvin Mudrick, who had observed in print a year earlier how "an embattled and exacerbated ghetto culture [had] contract[ed] into a coterie," such that "it is possible" (but only just barely, he implies) that one could "live in New York, be of Jewish extraction, and have intellectual abilities" and even "contribute to *Partisan Review* and *Commentary* — without joining the gang."[4]

Truman Capote, whose success with *In Cold Blood* (1966) had augmented his own literary celebrity, talked about a Jewish literary mafia more than anyone else. He explained the problem succinctly in a 1968 interview: "The Jewish Mafia in American letters . . . is a clique of New York–oriented writers and critics who control much of the literary scene through the influence of the quarterlies and intellectual magazines. All these publications are Jewish-dominated and this particular coterie employs them to make or break writers by advancing or withholding attention."[5] In Capote's account, the strategic points at which the Jewish literary mafia exerted its muscle were "the quarterlies and intellectual magazines" (like *Partisan Review* and *Commentary,* which Mudrick had named). Not coincidentally, sociologists in the early 1970s quantified the remarkable influence of "quarterlies and intellectual magazines" in the U.S. thought and culture of that time, calling these publications "where to find the intellectual elite." They listed the *New York Review of Books,* the *New Republic, Commentary,* the *New Yorker,* the *New York Times Book Review, Saturday Review, Partisan Review,* and *Harper's* as "the influential journals."[6] As Kerouac's comment suggests, though, other observers felt that the literary mafia had power over book publishers themselves, while Puzo was more concerned about the literary mafia's control of fellowships and prizes.

Still other observers saw Jewish readers and book buyers as the source of the problem. In a 1961 piece in the *New Leader,* an editor at McGraw-Hill and

—

novelist named Robert Gutwillig surveyed the contemporary book market and made the striking claim that "the Jewish audience" was "the single most important book and bookstore audience in this country"; indeed, Gutwillig claimed, "the book trade now strongly suspects that the Jewish audience is indeed the basic audience and, in fact, the only dependable audience" for hardcover trade books, with few exceptions. While one might think that an editor whose income depends on book sales might look to such a group with gratitude, Gutwillig did not see the situation as salutary: "any homogenous audience is bound to be parochial and unrepresentative of the feelings and ideas of the society as a whole." Moreover, he lamented, "the book business is becoming an adjunct of the advertising industry and is no longer an occupation for gentlemen."[7] A similar point was made at the end of the same decade by an eccentric academic, Ernest van den Haag, who in 1969 claimed that "a disproportionate number of books are bought by Jews and a disproportionate number of Gentiles do not buy books," which "may help explain the dominance . . . of the Jewish cultural establishment in literature."[8] Gutwillig and van den Haag did not cite any evidence for these claims, and there is no reason to believe that they were true; but while focusing on other nodes of the literary system, these observers agreed with Capote that Jews intervened in the development of U.S. literary culture by "advancing or withholding attention" so as to "make or break writers."[9]

This idea about a "Jewish mafia" in U.S. publishing circulated at least into the 1980s.[10] If it were just white Americans from Protestant and Catholic backgrounds, like Kerouac, Porter, and Capote, who complained about this Jewish literary mafia, it would be easy to dismiss the idea as an anti-Semitic myth, driven by the fears of Jews usurping white, Christian Americans' power that is familiar throughout the history of U.S. white supremacy and anti-Semitism. Such claims about nefarious Jewish control of U.S. publishing resound with one of the most common tropes of modern anti-Semitism in general—the trope that suggests that Jews conspire to establish control over communication media in order to forward their aims, a trope that recurs in all major modern anti-Semitic texts, including Edouard Drumont's *La France Juive,* the forged *Protocols of the Elders of Zion,* Henry Ford's *Dearborn Independent,* and, into the present, texts produced and circulated by both Islamic extremists and white supremacists.[11]

Yet a number of writers and editors who were themselves American Jews

—

also perceived a literary mafia at work in the U.S. in the 1960s and 1970s, and several of them went on the record about it. Norman Mailer helped to popularize the term, deploying it as early as 1960 in a reference to William Burroughs's *Naked Lunch,* and repeating it in the years that followed.[12] Mailer does not seem to have had a particularly *Jewish* literary mafia in mind in those references, but in the decade that followed, the term began to be attached to Jewish editors, in particular; in 1970, the *Boston Globe,* for example, casually referred to Jason Epstein, an editor at Random House, as "a *capo don* of the New York literary mafia."[13] Jerry Gross, who worked at Simon & Schuster, Warner Books, New American Library, and other houses and described himself as a "Jew-identifying Jew," remarked in 1973 that "the Jewish Establishment has taken over the game of the Old Boys' club."[14] Another Jewish writer, Meyer Levin, whose novel *Compulsion* had been a major bestseller in 1956, purchased a half-page advertisement in the *New York Times* on October 12, 1972, and started it off with a striking, all-caps headline: "CAN A LITERARY MAFIA AFFECT YOUR CHOICE OF BOOKS?" In the ad that followed, Levin explained that while the "Jewish literary mafia" he had encountered "includ[ed] some Jewish literati," he did not regard it as "exactly pro-Jewish": it discriminated against him and denied him reviews in "Time, Newsweek, Life or even the Saturday Review," because, as he understood it, this mafia judged him to be the wrong kind of Jew (a "too Jewish" and "nationalistic" one).[15]

Meanwhile, it was a prolific critic and experimental writer named Richard Kostelanetz, also Jewish, who produced the most expansive and detailed case against what he called the "literary mob" in a 1974 polemic, *The End of Intelligent Writing: Literary Politics in America.*[16] Over the course of more than four hundred pages, backed by substantial notes and bibliographies, Kostelanetz claims that by the 1960s, a "Jewish American group became the dominant literary-political force" in the U.S. (13). He characterizes that group as a "literary clique or mob" (78) and claims that it has "remain[ed] ultimately as powerful, self-protective, and avaricious" up to the time at which he was writing, in the early 1970s (80). Summarizing its influence, Kostelanetz remarks, "As the most efficient literary machine ever created in America, [this group] had unprecedented power to determine what writing might be taken seriously and what would be neglected or wiped out" (31), and he cites its "particularly comprehensive authority in upper-middlebrow political and literary criticism" (125). Kostelanetz lists 144 writers and editors by name as members of this "literary mob" (84–86), and though he often qualifies his critiques in one way or another—such as when he says that the literary "establishments" that concern him "are *not* 'conspiracies' but chains of interpersonal relationship based upon common sentiment and mutual interest" (3)—he also insists that "one definition of a 'conspiracy' is that all parties act toward a common goal, whether by design or by inadvertent cooperation that is only retrospectively apparent" (xvi) and that "to protest that the New York literary mob is 'not a conspiracy' does not prevent units of it from behaving like one" (99). The upshot of Kostelanetz's extensive, detailed critique is that this U.S. Jewish "literary mob" will have deleterious effects on what is published: "such a concentration of literary power is ultimately inimical to . . . the future of intelligent writing" (126).

Notwithstanding the sources and evidence that Kostelanetz marshaled, and some respectable scholars who have relied on and cited his work, critics dismissed his accusations and other critiques of a Jewish literary mafia as the fruits of envy or, at best, as resulting from misunderstandings about the ways in which writers, publishers, and critics go about their business.[17] The essayist and editor Joseph Epstein had been named among the lower tiers of Kostelanetz's list; writing anonymously in his first column as editor of the *American Scholar,* Epstein described *The End of Intelligent Writing* as "interesting above all for its false assumptions, its misperceptions, and its grand swerves away from reality," noting that Kostelanetz's "theory of an American Literary Mafia is untouched by any intelligence about intellectuals as human beings." Moreover, Epstein added that the idea that "an established order of older writers joined together systematically to impede new talent and fresh ideas may have a certain cogency for the frustrated and the talentless of high ambition."[18] If it were not sharp enough of a dig to imply that Kostelanetz wrote his book because he was "frustrated" and "talentless," after Kostelanetz responded with a letter to the *American Scholar,* protesting the column, Epstein replied that while Kostelanetz "wishes to give the impression that he writes in the boiling blood of outrage," his book and letter "can . . . be more accurately described as having been written in the juice of his

—

own sour grapes."[19] Similar sentiments were expressed by writers who felt that Kostelanetz either did not understand how things worked or was just jealous of others' successes.[20]

Other observers of the literary scene found this all silly and misguided. In the late 1960s, Gordon Lish and Curt Johnson were both editors of small literary magazines produced far from New York—Lish's was *Genesis West,* which he published in Palo Alto, and Johnson's was *December,* published in Chicago—and in their correspondence they treated the idea of a Jewish literary mafia as something of a joke. Discussing one publishing executive, Harvey Plotnick, the president of Regnery Publishers, Johnson, who was not Jewish, wrote to Lish, who was, "Yes, [Plotnick] is a Yid. . . . Didn't you ever hear about the conspiracy which goes back to the Protocols, . . . this world-, perhaps universe-wide conspiracy of Jews (which is what Yids are also called) which, in secret, has taken over everything[?]"[21] In another letter, riffing on the idea that their mutual friend Raymond Carver, who had recently spent time in Tel Aviv, might secretly be Jewish, Johnson joked, "If he is, that finishes him with me. Goddam Jews are taking over the writing of literature."[22] While Johnson's sarcasm may be difficult to detect when quoted this way, he makes clear how he really feels about the idea of Jewish literary mafia when he describes the problem as a "jewish conspiracy led by superjew, Geo[rge] Plimpton and fronted by superjewess (awful wd) Carolyn [Kizer]."[23] Plimpton and Kizer were influential and well-connected editors at the time who had grown up in wealthy, well-connected Protestant families; neither was Jewish. In an essay published in 1969, Johnson elaborated, heaping scorn on Plimpton for monopolizing grants from the recently established National Endowment for the Arts: "Our culture agency's tax-money grant was intended to ameliorate the obscure poverty of many writers, many mags," Johnson wrote. "As it happened, the cash has mostly gone to a New York few."[24] Johnson felt that the literary system had serious flaws, including a distinct bias toward New York (and it should be noted that he is cited approvingly several times in *The End of Intelligent Writing* and thanked among those who had "supported the book" in Kostelanetz's preface [xviii]), but he also recognized that to blame a "conspiracy of Jews" would be imprecise, hateful, and—what was even more unacceptable to a sharp literary editor like him—a cliché.[25]

—

Johnson thought the idea of a Jewish literary conspiracy was laughable, and the hyperbolic language of Capote, the drunken ranting of Kerouac, and the fierce polemic of Kostelanetz are not entirely reliable sources of information on the mechanics of U.S. publishing and the history of American literature. But, like other resilient anti-Semitic myths that distort genuine historical developments, these critiques of a Jewish literary mafia were not invented out of whole cloth or at random. They reflect, in their misleading way, a major transformation that had been taking place in U.S. literary culture, about which careful scholars and observers of that field have, to this day, had surprisingly little to say.

The Enfranchisement of Jews in U.S. Literary Culture

In the first decade of the twentieth century, it was both virtually impossible and virtually unheard of for a Jewish person, irrespective of their individual talents, to be hired for a job at a major U.S. publishing company or on the editorial staff of a widely circulated U.S. magazine or to be granted a professorship in an English department at a prestigious university. Some American Jews were by then publishing books with mainstream U.S. houses, and some Jews wrote for and even, in a few cases, held ownership stakes in major U.S. newspapers; but because of these exclusions from the publishing industry and literary scholarship, as a group Jews were largely denied what the scholar Richard Brodhead has called "literary access."[26] Developing a related idea, drawing on both the work of literary historians like Brodhead and somewhat more on the editorial theory of Jerome McGann, Rachel Malik has described the "horizons of the publishable, which govern what it is thinkable to publish within a particular historical moment." Malik rightly understands the "horizons of the publishable" as "complexly historical" and any single book as "a distinctive set of relations between publishing practices and other institutions and processes."[27] As Tillie Olsen has articulated especially well in *Silences,* taking the perspective of writers, the exclusion of a group of people from access to many (even if not all) literary institutions and opportunities profoundly reduces their ability to contribute to the development of what is publishable.[28]

To use another metaphor, we might say that at the beginning of the twentieth century, Jews were *literarily disenfranchised* – denied, on the basis of their collective identities, opportunities to participate in the literary system as individuals. Scholars use many different metaphors and terms to describe the positioning of minority groups in majority cultures, so as to capture the complexity of those dynamics, and my suggestion is that it is helpful to think of the change in Jews' situations that took place over the course of the twentieth century as their *literary enfranchisement*.[29] This term emphasizes that just as people who are granted the right to vote, after having been denied that right, are neither forced to exercise that privilege nor forced to vote for any one particular party or candidate, the literary enfranchisement of Jews emphatically did not mean that Jews who joined the industry shared ideas or beliefs with one another about what to do with their literary access; on the contrary, as many Jews came to work in the publishing business, they competed for customers and influence, and such competition led to vicious disagreements as well as brilliant collaborations. That said, by the late 1960s and early 1970s – not coincidentally the same period in which discourses about a "Jewish literary mafia" circulated most widely in the U.S. – the literary disenfranchisement of Jews had become a thing of the past. After the mid-1970s, it would be highly unusual for an individual to be denied a role in the U.S. literary system on the basis of their Jewishness.

American Jews' experiences, in this regard, were exceptional. Jews in the U.S. had not, by any means, started out as unusual in their literary disenfranchisement around the turn of the twentieth century; on the contrary, many other people in the U.S. were, at that point, likewise or even more thoroughly denied literary access, including African Americans, Native Americans, Asian Americans, Latinx people, disabled people, women, and even white European men from non-Anglophone backgrounds. All such people were routinely and without question not only denied opportunities to work as editors at prestigious U.S. publishing houses, magazines, and newspapers or as professors of literary studies at U.S. universities but also in many cases denied the educational opportunities that would have allowed them to acquire the knowledge and competencies necessary to be reasonable candidates for such positions and, as Brodhead emphasizes, even to desire them. For members of many of those groups, such disenfranchisement continued, in evolving forms, through the 1960s and 1970s, and in some cases, it distressingly persists into the present.[30]

—

For American Jews, though, literary enfranchisement began early – Ben Huebsch's establishment of a publishing house beginning in 1902 and Alfred Knopf's getting hired in the accounting department at Doubleday, Page & Company in 1912 are regarded as milestones – and continued to arrive in discrete waves, over the course of the twentieth century, as many different areas of U.S. literary culture opened to them. What constitutes literary culture in the U.S. or elsewhere changes over time, of course; the focus in this book is largely on the activities of trade publishers, on literary critics and academic literary scholars, and on magazines, journals, and newspapers to the extent that they published literary texts and reviews and discussions of literary texts. Booksellers, distributors, binders, printers, financiers, postal officials, legal professionals, and many other intermediaries also play crucial roles in constituting literary culture, but often their contributions are even more difficult to study than the work of editors and publishers is.[31]

A short survey may be helpful in establishing, in broad strokes, when Jews gained access to various opportunities within the U.S. literary field, especially because the literary field is much less formally constituted than many other professional areas, like law, medicine, or political office.[32] To begin with, there were no laws or formal policies imposing censorship on Jewish books or excluding Jews from reading or printing books or periodicals in the U.S. in the seventeenth, eighteenth, or nineteenth centuries, though such policies had governed Jews' opportunities in Europe, at times – for example, in Italy beginning in the sixteenth century and in the Russian Empire beginning in 1796 – and other minority groups in the U.S. did suffer under such restrictions, as noted, including Indigenous people, who were banned from speaking and being instructed in their native languages, and African Americans, who were subjected to antiliteracy laws banning them from learning to read or write.[33] With regard to the study of literature in the U.S., Jews and other non-Christians were excluded until the late nineteenth century from holding faculty positions at U.S. universities, though very little of what went on at universities before that time can be thought of as literary studies in the modern sense.[34] Before the mid-nineteenth century, a few American Jews, like Mordecai Manuel Noah, achieved prominence as editors, writers, or literary intellectuals whose work reached broad audiences, and a small number of Jewish publishers issued books for

—

general audiences; but it was very rare (if not totally unheard of) for an American Jew to achieve national prominence in an editorial capacity before the end of the nineteenth century.[35]

Beginning in the 1890s, though, Jews owned and edited major U.S. newspapers, including the *New York World* (beginning with Joseph Pulitzer's purchase of it in 1883) and the *New York Times* (beginning with Adolph Ochs's purchase in 1896); while these publications were extremely influential in a variety of ways, literary texts and criticism were a relatively minor component of their output.[36] Beginning in the first decade of the 1900s and intensifying in the 1910s and 1920s, American Jews founded, directed, and served as leading editors for major publishing houses, with key early houses founded by Jews including B. W. Huebsch (1902–25), Alfred A. Knopf, Inc. (1915–), Boni & Liveright (1917–33), Simon & Schuster (1924–), Viking (1925–), and Random House (1927–).[37] Publishers founded later in which Jews played leadership roles included Pantheon (1942–), Farrar, Straus & Giroux (1946–), Basic Books (1950–), Grove Press (1951–), and Fiction Collective/FC2 (1974–). By the 1940s and 1950s, even publishing houses that had reputations for being less welcoming to Jewish employees began to hire them and allowed them to rise to leadership positions, like Leonard Shatzkin at Doubleday.[38] Also beginning in the 1910s and 1920s, American Jews founded and served as the editors of respected, influential "little magazines" with circulations well under one hundred thousand, such as the *New Republic* (1914–), *Menorah Journal* (1915–62), *Seven Arts* (1916–17), the *American Mercury* (1924–81), the *New Masses* (1926–48), and *Partisan Review* (1934–2003), and Jews continued to be involved as founders and editors of such publications throughout the twentieth century and into the twenty-first.[39]

Jews' enfranchisement in other areas of literary culture took longer. While Jews pursued PhDs in literary studies in the U.S. soon after such degree programs were first established in the late nineteenth century, faculty positions in expanding English departments and other professional roles in academic literary studies were generally and with few exceptions denied to Jews into the 1930s.[40] Undergraduate and graduate students in literary studies were often made to feel, and sometimes explicitly told, that they could not expect to pursue jobs as professors of English or other literary studies because they were Jewish.[41] Only

—

in the 1950s and 1960s did it become uncontroversial for a Jewish man, and eventually a Jewish woman, to occupy such academic roles, and hundreds of hires followed, such that by the mid-1970s one estimate suggested that 13 percent of English professors at leading universities in the U.S. were Jews; by then, Jewish scholars were recognized as some of the most influential popularizers, theorists, and methodological pioneers in the field.[42]

The opportunity for Jews to assume editorial positions of significant influence at U.S. magazines with large, national circulations — and which often played important roles in publishing literary texts (especially poems, short stories, and serialized novels) and as venues for literary criticism — seems to have arrived relatively late. General interest magazines, low priced and fully illustrated, with circulations in the hundreds of thousands or millions, began as a phenomenon in the 1890s and grew in circulation into the middle of the twentieth century and included such titles as *Munsey's, McClure's, Cosmopolitan, Ladies' Home Journal, Reader's Digest,* the *Saturday Evening Post,* and *Collier's* (as well as the *Atlantic Monthly* and *Harper's,* which were founded earlier but increased their circulations during this period).[43] Such national magazines tended to have Protestant editors in chief, typically men who had been raised and begun their careers in the Midwest or South (except for the *Atlantic Monthly,* which showed a preference for Harvard graduates raised in New England).[44] The guiding idea seems to have been that to address a broad national market — and many editors of such magazines did address their readers directly, in chatty columns — an editor needed to be male and ethnically aligned with the white, Anglo-Saxon, Protestant U.S. majority.[45] A historian of Henry Luce's hugely popular magazines, for example, explains their staffing preferences this way: "In the late 1930s, Time Inc. employed few if any Jews on its editorial staff. It continued to hire more of its writers from the staff of the student newspapers at Yale and Princeton, . . . and the editors in New York were overwhelmingly Protestant products of elite universities."[46] Though one can point to occasional exceptions to this rule, the general tendency did not change until 1948, when Daniel Bell was hired at *Fortune* and Irving Howe was hired to write book reviews for *Time.*[47] The *New Yorker,* a widely circulated magazine founded in 1925 with plenty of influence in the U.S. literary scene, is one exception to this broad pattern, in that it had a Jewish cofounder and has had a number of Jewish editors over its life span.[48]

While there were surely at least a few Jews lower down on the mastheads of some mass-market magazines in the 1940s and 1950s, none of them seem to have played significant roles in shaping the culture or contents of the publications. Anti-Semitic advertisements for hotels that did not welcome Jewish and African American guests, declaring as much with phrases like "restricted clientele," were common in *Esquire, Harper's,* the *Atlantic Monthly,* and even the *New Yorker,* into the early 1940s.[49] The premise of *Gentleman's Agreement,* the celebrated 1947 magazine serial and bestselling novel by Laura Z. Hobson and award-winning film by Elia Kazan, is that a journalist at a major weekly magazine pretends to be Jewish so as to understand U.S. anti-Semitism — something he surely would not have had to do if any of his fellow writers or editors at the magazine were themselves Jews who could describe the anti-Semitism that they had experienced.[50] Into the 1950s, splashy mass magazine stories about American Jews — *Time*'s cover stories on Rabbi Louis Finkelstein and on the novelist Herman Wouk and *Look* magazine's 1955 feature "The Position of the Jews in America Today" — seem to have been assigned by non-Jewish editors and written by non-Jewish reporters with non-Jewish audiences in mind.[51] A well-intentioned article in *Reader's Digest* in April 1955 tells quite a tale, with its pronouns, about the way the mass magazine audience was imagined. Titled "The Jews among Us," the article offers a condensed history of Jews' experiences in the United States, from 1654 to the present, listing successful Jews in many industries and emphasizing American Jews' patriotism. It concludes as follows (emphasis mine):

> What of the future of the five million Jews now among *us?*
>
> If *our* history has any meaning at all, *we* can be certain that, as *they* progress through *their* fourth century in this land, the spirit that has united Jew and gentile in brotherhood will achieve new bonds of unity in a nation that has made *their* age-old dream of equality come true.[52]

Reader's Digest had a national circulation of over ten million in 1955; apparently its editors were not too concerned that some of those readers might be Jews.[53]

The situation seems to have changed for Jewish editors at mass-market magazines only in the mid- to late 1960s, with the founding of new magazines and with staff changes at others. A handful of Jews, including A. C. Spectorsky, Arthur Kretchmer, and Nat Lehrman, played major editorial roles at *Playboy*, which was founded in 1953 and peaked in circulation, at about seven million, in the late 1960s.[54] The *New York Review of Books* (1963–), edited by Barbara Epstein and Robert Silvers, and the *New American Review* (1967–77), edited by Ted Solatoroff, had subscriber bases slightly north of one hundred thousand, if only barely. Midge Decter was hired as executive editor at *Harper's*, under Willie Morris, in January 1968, and Gordon Lish began a celebrated run as fiction editor of *Esquire* in November 1969 – and both these Jewish editors played memorable and widely discussed roles, shaping the contents of those magazines and contributing articles and stories themselves. Such editorial roles at mass-market magazines were perhaps the last bastions of anti-Semitic hiring restrictions in the U.S. literary field, but by Decter's and Lish's time, in the late 1960s, barriers had fallen there, too: using data collected in 1970, the sociologist Charles Kadushin and his collaborators claimed that magazines with large and medium-sized circulations were "the American equivalent of an Oxbridge establishment," serving "as one of the main gatekeepers for new talent and new ideas," with the "power to make reputations," and, judging by which, Jews "compose about half of the American intellectual elite."[55] By then, as we have seen, the idea that Jews possessed too much power in literature and publishing, and wielded it inappropriately, had already begun to circulate in earnest.

All these advances in American Jews' literary access took place over a half century that saw enormous changes in Jews' social and socioeconomic status in the U.S. in general and a decrease in anti-Semitic restrictions on Jews in other sectors of U.S. business, like real estate, medicine, and higher education. Yet it is worth noting that the opening of U.S. literary culture to Jews' full participation far outpaced the elimination of anti-Semitic restrictions in other areas of high cultural prestige, including on executive boards of corporations and public institutions, in country clubs, and in the membership of social organizations devoted to the preservation of privilege for white, Christian, European Americans.[56]

The enfranchisement of Jews in U.S. literary culture also coincided with an unprecedented expansion of the U.S. publishing industry in the U.S. and abroad.[57] Though the size of the industry, measured in revenues and profits, did grow by leaps and bounds over the course of the twentieth century, this was not only a financial expansion; as scholars including Paula Rabinowitz and Loren Glass have argued, the midcentury U.S. paperback boom, for one example, democratized reading in the U.S., with expanding audiences making books and magazines increasingly influential in many different areas and aspects of U.S. life and even internationally, as the U.S. was taking on an increasingly dominant role in international politics and culture.[58] Jews had already, long before then, played important roles in the development of printing, bookmaking, and publishing in Europe and the Middle East—for example, the historian Kenneth Moss notes that "as of 1874 in Vilna, [Lithuania,] 12 of 13 publishing houses were owned and staffed by Jews"—but the enfranchisement of Jews in the globally expanding twentieth-century U.S. publishing industry had profound, widespread consequences for how people all over the world use books and think about literature.[59]

This transformation has not exactly been a secret, but neither has it been discussed in much detail by American literary historians and critics. As is true in a number of other areas of U.S. cultural history, journalists, critics, and cultural historians have tended to ignore or to mention only in passing this remarkable Jewish enfranchisement in the U.S. publishing industry, falling prey to what the intellectual historian David Hollinger has diagnosed as the "booster-bigot trap" that bedevils discussions of minority groups' influences in areas of mainstream culture.[60] Bigots (i.e., anti-Semites) have sometimes discussed the role of Jews in U.S. publishing, but more responsible scholars have tended to mention it only in passing. A minor but indicative example is John Hench's history of the Publishers Lunch Club, which attends thoughtfully to exclusions within social organizations for New York publishing professionals and which notes, without elaboration or citation, "the increasing presence of Jews and women at the top of the book publishing profession."[61] Major historical surveys of U.S. publishing mention Jews and Jewishness frequently in passing, but they do not offer any kind of sustained exploration of the role of Jews in the industry.[62]

Following Brodhead's call for a "history of literary access," this book explores the consequences for American literature of the enfranchisement of Jews in U.S. literary culture over the course of the twentieth century, and it does so without

—

accepting the simplistic conclusions that essentialism would propose.[63] Instead, it takes up the key question of how this major transformation of the industry influenced the development of American literature and literary culture. As such, I hope to contribute to a growing body of scholarship on the institutional history of American literature, as well as complementing the work of cultural historians who have explored Jews' influential roles in U.S. film, journalism, theater, music, and other fields.[64] Finally, I also hope to contribute — by providing highly textured and detailed microhistorical accounts of interactions drawn from archival and primary sources — to the understanding being forged by economists, historians, and sociologists, of "ethnic capital" and "minority economic niches."[65]

The Victim: Literature as Publishing History

While this book engages with the history of Jews' enfranchisement in U.S. publishing and literary culture, it is a work of literary studies more than a history of publishing per se. It draws on publishing history as a context to illuminate literary works, and it is premised on the idea that fiction and poetry often registered and indexed historical transformations in ways that were more insightful than other forms of writing. One exemplary case is Saul Bellow's second novel, *The Victim,* which he published in November 1947, midway through the half-century period of Jews' increasing enfranchisement in U.S. literary culture and a decade or so before the idea of a Jewish literary mafia began to circulate.

Though Bellow would eventually go on to win the Nobel Prize in Literature and become one of the most widely lauded of American authors, it has largely gone unnoticed that, at the beginning of his career, he wrote a novel that is, first and foremost, about a group of American editors and their personal and professional relationships. Bellow would later deride *The Victim* as one of his apprentice works and unworthy of serious attention, and it can be read as Bellow's reaction to complex questions about U.S. anti-Semitism in the wake of the Holocaust; but the book is also remarkable for the clarity and prescience with which it anticipated the reactions that would greet American Jews as they acceded to positions of increasing influence in U.S. publishing and literary culture.[66]

The Victim's protagonist, Asa Leventhal, is "an editor of a small trade mag-

—

azine."[67] His friend Daniel Harkavy is an editor at a different small magazine, called *Antique Horizons,* and his antagonist, Kirby Allbee, used to work as an editor at *Dill's Weekly,* a prestigious and popular "news magazine" housed in a sixty-floor skyscraper called the Dill Building (37).[68] Leventhal aspires to a more influential editorial role for himself: "What a break if I could land a job with an outfit like that" (36), he thinks, of *Dill's,* and Allbee arranges an interview for Leventhal there. When Leventhal is told that he is wasting his time applying for a job at *Dill's* because he has not previously worked at a newspaper (37), he responds, "That's a prejudice" and "Any outsider hasn't got a chance" (38–39). Critics and biographers have noted that Bellow's own unsuccessful interview in 1943 for a job at *Time*—where, as mentioned earlier, Jews were not generally hired until the end of that decade—inspired this crucial scene, and this suggests that the "prejudice" against "outsiders" to which Leventhal objects may, at least in part, be an anti-Semitic one.[69] Either way, the inciting incident for this novel is that a young Jew who aspires to an editorial job at a prestigious U.S. magazine is turned away because, as he is told, he is not the right kind of person for that sort of job.

The plot of the novel focuses on Leventhal's and Allbee's dizzying claims and counterclaims about each other's acts of prejudice and persecution. But where *The Victim* is most interesting with regard to the history of Jews' enfranchisement in U.S. literary culture is in its prescience about the kind of claims that would be made two decades later. What Allbee claims that he has lost and what he envies Leventhal for possessing and what he wants, with Leventhal's help, to regain is, quite simply, a job as an editor. Who gets such jobs, in the novel, depends entirely on "connections" and on "influence," terms that recur more than a dozen times throughout the book.[70] Leventhal "got his start in the profession" (16) thanks to a contact of his uncle's friend Harkavy, and toward the end of the novel, the narrator remarks, "That fall, one of the editors at Harkavy's paper, *Antique Horizons,* went to a national magazine and, through Harkavy, Leventhal got the vacancy" (256). The novel's noting that Leventhal got the job "through Harkavy" underscores what the novel has already made very clear: that when it comes to editorial jobs, merit has little to do with it, and what matters is whom you know.

Allbee, for his part, explicitly wants Leventhal to intervene on his behalf, in

—

recompense for earlier slights, to get him a job at Beard & Co., the magazine publisher where Leventhal works, and later through another of Leventhal's Jewish friends in Hollywood. "You must have connections," Allbee tells him (127). As Leventhal explains, Allbee seems to think that "it's all a Jewish setup" and that "Jews have influence with other Jews" (236). Leventhal's friend Harkavy recognizes this idea as an anti-Semitic canard, noting that it comes straight out of *The Protocols of the Elders of Zion* (263). The novel actually begins with an unsympathetic expression of this same idea by Leventhal's boss, who says that Leventhal is "like the rest of his brethren," who "always please themselves first" (3), a restatement of the classic anti-Semitic accusation of Jewish clannishness. (Allbee later reiterates this: "You people take care of yourselves before everything" [130].) Though Allbee comes "from an old New England family" (126) and "one of [his] ancestors was Governor Winthrop" (129), he has recognized by the end of the novel that he is "not the type that runs things" but "the type that comes to terms with whoever runs things" (264). In other words, whereas he had once assumed that as a white, New England Protestant, he had a privileged place in U.S. culture and specifically vis-à-vis editing, he now understands the situation has changed. As he says,

> The world's changed hands. I'm like the Indian who sees a train running over the prairie where the buffalo used to roam. Well, now the buffalo have disappeared, I want to get off the pony and be a conductor on that train. I'm not asking to be a stockholder in the company. I know that's impossible. Lots of things are impossible that didn't use to be. When I was younger I had my whole life laid out in my mind. I planned what it was going to be like on the assumption that I came out of the lords of the earth. I had all kinds of expectations. But God disposes. There's no use kidding. (232)

Jarring as it might seem, the analogy Allbee uses was not unknown in U.S. white-supremacist discourse (and it was invoked two decades earlier in Willa Cather's *The Professor's House*).[71] Allbee is specifically upset about Jews' engaging in the study and discussion of American literature; that is why he also complains about seeing "a book about Thoreau and Emerson by a man named Lipschitz" (129).

—

The irony of Allbee's complaint is that at the time that Bellow's novel appeared, in 1947, though some Jews were certainly succeeding as writers and though Jewish-owned publishing houses were increasingly central in U.S. literary culture, the privileged position of white Protestants in that culture remained quite powerful, and barriers to Jews' participation in it, in the form of university quotas and exclusionary hiring, had only begun to be dismantled.[72] Bellow was especially well positioned to see how things were changing, though, because he had studied anthropology, a field dominated at that time by attention to relationships and kinship networks.[73] Moreover, at that early point in his career, Bellow had published in the *New Republic,* where the critic Alfred Kazin was the literary editor, and in the *New Leader,* edited by the scholar Daniel Bell, both of whom shared Bellow's Yiddish-speaking, eastern European immigrant Jewish background. When Bellow had been invited to review for a widely circulated publication like the *New York Times Book Review,* he had been assigned books like Maurice Samuels's *The World of Sholom Aleichem.*[74] His letters to colleagues were frequently dotted with untranslated Yiddish phrases.[75] In other words, in this early stage of his career, Bellow was deeply enmeshed in a cultural and intellectual network of which many of the most receptive nodes were Jewish; one need not visualize him crashing on the sofa at his friend Isaac Rosenfeld's apartment, during his visits to New York, to get the picture.[76] Meanwhile, the same magazine, *Time,* that had declined to hire Bellow in 1943, at a moment when it had virtually no Jews on its editorial staff, allowed its reviewer, only one year later, to deride the protagonist of Bellow's debut novel as a "pharisaical stinker," using a term that can be defined as "marked by hypocritical censorious self-righteousness" but that also contains an obvious winking, pejorative reference, in typical *Time* style, to Jewishness via the Pharisees.[77] So Bellow had had immediate experiences in which Jewish editors were sympathetic to his writing while an institution that excluded Jews was not.

Kinship and Nepotism versus Objectivity and Merit

Bellow's novel was especially prescient in understanding that one of the crucial issues in the perception and treatment of Jews as they became American editors would be questions about kinship and responsibility. On the book's second page, the reader learns that "for a long time, Leventhal had had very little to do with his brother and his brother's family" (2), and later it is clear that Leventhal's brother has never been to his house (209) and indeed that "they had never, since childhood, spent an hour together" (212). Nonetheless, Leventhal's sister-in-law asks him to come to their home on Staten Island because one of her children is sick, and he goes. When he arrives, he finds that his nephew, who opens the door, "[does] not know him" and asks, "Who are you?" (4). Leventhal does not blame the boy and goes on to observe that, physically, he resembles his mother, with "only his slightly outcurving nose belong[ing] to the Leventhals" (5). While this incident suggests, on the one hand, how tenuous family relations are, such that there is little linking an uncle and his nephew despite some shared genetic material, it also suggests the ways in which family exerts a claim on Leventhal, their estrangement notwithstanding.

Leventhal's brother, Max, feels judged by his family; he thinks that they think he "should have married a Jewish girl" (215), referencing a demand for endogamy that is one of the clearest and most prevalent forms of homophily in many human cultures. Leventhal denies that he feels that way, but he is far from feeling insensitive to the claims of familial bonds: reconnecting with his brother becomes a powerful emotional experience for him (218), and Leventhal later reflects that "he would go to any lengths to save" his nephew (238). When one character, late in the novel, rehearses a cliché, "Don't you want to provide for the people you love?" (227), it suggests how conventional it is, and how commonsensical, that one should feel especially bound to help those people with whom one has intimate ties. After all, as Leventhal realizes, there are too many people in the world, "innumerable millions" (164), for one to be able to do right by all of them, and if the key commandment of Western religion is to "love thy neighbor as thyself," the question remains, as Allbee says, "Who the devil is thy neighbor?" (173–74). Is it really wrong, the novel seems to wonder, if the neighbor we "love" (and thus want to "provide for") is sometimes one of our kinspeople, family members, coethnics, or coreligionists? While such questions, about one's obligations to kin and to strangers, have always been a major issue in Judaism and in Western moral philosophy, they were especially pressing for American Jews, in a daily sense, at the moment Bellow wrote his novel, as

—

19

both dawning perceptions of the genocide of European Jews and advocacy for a Zionist state gave questions about Jews' duties to other Jews around the world (both their relatives and those to whom they had no connection other than a shared Jewishness) immediate, concrete, and world-historical stakes.[78]

Obviously the kinds of questions that may have been on the minds of Bellow's readers — for example, whether the U.S. should intervene in a foreign military conflict to save the lives of one's cousins or whether it is ethical within modern secular nationalism to grant special rights to citizens of a state on the basis of their religious or ethnic identities — have consequences much more dramatic than questions about who publishes or reviews or reads which novel or poem. But for people like Bellow, whose lives were spent writing, reading, and editing, the question of whether one had a literary responsibility to one's *landslayt* (fellow ethnics) would have been the small scale on which they acted out their beliefs about whom they were responsible for and how. Concerns about the exercise of that kind of literary responsibility — Jews giving too much preference to people like them — drove the critiques of the Jewish literary mafia. Not coincidentally, in Norman Podhoretz's memoir *Making It* (1967), on which many critiques of the literary mafia rely for information, he called the group of Jewish writers, critics, and editors who became influential in U.S. letters in the 1950s "The Family," using a term that evoked the mafias of U.S. organized crime.[79] In line with this description, critics of a putative Jewish literary mafia presumed kinship relations between all Jews, and they objected above all to literary professionals privileging such kinship instead of relying on putatively meritocratic, ideological, or aesthetic criteria.

As if wary of such critiques, editors, publishers, and other cultural gatekeepers very often claim that they make their decisions on objective or meritocratic bases, and some literary scholars decry the notion that their taste has been influenced by who their kin or ancestors happened to be. It is not unusual to suggest, for example, that literary-prize judges should put aside "group pleading" and simply "choose the year's 'best' novel."[80] Similar statements are no more surprising when voiced by influential editors. In 2013, I asked Deborah Treisman, the fiction editor of the *New Yorker* — then, as now, probably the most influential U.S. venue for short fiction, with regard to launching a writer's career — whether the fact that both she and David Remnick, the *New Yorker*'s editor, are of at least partial Jewish descent might have anything to do with the magazine's remarkably strong support for Jewish writers. She replied that her "aim is to be receptive to fiction that is powerful, eloquent, and original, regardless of its plot or its preoccupations": "We try to cast the net very wide when it comes to what we publish, and what we look for in a story is, of course, evidence of talent and inspiration, rather than ethnic, cultural, or religious concerns."[81] Many other contemporary editors, and many who were active and influential in the twentieth century, have made or, if asked, *would* make similar claims about their tastes and what they seek in submissions as "objective" and unrelated to their own backgrounds and focused on purely, if vaguely defined, "literary merit."[82]

Contemporary literary scholars, trained and practicing a couple of generations after New Criticism went out of fashion, might be expected to reject such claims of literary objectivity, but they do not always do so.[83] Walter Benn Michaels, one of the most influential contemporary academic scholars of nineteenth- and twentieth-century American literature, has repeatedly made a point of asserting that his own ethnic, racial, and religious background is immaterial to his interests or arguments. Though he acknowledges that he "is . . . Jewish" and though "some of the things he does," like eating "lox and bagels" and gesturing when he talks, "are stereotypically associated with Jews," he is emphatic that a "description of [him] as Jewish . . . doesn't really tell you very much."[84] One of the specific things it *really* does not tell you anything about, he insists, is his taste in literature: "My great-grandparents could read only Yiddish. Am I supposed to feel a stronger connection to Abramovich's 'Kliatche' ('Mare'), a book I never heard of until I looked up Yiddish classics on the Web two minutes ago, than, say, to 'Vanity Fair,' a book my ancestors wouldn't have understood one word of? . . . Obviously not."[85] Michaels has specific, sympathetic reasons for making this claim (he thinks the really important fact about any individual living under capitalism is not who their ancestors were but how much money they make, because our most pressing problem is economic inequality), but a number of other prominent literary critics with different politics and personalities have agreed that it would be "obviously" mistaken to imagine that a person's family background, religion, or ethnicity might affect what it is that they like to read, write, buy, edit, or publish.[86]

It is this idea that editors and scholars espouse — that a person's literary tastes

—

21

need have nothing at all to do with their own cultural or ethnic background and that one can judge literature in a purely disinterested, meritocratic way — that makes the critique of a literary mafia circulated by Capote, Kostelanetz, and others conceivable and speakable. Kostelanetz has no trouble remarking that because of conspiracies in the publishing business, one cannot find "a first-rate novel" (192) or that editors are not able to attend to "the best manuscripts" (205) that come across their desks, as if there were a simple, widely accepted rating scheme by which literary works could be assessed as "first-rate" or "best." This idea of literary objectivity or meritocracy makes it possible for some observers of the literary scene to believe that there could be a respite from the machinations of a corrupt literary mafia, in the sense that editors and reviewers could perhaps stop playing favorites and just choose the books that are, according to a shared standard, the most deserving. It is the same idea relied on anytime anyone proposes that a literary agent looking for their next client or a publisher choosing between forty submitted manuscripts or a reviewer selecting among several novels they might review or the judges of a literary prize picking their winner for this year should simply choose the one that is best, most beautiful, or most excellent. If Capote and Kostelanetz had, on the other hand, been willing to acknowledge that every literary gatekeeper, every critic, and every individual reader regularly draws on their own background and experiences, in one way or another, in forming their judgments and developing their idiosyncratic tastes, it would be harder for them to criticize such people, either individually or collectively, for at times favoring books by people who are like them or for hiring people who remind them of themselves.

Of course, most people reading this will agree that there is no such thing as literary objectivity or a truly "best" or "most beautiful" book, poem, or story — and especially if they have read slush or served as a judge of a literary prize or been an acquisitions editor or a book reviewer (or, perhaps, if they have served on job-search committees at a university).[87] If one has had those experiences, one will probably agree with Gregory Jay that "the power of a text to move a reader is a culturally produced effect" and that "literary 'taste' is not natural but taught, and taught in a way that reproduces values that go beyond aesthetics."[88] And thanks to cultural sociologists, one need not accept such a claim on faith, either. Their work on literary taste and publishing consistently suggests that

—

"book publishing" is "an exceedingly personal business dependent on interpersonal ties and loyalties" and that "reading a book is no innocent act of individual style" but "a project flowing from a habitus forged in particular conditions of existence."[89]

Drawing on empirical studies of contemporary literary professionals in the U.S., Clayton Childress shows how literary agents rely on "cultural matching as a winnowing strategy," as a way of finding within the thousands of authors whose submissions they might read the ones that they should take on as clients, and in a study of contemporary book reviewing, Phillipa K. Chong shows how "editors and reviewers alike [employ] homophilous logic as a way of predicting suitable matches between books and reviewers."[90] The work of these and other cultural sociologists makes clear that the key "twinned problems" of gatekeeping in the literary field in the postwar U.S. have been "oversupply and fundamental uncertainty over quality," and the best way that professionals have found to "manage" those problems is a "reliance on interpersonal relationships" (even though that inevitably leads to "conflicts of interest").[91] As another group of sociologists phrased it, in the 1980s, "The enormous number of manuscripts received by any editor" makes necessary "prior screening by friends, by friends of friends, by agents with whom an editor feels comfortable, by professors who intercede for their protégés, and by a host of other informal 'brokers.'"[92] When doing the work of cultural gatekeeping around literature, people regularly privilege the opinions of people whom they perceive as connected to or resembling themselves, in one way or another; they thus practice a form of what Frank Parkin, drawing on Max Weber, called "social closure."[93]

This aspect of U.S. publishing should not be surprising, given how much nepotism, cronyism, and racism operate in so many aspects of life in the U.S. (and how false the idea of meritocracy has been shown to be, in general), even in those areas with less "radical quality uncertainty" than literature.[94] Indeed, even in professions where we might expect the very least uncertainty and in which we would place objectivity at a premium — for example, in the administration of the law and medical care — it has been demonstrated that the identities of professionals and of those whom they serve have profound and often tragically unjust effects.[95]

That said, it is also misleading to assume, as critics of a Jewish literary mafia

—

have done, that literary professionals will act *simply* and *straightforwardly* (or *predictably*) according to homophilous logic. Such simplifications are quite understandable; simplifications are common heuristic tools, and they have helped scholars studying the development of ethnic niches to uncover valuable insights about how and why immigrant and minority communities, around the world and throughout human history, have derived benefits from carving out niches in particular industries. (The concentration of Jews in U.S. publishing by the mid-twentieth century can certainly be understood as one such ethnic niche.) Much of the scholarship on the economics and history of such ethnic niches relies, deliberately, on simplified (sometimes mathematical) models of interactions that understand the benefits of shared membership in a minority group without nuance or complexity, and such simplifications even creep into economic and cultural history. Michael Cohen's excellent, richly detailed study of Jews' niche in the U.S. cotton industry in the nineteenth century, for example, concludes that "shared ethnicity fostered . . . networks of trust," which is undeniably true. In describing how this happened, though—claiming that "Jews, much like other ethnic minorities, trusted one another more than they trusted strangers with whom they had no connections"—Cohen misleadingly simplifies the dynamics at work.[96] While people do occasionally tell stories about a Jew offering assistance to another Jew, irrespective of any other information about that person, what actually seems to have worked for Jews and other minorities, in cases Cohen studies and in other ethnic niches, is that shared ethnicity brings with it a wide range of effects that encourage minority-group collaboration, including "lower transaction and communication costs," "less noise in productivity signals," "better match quality," "better resource access," and, with regard to trust specifically, enhanced information about whom *not* to trust and strengthened enforcement mechanisms through which breaches of trust can be sanctioned.[97]

This may seem like a minor distinction, but it is not. Jews did not, and do not, succeed by trusting other Jews *because* of their Jewishness, per se. Rather, as Shelley Tanenbaum shows in a study of loan societies in the U.S., Jews have used shared ethnicity to develop a wide range of carrots and sticks to engender and reinforce trust.[98] This does not confer a blanket advantage to everyone in the minority group. It means, among other things, harsher and swifter exclusion of any group members perceived as untrustworthy: indeed, thanks to efficient

—

24

information sharing among ethnic networks, an individual judged untrustworthy by one institution or in one city might find themselves quickly and summarily excluded from opportunities by other unrelated institutions in other places.[99]

By the same token, the homophily acted on by players in the literary scene is not simple or indicative of a benefit for every member of the group. It has never meant that Jewish editors simply want to publish Jewish writers. No editor has ever said, "Hey, since I'm Jewish, I'll publish any Jewish writer who comes along, no matter how terrible their work may be!" On the contrary, because of the phenomenon that Sigmund Freud labeled the "narcissism of minor differences," when two people share quite a bit of background or preferences, a disagreement between them on a relatively small aesthetic or political question can be experienced much more intensely than the same disagreement between two people with much less in common.[100] Moreover, any two editors or writers who may be perceived as sharing a background and tastes, in broad strokes, are as likely as not to turn out to make fiercely different choices when it comes down to individual novels, poems, or stories; as sociologists studying taste have pointed out, issues of scale complicate their analyses of taste to a significant degree (two editors' preferences might be judged as similar at, say, the genre level — both enjoy literary fiction with some fantasy elements — but be entirely different and contradictory at the book level).[101] Homophily, as it operates within U.S. literary culture, has complex consequences, because the identities and preferences with which it interacts are irreducibly complex and cannot be expressed in simplified models. (That gross oversimplifications are the stock-in-trade of anti-Semitic conspiracy theorists and white nationalists, who seem to be thriving in the contemporary U.S., is another reason, as if one were needed, that responsible scholars should avoid them.)

Some critics, and especially those engaged in refuting the claims of Capote and Kostelanetz, seem to believe that because the homophily that governs literary decision-making is so complex, what we are left with is, more or less, a meritocracy, or as close to one as we could hope for.[102] But that does not follow, either. This book proposes that one of the major tasks of U.S. literary history — if it is to be attuned not just to the history of publishing in general but also, specifically, to the exclusionary, sometimes white-supremacist tendencies of U.S.

—

publishing's past and present—must be to explore the specific ways in which a wide variety of homophilous logics and strategies have operated in the creation, production, and reception of American literature and literary culture. That is what this book, *The Literary Mafia,* aims to do throughout its chapters and close readings: to describe and explore one complex set of homophilous logics that had major effects in the history of U.S. literary culture. In other words, this book attends to the ways that the relationships a major subset of U.S. literary professionals have had with people linked to them through kinship of one sort or another—in particular their *landslayt,* their students, their spouses and partners, and their children—influenced and conditioned their tastes, decision-making, and creative expression.

Was There a Literary Mafia?

It may seem strange that this book takes its title from a myth that it deems false and even pernicious. If there was not a Jewish literary mafia in the postwar U.S., why recirculate that term? It is true that this book disagrees with those observers, like Capote and Kostelanetz, who claimed that a Jewish literary mafia took control of American literature in the 1960s. But it also recognizes that their claims, marginalized as they have been in the work of most scholars and critics, have done less damage to the way we tend to think about U.S. literary history than the knee-jerk reactions to them and the arguments used to counter them have.

As much as, throughout this book, I reject simplistic complaints about a Jewish literary mafia in the U.S., I also aim to correct the accounts of the more numerous critics and literary professionals who assert or assume that U.S. literary culture functions as a meritocracy in which objective professionals, whose backgrounds make no difference in their decision-making, strive to ensure that the best, most excellent work flourishes. I likewise hope to challenge an even larger group of contemporary observers (both publishing professionals and literary scholars) who, in their efforts to avoid offering any support to anti-Semites who might take comfort in claims like Kostelanetz's, have tended to ignore or minimize the roles played by Jews in the modern history of U.S. publishing.

—

Denying that literature is, or ever has been, objective or meritocratic does not imply that it is meaningless or unworthy of our attention. On the contrary, what we read (and write, edit, publish, and review) has to do with who we are and who we are connected to, and that should make it more, and not less, meaningful. Nor does crediting Jews for their roles in the development of American literature — as publishers, editors, critics, and scholars who helped so much of twentieth-century American literature see print and reach audiences — somehow render the U.S. literary field parochial or subjugate it to a public-relations effort on behalf of a minority group. Unless one views the history of publishing and U.S. literary development in the twentieth century as a record of blameless editorial perfection, it is hard to see how crediting Jews for playing a major role in it can be anything but a mixed bag for them. To put a finer point on this, Jewish individuals supported much of the aesthetic and industrial innovation that made American literature and U.S. publishing globally influential in the twentieth century and helped give us many literary works that continue to inspire, compel, and challenge readers today. But Jews were also for the most part complicit in the U.S. publishing industry's and literary field's misogyny and white supremacy, and they can be understood to have supported social closure that made it more possible for Jews than for members of many other U.S. minority groups to envision and pursue literary careers for themselves. This is not a story of Jewish triumph or of Jewish perfidy — it is just a story about American literature in the twentieth and twenty-first centuries, for better and worse.

—

CHAPTER 1

JEWS EDITING JEWS

Literary Gatekeeping among *Landslayt*

Jews and the National Book Award, 1954–1974

For anyone with a suspicion that a Jewish literary mafia was meddling in U.S. letters, what happened the night of March 23, 1960, would have smelled a little fishy. That Wednesday night, at the Hotel Astor in New York, a thousand "authors, critics, librarians, and book industry people" gathered to present the tenth annual National Book Awards. The fiction prize was awarded that night to a twenty-seven-year-old, "the youngest writer" ever to win it. The winner, Philip Roth, was honored for his debut book, the collection of short stories *Goodbye, Columbus.*[1]

There was not anything especially suspicious about Roth's book in and of itself or about the prize ceremony. But surely it would have been noticeable to anyone who was paying attention that Roth's book had been chosen over many worthy finalists—no fewer than sixteen, written by such respected American authors as Louis Auchincloss, William Faulkner, Saul Bellow, John Hersey, Shirley Jackson, John Updike, and Robert Penn Warren—and that it was strikingly similar, in form and content, to the previous year's winner. Roth's book consisted of a novella and five short stories, all peopled by American Jews, and the 1959 winner, Bernard Malamud's *The Magic Barrel,* was likewise a collection of short stories about American Jews. Remarkably, a single magazine had been the original venue for almost half of these prize-winning stories (five of Malamud's,

—

between 1950 and 1958, and two of Roth's, in 1957 and 1959): *Commentary*, which was published by the American Jewish Committee and, as mentioned in the introduction, often named as an organ of the Jewish literary mafia.[2] If a clique of literary Jews were shamelessly conspiring to support one another's work over everyone else's, would this not be exactly the result one would expect?

Moreover, the National Book Awards seems like a crucial site at which a conspiracy within the U.S. publishing business could exert itself. Unlike other major U.S. and international literary prizes, such as the Nobel, Pulitzer, and the Booker, which were founded and funded by people or institutions without a direct financial interest in bookselling and overseen by boards with varied interests, the National Book Award was created by the publishing industry itself, with initial sponsors including "the American Book Publishers Council, American Booksellers Association and the Book Manufacturers Institute." The launching of the prize on March 16, 1950, celebrating books from 1949, was, as James English, Evan Brier, and others have shown, an attempt by the book industry, which had thrived and expanded during World War II, to bolster the cultural and commercial position of books in the postwar era.[3] That this was not only the book industry's response to the rise of television and film but also an alternative to prizes like the Pulitzer and Nobel, over which, frustratingly, publishing professionals exerted very little control, was no secret: the first article on the prize in the *New York Times* ran under the headline "Book Trade Plans to Honor Writers," and the article highlighted the prize as an example of extraordinary cooperation within the industry.[4] From the prize's founding, it aimed to promote literary quality (and, in the terms of the period, to celebrate literature that was more "highbrow" than "middlebrow"), in part to distinguish itself from the other major U.S. literary prize, the Pulitzer, which, as one scholar has noted, had a tendency in that period to reward "bestselling popular fiction" rather than critically acclaimed literary fiction.[5]

The National Book Award did not immediately establish itself with American readers — as late as 1959, the *Los Angeles Times* book critic Robert Kirsch noted that "most Americans are unaware of the National Book Awards" and that "the interest engendered seem[s] confined largely to those initially involved either in the writing, production or sale of books" — but the prize did eventually succeed in positioning itself as an arbiter of U.S. literary quality.[6] In 1974, Joyce

—

Carol Oates called the NBA "the most distinguished American literary honor"; in 1988, forty-eight African American writers and academics grouped it, with the Pulitzer, as one of the "keystones to the canon of American literature"; and in 1991, in an essay highly critical of decisions made by the award's judges, Carol Iannone nonetheless acknowledged "the distinction conferred upon . . . an NBA finalist."[7] Of course, as James English persuasively argues in *The Economy of Prestige,* critiques of award recipients or complaints about deserving artists having been passed over, like those contained in the 1988 open letter and in Iannone's article, reinforce rather than undermine a prize's prestige.[8] Meanwhile, even as quality was always emphasized, the awards were from the beginning intended to function as a marketing tool that would benefit publishers and booksellers. "The National Book Awards Sell Books," a promotional flyer for the 1959 awards put it—and in many cases, they did.[9] In a study of literary celebrity, Joe Moran summarizes the function of the prizes succinctly: they "help to create a kind of 'major league' of literary heavyweights by stimulating sales and inspiring media coverage, while also appealing to the existence of higher values which surpass mere commercial considerations."[10]

Many of the National Book Awards given in the 1950s functioned, unsurprisingly, to consecrate and publicize the work of established writers. This benefited both publishers and booksellers, who stood to profit from such publicity for authors whose books they already published or stocked. William Faulkner won the National Book Award for Fiction twice, in 1951 and 1955, and this followed the rehabilitation of his reputation by *The Portable Faulkner* (1946) and his Nobel Prize for Literature in 1949. John O'Hara's reputation was well established by the time he won the 1956 National Book Award, and the same could be said for Wright Morris, the recipient of the 1957 prize. But the National Book Award could also lend symbolic capital to what might otherwise have seemed a temporary vogue or passing fad in the book market; this turned out to be especially true for the literary subgenre sometimes called American Jewish literature.

The postwar decades have often been described as a "breakthrough" moment for American Jewish writers, but it is difficult to put one's finger on what concretely distinguishes the literary successes of Jewish authors in the 1950s, 1960s, and 1970s from their predecessors of the 1890s through the 1940s, a number of whom also achieved commercial and critical successes.[11] One of the clearest reasons why the postwar decades felt different, to many critics and observers, from the prewar ones is that the National Book Awards, which figured themselves as speaking to and for an entire nation of readers, awarded prizes to Bellow in 1954, Malamud in 1959, and Roth in 1960.[12] Doing so, the awards' judges and administrators as much as declared that writing about American Jews (fiction peppered with explicit references to rabbis, synagogues, Jewish holidays, and Yiddish syntax and speech, as well as dozens and dozens of occurrences of the word "Jew" in and of itself) could be consecrated not just as the respectable output of an American minority subculture, aimed at a parochial, limited audience, but, more broadly, as the very best of American literature. This message was cemented when the National Book Award for Fiction was awarded to Jewish writers again in 1965, 1967, 1969, 1971, and 1974 — to Bellow (twice more), Malamud (once more), and the Jewish immigrant writers Jerzy Kosinski and Isaac Bashevis Singer once each — reflecting the publishing industry's emphatic judgment that fiction by and about Jews could be understood as representing "the most distinguished American books."[13]

The question raised by this history, in the context of critiques of a Jewish literary mafia, is whether the people responsible for these National Book Award decisions were Jewish critics, writers, and editors who shared values and socialized together; if so, that would lend some credence to the claim that a Jewish literary mafia operated in U.S. letters in the postwar decades.

But it turns out that is not the story told by the judging panels that actually selected Malamud's and Roth's books. Only one Jewish critic, Alfred Kazin, sat on the 1959 committee that selected Malamud's *The Magic Barrel*, and none sat on the 1960 committee that chose Roth's *Goodbye, Columbus*. Jewish writers and critics did judge the National Book Award for Fiction regularly in the 1950s and early 1960s — among them the novelists Budd Schulberg and Herbert Gold and the critics Leslie Fiedler and Harry Levin — but these served on the panels that awarded prizes to James Jones, Wright Morris, Walker Percy, and J. F. Powers, respectively.

There were two particular years, in the first three postwar decades, in which judges' Jewishness seems that it could have been a factor in deliberations for the National Book Award for Fiction. In 1954, the prize went to Saul Bellow's

—

The Adventures of Augie March, and the judges who selected that book included the Jewish critic Leon Edel, famed for his biographies of Henry James, and Mary McCarthy, who grew up with a Jewish grandmother and was a major figure among the New York Intellectuals.[14] The presence of McCarthy and Edel on the panel does seem like a significant advantage to Bellow; McCarthy and Bellow "saw a good deal" of each other in Paris, between 1948 and 1950, which was also the period during which Bellow wrote *Augie March,* and according to Edel's recollection, McCarthy "was so convinced the prize should go to *Augie* that she declared there was no reason [for the judging committee] to meet at all." Edel later recalled of his own motivations, "Bellow was a friend of mine and I was all for his getting the award."[15]

Yet it is worth noting that the other three judges on that committee, while well-established critics and writers who published regularly in major reviews, appear nowhere in Kostelanetz's survey of the putative Jewish literary establishment and do not seem to have had powerful links to anything that could be considered a Jewish literary mafia. They were David Dempsey, who wrote a chatty column for the *New York Times Book Review;* Arthur Mizener, a professor at Cornell whose biography of F. Scott Fitzgerald had appeared in 1951; and Gerald Sykes, who on the basis of two novels, *The Nice American* and *The Center of the Stage,* had been called in 1952, by a *New York Times* reviewer, "one of the most promising and exciting" of emerging novelists.[16] There may have been all kinds of personal, even biased reasons that one of these judges would have supported Bellow's novel — and according to Edel's recollection, their decision was ultimately unanimous — but one could not easily claim any Jewish collusion was at work.

The previous year's panel is a different story. For the 1953 fiction award, the panel of five judges included Martha Foley, a non-Jewish journalist and cofounder of *Story* magazine; Howard Mumford Jones, a non-Jewish Harvard English professor; and three younger Jewish writers: Kazin, Irving Howe, and none other than Saul Bellow himself. Even setting aside the peculiar fact of Bellow's having judged a major national prize exactly one year before he himself won it, this panel looks a little suspicious. Bellow, Howe, and Kazin certainly knew one another, wrote for many of the same magazines, and had many friends in common. This committee had eleven finalists to choose from, including Er-

—

nest Hemingway's *The Old Man and the Sea*, novels by Jean Stafford, John Steinbeck, and William Carlos Williams, and Peter Martin's *The Landsmen*, a novel of nineteenth-century Jewish life in eastern Europe whose very title clumsily evokes Jewish kinship relations and that one reviewer remarked would have "a special . . . claim upon those who have intimate knowledge . . . of the ringed life of the captive Jew in Europe."[17] Yet instead of giving the prize to any of those books, the jury awarded it to Ralph Ellison's *Invisible Man*. As Ellison's biographer Arnold Rampersad phrases it, Ellison "was lucky in having three young, progressive Jewish writers as a majority on the panel," two of whom, Kazin and Bellow, he "counted . . . among his friends."[18]

In other words, the only time that either of the two most respected national U.S. prizes for fiction, the Pulitzer or National Book Award, went to an African American novelist between the 1950s and the early 1980s was on an occasion when there happened to be a majority of Jews on the judging panel. It does not seem a stretch to suggest that in addition to Kazin's and Bellow's friendship with Ellison, a perspective or affinity shared by three writers from similar Ashkenazi Jewish backgrounds could have been expressed in their decision — and Howe, Kazin, and Bellow all do appear by name among the first two, inner layers of Kostelanetz's "New York Literary Mob."[19] But at least in this case, the result of their shared perspective was not the promotion of work by someone from a similar Jewish background or someone seen as a member of the literary mafia at all.[20]

Instead, this moment of potential collusion reflected three writers' agreement about the value of the aesthetic project of another minority writer, possibly a shared sensitivity to the project of a writer, like Ellison, who saw himself as writing into the mainstream of U.S. culture but was grappling with his relationship to minority experience and to a history of persecution and literary marginalization. Howe, Kazin, and Bellow's decision, made with Mumford Jones and Foley (apparently overpowering Jones, who wanted to award the prize to Hemingway), was profoundly influential: it transformed Ellison's career and in some sense African American literature as a field. As Rampersad phrases it, it was "winning the National Book Award — not the publication of *Invisible Man* itself" — that "transform[ed] . . . Ralph's life."[21] One cannot overstate the central, if complex, importance of the commercial and critical success of *Invisible Man*, marked

—

especially by its winning of the National Book Award, and subsequent sales, within the history of African American literature as it is currently understood.[22]

It mattered, then, that Jews like Howe, Kazin, and Bellow were given the opportunity to serve as judges for the National Book Awards, but not because Jewish judges prioritized or promoted the work of Jewish writers. The judges who awarded eight National Book Awards for Fiction over two decades, between 1954 and 1974, to Jewish writers writing about Jews, turn out to have been mostly non-Jews, based outside of New York's literary circles. That a Jewish majority on the fiction panel led to a landmark for African American literature suggests something very important about Jews' growing influence in U.S. publishing: the consequences were often surprising and by no means simply increased support for Jewish literature per se.

Even when Jewish literary gatekeepers did turn their attention to writing by and about Jews, though, they did not simply green-light at random every Jewish text they encountered. The rest of this chapter concentrates on two editors employed, in different decades, by one of the premier U.S. publishing houses and the longest surviving one founded by a Jewish family: Alfred A. Knopf, Inc. Knopf was unusual in that, unlike many other firms founded by Jews in the first decades of the twentieth century, it employed mostly Jews as editors in its key editorial leadership positions, and so it offers a series of cases in which one can see the unexpected and complex consequences of Jews' literary enfranchisement.

Jewishness at Knopf

The company that Alfred and Blanche Knopf founded and ran has been acknowledged as mattering in the history of U.S. publishing and U.S. culture for many reasons, including the firm's leading role in setting standards of book design and its commitment to the translation of European and world literature.[23] Alfred and Blanche were Jewish, and their publishing house was led consistently by Jewish editors for many decades after its founding; so it also serves as a fascinating site for exploring the roles of Jews in the book business: How did Jewish editors make decisions about what to publish or not publish?

How did their editorial choices help to shape "the horizons of the publishable" in the U.S. in general and more specifically with regard to literary representations of Jews and Jewishness? And the bottom line: Did the Jewish ownership and directorship of this prestigious and influential company, from its founding and into the postwar decades, make it easier for Jewish writers to get published there, win prizes, and find their readership? Could it be said that Knopf functioned as an instrument, purposefully or not, of a Jewish literary mafia in the United States? As in the case of the National Book Awards, the answer is that while Knopf did place Jews in positions of power and influence in American literature, the results were not always what one might expect, and they were certainly not an aggressive promotion of works by the interconnected and mutually supportive Jewish writers targeted by Kostelanetz.

Alfred and Blanche founded their publishing company with the help of Alfred's father, Samuel, in 1915. Samuel had immigrated from Poland as a child in 1871 and in the early years of his career sold clothing and furniture before turning to advertising; he was successful enough in that field to raise his children in some luxury in Harlem and Fort Washington. His son Alfred was raised as a Reform Jew, attended services at Temple Israel of Harlem, and was confirmed at Temple Beth-El on the Upper East Side before the family was accepted at the prestigious Temple Emanu-El.[24] Blanche Wolf, meanwhile, was born to a family of German Jewish immigrants who had made fortunes in cattle exporting and millinery and who looked down on Alfred, when Blanche first met him, as a "Russian Jew."[25] While scholars and biographers have emphasized that the Knopf family was not religiously observant and sometimes spoke disdainfully about "Jewish Society," there is also evidence of the family's ongoing links to Jewish culture: for example, Samuel—who, as director and treasurer of Knopf, maintained "control over editorial decisions, salaries, and other matters," such that "Blanche and Alfred frequently deferred" to him, if not always willingly, until his death in 1932—was a member of the Jewish Publication Society at least from the turn of the century.[26] Although Ben Huebsch got his start in the field a little earlier, Alfred also regularly receives credit for breaking the barrier against Jews in U.S. trade book publishing.[27]

Notwithstanding the Knopf family's Jewishness, the publishing house that Alfred, Blanche, and Samuel founded in 1915 was decidedly nonsectarian.

—

Throughout its history, it has been known for publishing ambitious, critically acclaimed literature, and the fact that its editors have actively, and successfully, sought to publish more winners of the Nobel Prize in Literature than any other U.S. house speaks volumes about how the house wishes to be perceived.

At the same time, whether because of Samuel's interest or because there was a market for such books, beginning in Knopf's earliest years, it published both fiction and nonfiction that took Jews as primary subjects. In the 1910s, 1920s, and 1930s, these almost always focused on Jews in Europe or elsewhere: nonfiction titles included Albert M. Hyamson's *Palestine: The Rebirth of an Ancient People* (1917), a paean to Zionism; and Abraham L. Sachar's *A History of the Jews* (1930), a standard textbook introduction that went through multiple editions. As for fiction, the house published the British Jewish novelists Gladys Bronwyn Stern and Louis Golding, as well as translations of European Jewish authors who wrote in Russian, Hungarian, German, and Yiddish: Isaac Babel, Max Brod, Ludwig Hatvany, Sholem Aleichem, and I. J. Singer. What Knopf did not do, before World War II, was publish fiction or nonfiction about American Jews. All the American authors who wrote most successfully in English about Jews in the United States in those years, including Abraham Cahan, Anzia Yezierska, Samuel Ornitz, Ludwig Lewisohn, Waldo Frank, Henry Roth, and Jerome Weidman, published with other firms, such as Boni & Liveright, J. B. Lippincott, and Harper & Brothers. As if to underscore this tendency of Knopf's books to focus on Jewish life outside the U.S., when the firm published a novel in the 1930s about the current, imperiled state of world Jewry, including Americans, it was set, fantastically, on the approach to the Gobi Desert.[28]

Why did Knopf's editors find contemporary literature by and about European Jews worthwhile but studiously avoid books about American Jews' experiences? The thinking that drove this set of publishing decisions can be gleaned from the editorial discussion around a book titled *Commentary on the American Scene,* which was considered by the Knopf editors beginning in 1951. Elliot Cohen, the editor of *Commentary* magazine, submitted a collection of essays that had appeared in the magazine's "From the American Scene" section, with the aim of seeing them printed together as a book. The first Knopf staff member to evaluate the project, the non-Jewish publicity director Bill Cole, evinced enthusiasm and praised the collection for its "unity of content and literary excellence that altogether make a rich and informative picture of Jewish life in America from the time of the great immigrations to the present." Cole concluded his report, dated May 10, 1951, by speculating about the possibility of a wide market for such a collection: "It should be of great interest to all Jews, to intelligent and inquiring gentiles, and perhaps even to the *goy polloi*" (the last phrase playing on the Yiddish term for a gentile and the colloquially common Greek term for the masses).[29] Cole's optimism about the project inheres precisely in his belief that the material would benefit from a Jewish market for books while also standing a chance, at least, of attracting the attention of non-Jewish readers, the evidence for which assertion is himself.

The firm's editor in chief, Harold Strauss, was not so sure. A Jewish graduate of the Horace Mann School and Harvard who had come to the Knopfs' attention while reviewing books for the *New York Times* in the mid-1930s, Strauss was a well-read admirer of both Anglo-American modernism and European Jewish literature, and he served as the top editor at Knopf from 1942 to 1966.[30] He agreed with Cole about the *Commentary* project's "intrinsic quality," calling it "the best available over-all picture of the life of Jews in America." And, in assessing the book's commercial prospects, he acknowledged that "the Jewish market has become quite a good one," but, he elaborated, only "when a book coincides with one of the major Jewish emotional orientations — e.g., the establishment of the state of Israel; the extermination of the Jews of Central Europe; clinical studies of and attacks on the causes of anti-Semitism."[31] Strauss's concern was that the project "fits into none of these major categories." Moreover, Strauss went on to suggest how his personal perspective on Jewishness factored into his reaction to the project, noting, "[The book] has strong nostalgic values for some of us, but it treats the Jews as separate communities in America; and many Jews are unwilling to think of themselves in that way." He concluded his report by casting skepticism on Cole's suggestion that the book would have an audience among non-Jews: "finally, although the book is likely to get a very good press, I cannot imagine that there will be any great number of non-Jews, Mr. Cole's example not withstanding, who will be interested enough to buy it."[32] With the turn to the first-person plural ("some of us") and the condescending reference to Cole, Strauss makes clear that when he describes the "Jewish market," he is projecting rather than reporting.[33] He relies on his personal sense of what would appeal

—

to Jewish readers, demonstrating his belief that his own Jewishness qualifies him as an authority in making such a reckoning.

It is no surprise that a Jewish editor like Strauss would assert his authority this way when a book about Jews came under consideration, but this case is suggestive of the specific ways in which the presence of Jews on the Knopf editorial staff influenced what the publishing house eventually published. It does not indicate that these Jews on the editorial staff made it easier for manuscripts treating Jewish topics to be accepted. On the contrary, the case of Knopf suggests that in some instances at least (and as is familiar from the history of Hollywood and other fields), the presence of Jews in editorial roles led to more eccentric or tougher standards being applied to such submissions.[34]

Indeed, in the mid-1950s, Knopf editors considered manuscripts from the critic and fiction writer Leslie Fiedler and the Canadian novelist Mordecai Richler, and both cases illustrated the possibility of a book's attention to Jewishness dismaying Knopf's editors. Strauss evaluated a manuscript by Fiedler, which has never been published, in March 1954 and found much that was lacking: "Parts of it are immensely powerful," Strauss wrote in a letter to Fiedler; "parts of it are very weak, and all of it is repulsive." Among other problems (including its wandering from its main theme, its unsympathetic protagonist, and that "the book would not escape censorship in its current form"), Strauss noted that "the Jewish material is totally irrelevant": "The scene in which the uncle shows up has for me no connection with the rest of the book, and so do many of [sic] discussions of things Jewish."[35] This suggests the degree to which, for Strauss, "Jewish material" required justification and had to fit into the parameters he and his colleagues were establishing for it. When proofs of Mordecai Richler's second novel, *Son of a Smaller Hero,* soon to be published by André Deutsch in London, were sent to Blanche Knopf in May 1955 for possible U.S. publication, she replied, regretfully, that "it is almost impossible these days to do anything with a novel of this kind over here, except lose money and get nowhere with the author's next book." She may have meant something other by "a novel of this kind" than a novel about Jews; but one of the reports on the novel she had been sent emphasized that "the Jewish family . . . is as much a subject [of the novel] as the rebellious youth," so it seems entirely plausible that she was objecting specifically to that aspect of the book.[36] Fiedler never published with Knopf, and Richler would not do so until 1971.

On the other hand, in the 1940s, Alfred recognized the sales potential of books that would appeal to "Jewish groups," and one manuscript that reportedly elicited "very extraordinarily great enthusiasm on the part of [Blanche]" in the mid-1950s was a memoir by the musical impresario Samuel Chotzinoff that tells a typical story of a Jewish family's immigration and early years in the United States (and so does not seem to fit into Strauss's list of "emotional orientations").[37] It is not by any means the case, then, that Knopf avoided publishing books treating Jewish subjects or that the house was entirely faithful to the approach Strauss outlined in his response to the *Commentary* collection. Still, a survey of novels that Knopf published in the late 1940s and early 1950s suggests that its publishing program mostly did align with Strauss's eccentric sense of "major Jewish emotional orientations."

In the late 1940s, anti-anti-Semitic literature became quite popular in the U.S. in response to the growing awareness of the Holocaust.[38] Participating in this trend, Knopf published a series of novels mostly set outside the U.S. and focusing squarely on the Holocaust and anti-Semitism, including Jacob Wechsberg's *Homecoming* (1946), about an American Jewish soldier who finds the Jewish population of his hometown, in Czechoslovakia, decimated; Robert McLaughlin's *The Side of the Angels* (1947), about a non-Jew who falls in love with a Jewish girl; Leo Katz's *Seedtime* (1947), about pre–World War I pogroms in eastern Europe; Haakon Chevalier's *For Us the Living* (1949), about Nazism in California in the 1930s; and John Hersey's bestseller *The Wall* (1950), about the Warsaw Ghetto uprising. Perhaps the most lasting books dealing with Jews published by Knopf in the first decade after the war were challenging, complex literary texts with deep and unpredictable engagements with Jewish history and culture, by the Yiddish writer Isaac Bashevis Singer (*The Family Moskat* [1950]) and the Canadian poet A. M. Klein (*The Second Scroll* [1951]), and both were set, consistent with Knopf titles treating Jewish subjects in earlier decades, outside the United States.

In addition to narrowing the possibilities of what Jewish literature could look like, the influence of Jews at the highest level of Knopf's editorial staff also

—

fascinatingly allowed the firm's writers higher tolerance for controversial literary representations that some readers considered anti-Semitic. Evidence from the firm's early years suggests that the Knopfs had an unusually high tolerance for such material from the beginning. Alfred, Blanche, and Willa Cather frequently told the story of how Cather, already an established writer who had published with the venerable Houghton Mifflin, came in to meet Alfred and to ask him to be her publisher, one day in late 1919 or early 1920, because she liked the look of Knopf books and appreciated the house's advertisements. When Blanche told the story, she noted that she herself was sitting at the switchboard when Cather called to set up an appointment, though in other versions Cather just appeared at the offices unannounced.[39] What does not get mentioned in the retellings of this key moment in the house's history is the story that Cather published just a few months earlier, in the August 1919 issue of the *Century*. Titled "Scandal," it was, in the critic Donald Pizer's words, one of Cather's "most well-known anti-Semitic stories."[40] The form that the story's anti-Semitism takes is in depicting a wealthy, dandyish Jew who unscrupulously manipulates non-Jewish women artists for his own benefit. Though this suggests that Cather felt that parvenu Jews in the arts posed a threat to women like herself, she does not seem to have connected her portrait of Siegmund Stein, "one of the most hideous men in New York," to the new Jewish publisher she decided to work with.[41] Nor does this portrait seem to have bothered Alfred, Blanche, or Samuel — all of whom "developed sincere friendships" with Cather in the years that followed — as the story was quickly reprinted in the first of Cather's books to be published by Knopf, *Youth and the Bright Medusa* (1920).[42]

Another example was Knopf's apparent enthusiasm for T. S. Eliot's poem "Burbank with a Baedeker, Bleistein with a Cigar." The Knopfs published this poem alongside "The Lovesong of J. Alfred Prufrock" and many of Eliot's other celebrated early poems in a collection of Eliot's work called *Poems* (1920), but it was also included as a representative selection of Eliot's work in *The Borzoi 1920*, a celebratory volume that Alfred described as "a permanent record" of the company's "first five years' publishing."[43] "Burbank," notoriously, contains a vicious caricature of a man named "Bleistein," including a description of a cartoonish physical stereotype ("A saggy bending of the knees / And elbows, with the palms turned out, / Chicago Semite Viennese") and, most infamously, the lines, "The rats are underneath the piles. / The jew is underneath the lot."[44] While these lines have been at the center of critiques of and debates about Eliot's anti-Semitism for many decades, in 1920 someone at Knopf — probably Alfred and Blanche themselves — seems to have felt no doubt that "Burbank" was a poetic triumph that should be emphasized as a highlight of their early years in the publishing business.[45]

A refusal to shy away from work considered anti-Semitic continued into the firm's later years. Again in 1930 and then as late as 1945, when books by H. L. Mencken and Raymond Chandler, published by Knopf, were criticized for allegedly anti-Semitic representations, there is no evidence of consternation on the part of Alfred or Blanche, and on the contrary, the authors pointed to the Jewishness of their publisher and Alfred's support of their work as Exhibit A in their defense.

In a passage in Mencken's book on religion, *A Treatise on the Gods,* published by Knopf in 1930, he described Jews as "very plausibly . . . the most unpleasant race ever heard of" and as lacking "many of the qualities that mark the civilized man."[46] Speaking to an interviewer for a Jewish newspaper, in response to the controversy this caused, Mencken emphasized the Jews in his professional network, beginning with Alfred himself: "Here I have a Jewish publisher," he said, "a Jewish assistant, a Jewish proof-reader, a Jewish secretary."[47] A few weeks later, Alfred struck a conciliatory tone, suggesting in a letter to Mencken that the book's especially strong sales might have been explained in part by its selling well "to the very Jews who are objecting to that paragraph."[48] Alfred was apparently not the sort of cultural executive who worried about outcries from what Mencken called "professional Jews."[49] As Amy Root Clements explains, based on her reading of Alfred's unpublished autobiography, Knopf "approached the topic of Mencken's attitude toward Jews with nonchalance" and with a sense of humor.[50]

The case of Raymond Chandler's *The High Window* (1942), some fifteen years later, was similar. In 1945, after a twenty-five-cent edition of the novel had been published by Grosset & Dunlap, Chandler received "about a dozen letters" complaining about the way he had referred to Jews in it.[51] A couple of characters are identified as Jewish by the narrator, including "an old Jew in a tall black skull cap" in a pawn shop and "Dr. Carl Moss," who is described as "a big

—

burly Jew with a Hitler mustache, pop eyes and the calmness of a glacier."[52] The line that seems likely to have raised the strongest objections is a bit of dialogue spoken by Chandler's protagonist and narrator, Philip Marlowe, about the atmosphere of a private Hollywood club, in which, he remarks, "everything runs so true to type," including "the fat greasy sensual Jew with the tall stately bored showgirl."[53] Like Mencken and many others in similar situations, Chandler responded to the criticism with a list of his associates, this time with Alfred as the topper: "I have many Jewish friends," he writes. "I even have Jewish relatives. My publisher is a Jew." He also mentions that one of the Jewish characters in the book, Dr. Carl Moss, "is a portrait of [his] publisher, Alfred Knopf."[54] Moss is one of very few characters in the novel whom the protagonist, Marlowe, feels he can trust and whose wisdom and savoir faire outstrips Marlowe's; the character can be understood as an homage to the publisher who was in large part responsible for lifting Chandler out of the ranks of genre writers into a higher level of literary prestige. But it remains curious that Chandler felt it necessary to point out the doctor's Jewishness and suggests the degree to which Alfred Knopf's Jewishness did somehow matter to Chandler. So does Chandler's two-page letter, dated March 22, 1945, addressed to "Dear Alfred," in which he explains that he does not "see any point in answering" another of the letters and denies, at length, that he can be considered an anti-Semite.[55] The letter reads as if Chandler needed to prove at least to Alfred, a Jew who will listen to and believe him, what he cannot prove to his unsympathetic Jewish correspondents.

Interestingly, in both cases, the texts were eventually changed to eliminate the passages to which readers had objected—though not, it seems, because Alfred, Blanche, or any Knopf editors insisted. Mencken himself chose to make revisions to *A Treatise on the Gods* in the fall of 1945, probably influenced by his awareness of the genocide of European Jews and how his own remarks about Jews might be understood in that context. Chandler's text was revised in a 1976 Vintage Books paperback edition, more than a decade and a half after his death. Mencken's revisions were subtle, and *The High Window* was modified by simply replacing the word "Jew" with the word "man" in the spots to which readers had raised objections.[56] In both cases, the revisions suggest that the original complainants, oversensitive as their concerns may seem, must have had a point:

—

neither book suffers noticeably in its meaning or effect because of the revision of the putatively offensive passage, which suggests that the original versions can be understood, in some sense, as gratuitous. That being said, these authors were insulated from pressure when the critiques first arose, precisely because, as they both pointed out to unsympathetic correspondents, their publisher was a Jew.

Perhaps even more telling, with regard to what the Jewishness of Knopf's publisher and editorial staff may have made possible for their authors, are the early novels of Harold Robbins, who would go on to become perhaps the most notoriously commercial, bestselling American writer of the twentieth century. In *Never Love a Stranger* (1948) and most famously *A Stone for Danny Fisher* (1952), Robbins represented Jews in ways that could be criticized as reinforcing stereotypes or providing fodder for anti-Semitism, without much literary merit to defend them.[57] One critic has observed that "Harold Robbins never overlooks the Jew in his books and they are, invariably, a rather poor and revolting lot," and in *Commentary,* in 1953, Meyer Levin compared the representation of Jewish criminals in *A Stone for Danny Fisher* and other contemporaneous novels featuring Jewish gangsters to "the all-powerful Jew of secret world conspiracy, the archetypal Jew of *Der Stürmer* and the Protocols of the Elders of Zion, who from some hidden chamber pulls the strings of world intrigue."[58] These were not entirely fair characterizations of Robbins's novels — *Never Love a Stranger* decries the rise of anti-Semitism and racism in the 1930s and features a saintly Jewish aunt who can do no wrong — but they reflect the discomfort that some readers and writers felt with the introduction of Jewish characters into commercial, salacious fiction at a time when anti-Semitism had led to the murder of millions.[59] Other writers felt that these circumstances impelled them to make different choices; Arthur Miller, for example, wrote in 1948, "I gave up the Jews as literary material because I was afraid that even an innocent allusion to the individual wrong-doing of an individual Jew would be inflamed by the atmosphere, ignited by the hatred I suddenly was aware of, and my love would be twisted into a weapon of persecution against Jews."[60]

If potentially troublesome representations of Jews like the ones found in Robbins's books were by no means unique to books published by Knopf, they

—

may have been more imaginable there, in the years immediately after the Holocaust, than at some other presses, where on the one hand a persistent anxiety about parochialism and on the other hand a fear of giving offense may have constrained the publishing of novels with unsavory Jewish characters. Strauss praised the manuscript of Robbins's *A Stone for Danny Fisher,* when it was submitted, as "a book about New York Jewish life on the Lower East Side," while the front-flap copy on the dust jacket of the published book boasted of its depiction of "the seamy life of New York, . . . the way to make a shady buck by playing along with gamblers and mobsters, the unbridled lusts and passions of slum life."[61] The close juxtaposition of those two qualities — "Jewish life" and "unbridled lusts and passions of slum life" — did not seem to trouble anyone at Knopf in the way they troubled Levin. Perhaps not coincidentally, in the plot of Robbins's novel about Hollywood, *The Dream Merchants* (1949), accusations of anti-Semitism prove to be a red herring used by a feckless villain to manipulate his gullible, Jewish immigrant father.[62] The lack of consternation on Alfred's part, in 1920, 1930, and 1945, when putatively anti-Semitic works were published by Knopf authors, and critics or readers complained, strongly suggests that any concerns about Robbins's representations of Jews would not have rattled the founder or his editors in the 1950s, either.

These dynamics at Knopf may have been, like other aspects of the company, distinctive. Other publishers may have been less likely to rely on Jewish editors as their gauges of the Jewish market and what it wanted, and they may have been less likely to defend work like Mencken's, Chandler's, and Robbins's that smacked to some readers of anti-Semitism.[63] Yet the company offers one clear picture of a possible set of consequences of Jews' editorial influence at a major U.S. publishing house. It mattered that Jews were prominent as literary gatekeepers at Knopf not because, in some simple sense, that made it easier for Jewish writers to find support there but because of specific effects that these editors' decisions had on what was seen as marketable, prestigious, and defensible in U.S. literary culture. The empowerment of these gatekeepers made particular kinds of writing about Jews — rooted in Europe and the Middle East, focused on anti-Semitism, and unbowed by the possibility of being criticized as anti-Semitic — much more possible at Knopf and, through the company, in the U.S. in general.

—

"Der Knopfer Rebbe":
Gordon Lish and Ethnic Literary Solidarity

The first half century of Knopf's operations illustrates that even when editors saw themselves having a special connection to, or as acting as representatives of, a Jewish market or audience for books, the way that they would interpret that connection or responsibility was neither simple (they did not indiscriminately publish any writing about Jews) nor entirely predictable (Knopf's focus on books about Jews in Europe and the Middle East, for example, was hardly inevitable). Another editor associated with Knopf, much later—in the 1980s and 1990s—fills out this picture further. Even when a gatekeeper seems to have set out to privilege people who share his background, unapologetically, out of a sense of shared purpose with them, this editor's record suggests that the results are still not predictable—at least not in the simplistic way that the critics of a Jewish literary mafia imagined. The editor, the notorious Gordon Lish, furnishes an exemplary case of how an editor's Jewishness mattered, a case that has been strangely neglected in the many journalistic profiles of Lish and academic studies of his editorial career.

Unusually, Lish's name is probably already familiar to any scholar of postwar American literature and to many casual readers, too. A 2015 *Paris Review* interview with Lish, under the heading "The Art of Editing," begins by noting, without exaggeration, that "not since Maxwell Perkins has an editor been so famous—or notorious—as a sculptor of other people's prose."[64] Lish, who at least from the moment he took the position of fiction editor at *Esquire* in 1969 has been an inveterate, skillful, and amusing self-promoter, is the kind of literary celebrity whom the writers and editors of hip magazines have deemed worthy of profiling, in almost exactly the same way, again and again, for three decades.[65] His notoriety increased in the 1990s, when journalists examined the manuscripts Lish sold to Indiana University Bloomington and began to publicize the extent and intensity of his edits to the short stories of Raymond Carver, whom he supported and published at *Esquire,* McGraw-Hill, and Knopf. Many academic articles have followed, arguing about the effect of Lish's edits on Carver's work, and these edits have become the proverbial example of an editor's power, for better or worse, to transform the work of the writers he edits (the postwar

—

equivalent of Perkins's edits of Thomas Wolfe).[66] It is no surprise, then, when Lish pops up in one of the most influential recent studies of postwar U.S. fiction, Mark McGurl's *The Program Era*, as the figure who, on the basis of resonances between a textbook he wrote as a work for hire in the early 1960s and the fiction he edited and wrote later, provides evidence for McGurl's claim that "American literary minimalism is at least partially a product of the corporate educational technology and textbook business of the 1960s and 1970s."[67] In a more recent article, Lish's authorized biographer David Winters laments Lish's "reception," by McGurl and others, "almost exclusively as an advocate of literary minimalism," which Winters understands, quite correctly, as the result of such critics remaining perplexingly "unaware of the stylistic and thematic diversity of the writers [Lish] taught, edited, and influenced."[68]

Even as Winters and others have begun to revise understandings of Lish's work and legacy (and it should be noted that one element of that revision focuses on allegations about Lish's practice of taking his "female students . . . to bed," which will be treated in chapter 3), the effect of Lish's Jewishness on his editorial practices has not been treated in any depth.[69] On the contrary, if not completely ignoring it, both journalists and literary critics who have written about Lish have regarded his Jewishness as the least remarkable thing about him. This might be understood as making good sense, given how absolutely natural and normal it seemed, by the 1970s, that an influential literary editor at a U.S. publishing house would be Jewish. Moreover, many of Lish's predecessors and contemporaries in the editorial field — an apposite example is Robert Gottlieb, who hired Lish to work at Knopf — generally took pains to deny that Jewishness was a significant factor in their decision-making or experiences and to claim that it was not something necessary to discuss at length or dwell on.[70] Yet Lish, by contrast, has insistently reminded his interlocutors of his Jewishness, has returned to it often as a subject for his own writing, and, as it turns out, has embraced it as a factor in his editorial practices.

In published interviews, Lish has drawn attention to his Jewishness insistently, even though interviewers typically do not raise the subject themselves. In the 2015 *Paris Review* interview, for example, when Lish is asked why he had been expelled from the prep school Andover as a young man, he answers, "Fighting, fighting. Some fellow, or fellows, called me a dirty Jew, and I was a fighter."

—

As vague as this answer is—Was he picked on by one or more people? Were they his fellow students or just "fellows"? Did it happen once or frequently?— Lish insists on specificity when it comes to the nature of the provocation. He does not say that kids made hateful or racist remarks to him or that they picked on him because of his religion: he says, specifically, that they called him a "dirty Jew." Later in the same interview, when he is asked why he feels more drawn to editing than to other literary activities, another remark helps to explain why he would be so specific about the epithet in telling the story of his childhood: "Words seem to me safe sites for me to inhabit. . . . I'm afraid of my children. I'm afraid of my wives. I'm afraid of my friends, of my father, of you. . . . I expect I'm just a fearful fellow, paranoid. It has lots, I'd guess, to do with my size, my skin, my sense of being Jewish. But when I read, when I edit, or revise, I don't fear anything in the least. I feel at home, at peace, assured."[71] Here, unprompted, Lish explains his affinity for editorial work as a reaction to the fear and "paranoia" he experiences because of his "size," "skin" (Lish has suffered, throughout his life, from psoriasis), and "sense of being Jewish": as directly and explicitly as is possible, in other words, Lish says here that he became an editor because he is Jewish.[72]

In a different interview, also published in 2015, Lish offers a related formulation of his feelings about who he is and the work he does: "Fiction matters to me more than anything else in the world. It matters to me more than my life does. It's like saying I'll die for being a Jew, I'll be killed for being a Jew. Or I'll be killed for having psoriasis. These particularities come closer to naming and identifying me than anything else, and my feeling about prose fiction is that it's on a par with these concerns."[73] Again, this statement could not be more explicit: Lish, in his self-understanding (his "naming and identifying" of himself), is, quite straightforwardly, a Jew with psoriasis who edits fiction. And this sense of himself as a Jew pervades Lish's attempts to articulate his feelings about editing. Describing a fiction-writing workshop that he observed at the University of Texas, which was unbearable to him, he says, "here was someone coming into my synagogue, as it were, and desecrating the whole place."[74] On his editing of Carver's stories and how it has come to be perceived, he comments, "I fashioned a golem that would be cheered to see me destroyed."[75] Dismissing a question about how he thinks about his reputation, he observes, "My . . . in Yiddish

—

it's *nachas;* my joy comes from making the thing."[76] On each of these occasions and countless others, Lish reaches for a Jewish analogy or a Yiddish word to suggest how deeply and intensely he feels, both about life or the world in general and specifically about his work in the field of literary editing.

Lish's sense of Jewishness as central to his identity, expressed in these interviews, aligns straightforwardly with the concerns of his published writing. Though always recursive, provocative, and more focused on voice and language than plot or character, a good number of Lish's short stories, such as "Resurrection" (1984), "Fish Story" (1989), and "Three Jews on the Way Home from a Class" (1997), make the Jewishness of their characters explicit. In the case of his most highly praised novel, *Peru* (1997), as Martha Bayles notes in the *New Republic,* "the vocabulary of war, Jewishness and the Holocaust are scrupulously"—which is to say, noticeably and significantly—"omitted."[77] With regard to his positioning as a writer, Lish does not seem to have minded being grouped among American Jewish writers; he contributed to David Rosenberg's anthology *Congregation: Contemporary Writers Read the Jewish Bible* (1987), which was described, in Edward Hirsch's review on the front page of the *New York Times Book Review,* as premised on the notion of "a broad community of American Jewish writers who share an identity, however conflicted or attenuated, as well as a cultural heritage"—and, though Lish certainly ranked among the most "conflicted or attenuated" of them, he was still willing to contribute to Rosenberg's "sequel," *Testimony: Contemporary Writers Make the Holocaust Personal* (1991), if again with a highly irreverent essay that questioned the whole enterprise.[78] If he had wanted to distance himself from "a broad community of American Jewish writers," he could have just said no.

In fact, much more than has been acknowledged, Lish's entire project as a writer of fiction seems to have originated in and derived its ongoing energy from concerns about Jews, editing, and influence. The stunt with which Lish first gained a national readership for his own fiction has often been recounted: in 1977, as fiction editor of *Esquire,* he published an odd pastiche of J. D. Salinger's fiction without a signature, under the title "For Rupert, with No Promises."[79] Having successfully attracted a great deal of attention and speculation that Salinger himself might have written the piece, Lish then revealed himself as the author of the story. He claimed the following year in the *New England Review*

—

that he had "stopped writing fiction when [he] was nineteen" and that "For Rupert" had been his first attempt to do so since then.[80] (This was not exactly true, but it is the kind of myth that Lish likes to create.)[81]

What has not been discussed in retrospective accounts of the stunt is Lish's explanation that Cynthia Ozick's story "Usurpation—Other People's Stories," which he had edited for *Esquire* in 1974, inspired him to write "For Rupert."[82] Ozick's well-known story takes up the question of influence among Jewish writers (tracing a Jewish writerly lineage backward from Bernard Malamud to the Hebrew writers S. Y. Agnon and Shaul Tchernichovsky and then to the medieval Hebrew poet Solomon Ibn Gabirol), and as if to ensure that no one could miss the reference, Lish invokes Ozick's story unmistakably, if without naming her or the story itself, referring to "an American writer, a woman," and the story "she brought forth into the world about two years ago," which "begins as a story that this writer has stolen from another writer."[83] Following this, Lish includes in "For Rupert" an anecdote taken directly—mostly paraphrased but with some dialogue reproduced verbatim—from Ozick's story, about a father in a concentration camp who consults a rabbi about whether it is acceptable for him to have bribed a Nazi to substitute another child for his own son's place on the list of inmates to be murdered the following day.[84] In addition to usurping Ozick's usurpation—that is, stealing from her a focus on writers stealing from other writers—"For Rupert" also constitutes a radical act of creative editing, in which Lish as editor and hidden author, inspired by an Ozick story in which a young American grapples with the influence of celebrated Hebrew authors who are closer to the linguistic and textual traditions of Jewish culture, cuts a little bit of closer-to-Jewish-texts-and-tradition Ozick and pastes it into the much-further-from-Jewish-texts-and-tradition (putative) work of Salinger.

Lish followed that first Salinger metafiction with a second, "For Jerome with Love and Kisses" (1983), which is among his most acclaimed fictions—it won an O. Henry Award and was singled out for praise in reviews of his 1984 collection *What I Know So Far*—and which makes even clearer that Lish's interest in Salinger is in large part motivated by a fascination with the latter's relationship to the field of American Jewish literature.[85] Narrated in the form of a letter from Sol Salinger, the writer's father, to his famous son, the story supposes that the parents of several dozen of the most well-known Jewish writers in the United

States – including Bellow, Roth, Malamud, Ozick, Wouk, Uris, and many others down to commercial successes like Judith Krantz and somewhat more obscure novelists like Norman Fruchter – live together in an apartment community in Florida, comparing notes about their offspring. Sol Salinger's main complaints against his son, articulated in a cartoonish Jewish dialect (complete with Yinglish words like "mensch," "tookis," "shtarkers," and "kishkas"), are that he publishes under his initials rather than his full name (J. D. rather than Jerome David) and that he has no interest in appearing on Merv Griffin's talk show. The story's punch line is that the one parent in the residential community suffering even more than the elder Salinger is one Mrs. Pinkowitz, whose son, Thomas, has gone so far as to change his last name to Pynchon. Self-mocking and satirical as the story may be – and possibly a little sloppy with its literary history, too – there can be no doubt that it evinces a deep fascination with what Hirsch's review called "a broad community of American Jewish writers": Lish's Seavue Spa Oceanfront Garden Arms and Apartments, where the story has Sol Salinger living, is a fun-house-mirror reflection of such a "community."[86]

As unusual a fiction as "For Jerome with Love and Kisses" is, it cannot be dismissed as a one-off within Lish's oeuvre. On the contrary, one of that story's signal stylistic elements became a regular feature of the fiction Lish would publish over the following several decades: the uncomfortable, exaggeratedly verbose retelling of familiar Jewish jokes. A handful of these jokes appear in "For Jerome," and many more of them form the basis for an experimental novel, *Extravaganza: A Joke Book,* which Lish published in 1989. Lish continued the practice in stories published in the following decade, including "Squeak in the Sycamore" (1995) and "Narratology to the People!" (1997).[87] All of which is to say that Lish, as a writer of fiction, insistently placed Jewishness at the very center of his work.

Lish also happens to have been unabashed, to say the least, about wielding literary influence and his power to make editorial decisions based on his tastes. Very soon after taking his job at *Esquire,* he was already joking publicly about his position of power in the "New York Literary Establishment."[88] Less comically, he was never embarrassed to select his favorite students for publication and to praise them extravagantly, a practice that started at *Genesis West,* which had a regular feature in which teachers presented the work of their students (Lish

—

himself introduced the work of a student of his named Opal Belknap). This tendency intensified when he was at Knopf and editing the *Quarterly*. Unlike many other editors, Lish expressed no hesitation about the justness of relying on his own predilections when making editorial decisions, and he had no compunctions about selecting for publication, and advocating for, writing by people he knew.[89]

Consistent with all these attitudes, Lish in his role as an editor sought out, advocated for, and defended the work of Jewish writers. He did so throughout his editorial career, from the 1960s to the 1990s, during which time he exerted his authority over several literary journals and magazines, small and large (*Genesis West, Esquire,* and the *Quarterly*), at two book publishers (McGraw-Hill and Knopf), and as the editor of three significant fiction anthologies. Lish's choices about what to publish, how to publish it, and how to talk about it all regularly reflected the same fascination with Jewishness that played out in his own fiction.

Lish was especially conscious of his own Jewishness because he entered the editorial field not among book editors and publishers in New York, where many other Jews had worked for decades, but in the field of high-prestige literary periodicals, where his sense was that the people in power were Ivy League–trained Protestants like George Plimpton (of the *Paris Review*) and the poet and editor Reed Whittemore. "It was an us-and-them paradigm," he explained in a 2018 interview, "that bore in on me in the course of my deliberations or in the expression of my affections as an editor, throughout the course of my career as an editor. No question about it." He recalled that on his first day in the *Esquire* offices in 1970, the fiction editor who was turning the reins over to him, Rust Hills, called out for the benefit of anyone within earshot to say that Louis Auchincloss, the paradigmatic WASP novelist, "is on the phone, and he would like to know, What nationality is the name Lish?"[90] The same year, Lish passed along for the consideration of his boss, Don Erikson, an excerpt from Wallace Markfield's forthcoming novel *Teitelbaum's Window* (1970) with enthusiasm and a self-conscious note about "the density of the Yiddish and the extent to which it limits the audience." Erikson wrote back that he could "see as many reasons for doing it as not doing it; as for the latter, one major one might be that, god damn it, it's time now the jews stopped yammering on in this way."[91]

—

This sort of resistance did not deter Lish but seems to have spurred him on. Jewish writers aroused a special kind of attention in Lish as he perused submissions and slush piles: "One had a weather eye out for [Jewish writers], by name," he said, "and once one had entered into the work, one found reasons to keep on looking at it."[92]

But Lish did not support all Jewish writers, indiscriminately, as a member of a Jewish literary mafia might. On the contrary, the Jewish writers he favored were not the ones who were most prominent in U.S. culture. He did publish Philip Roth and Isaac Bashevis Singer, with more or less enthusiasm, but he adored the work of Harold Brodkey, Harold Bloom, Leonard Michaels, and Stanley Elkin.[93] Of all the Jewish writers Lish supported and published over the decades, none received more enthusiastic support than Grace Paley and Cynthia Ozick. From the very founding of his magazine *Genesis West,* in 1962, Lish made it clear that Paley's fiction was one of his foremost causes: he published one of her stories, titled "A Gloomy Tune," in his debut issue, remarking in the issue's contributors' notes that her 1959 collection of stories *The Little Disturbances of Man* "has been praised as a work of unqualified genius" and that she "was recently the subject of a panegyric by Harvey Swados."[94] At every opportunity Lish sung Paley's praises: in the magazine's third issue, advising readers that they could receive a free copy of the first issue, Lish noted that the issue contained "an inordinately executed [*sic*] piece of prose by Grace Paley, author of [a] remarkable collection of short stories."[95] In his fifth issue, Lish published a short critical essay on Paley by the critic Irving Malin, which is, strikingly, the only critical essay that ever appeared in *Genesis West;* meanwhile, in that issue's contributors' notes, Lish remarked, "Grace Paley, the subject of [Malin's] essay in this issue, is regarded by many as the finest short story writer in America." Comically, Malin's piece begins with the statement, "It is surprising that Grace Paley has not yet received any significant critical attention": this highlights the strategic vagueness of Lish's praise (Lish does not say exactly who were the "many" who regarded Paley as "the finest short story writer in America").[96] In the sixth issue of *Genesis West,* in an interview with Herbert Gold, Lish pointedly asks whether Grace Paley would be included in a hypothetical anthology of 1960s fiction if Gold were asked to edit one; she would, Gold assures him.[97]

Finally, as if to underscore his devotion to her work and its centrality to his ed-itorial ambitions, in the final issue of *Genesis West,* in 1965, Lish published two pieces of Paley's fiction: "Living" and, remarkably, for a second time in the same journal, the story that was now titled "Gloomy Tune."[98] The editorial note that begins the issue, which Lish remarks was composed "at presstime" and an-nounces that the journal will cease publication, thanks some of the donors and collaborators who helped him to publish *Genesis West,* as well as Grace Paley: "because I love that person."[99]

Genesis West published many other writers and had a variety of editorial interests and aims, but it is clear that Paley was never far from Lish's mind as a model of the kind of prose fiction that most excited him. She remained on his mind at the end of the decade — he included her story "A Subject of Childhood" in the innovative print and audio anthology he edited, *New Sounds in American Fiction* (1969).[100] When he started as fiction editor at *Esquire* in 1970, he re-mained loyal to Paley. In a 1971 note to his boss, Don Erikson, he explained that he is "a sucker for Paley's sort of thing" and that "the best of her stories are among the best stories in the language."[101] Two years later, Lish passed along a Paley story to a colleague, opening his note, "Behave yourself: I am turning over a story by Grace Paley. This is a rare treat. . . . Do your best to be worthy of her." He goes on to explain that publishing Paley's stories in *Genesis West* "was the proudest event in [his] life" and, by way of conclusion, notes, "Paley is a master AT WHAT SHE DOES, and you're going to hear a strong man cry if I get any-thing less than cheers in this thing."[102]

Lish's commitment to the work of Cynthia Ozick went even further. When Lish arrived at *Esquire* at the beginning of 1970, she was not yet on his radar — she had published only one book, the long novel *Trust* (1966); some poems; and a couple of stories in small magazines. Soon after Lish settled into his po-sition as the magazine's new fiction editor, Ozick's agent sent along a few of her short stories, which Lish promptly rejected but with typically effusive kindness. Ozick recognized from the first that *Esquire,* known for pinups and men's life-style features if also for serious reporting and fiction, was not the most natural venue for her work, but she suspected an affinity with Lish on the basis of the prose in his rejection letters. She was working on a long story but told him it was "in every sense inappropriate for *Esquire*," and she suspected that Lish "wouldn't, or couldn't, take 'Virility' . . . because how would it look for *Esquire* to print a Women's Liberation–theme story?"[103]

Lish did not end up publishing that particular story, but the main reason Ozick felt her work was not suited to *Esquire* was not really feminism; she was not especially in step with second-wave feminists. The real barrier, she felt, was her commitment to a particular kind of Jewish writing, dense with textual and historical allusions and linguistic complexities and deeply engaged with a non-assimilating or inassimilable Jewishness. Sending him the story "Usurpation" in October 1973, she did not beat around the bush: "The story," she wrote, "is both too long and too Jewish for *Esquire*."[104] When he published it, she was astonished: "I know (and you know) that there is no other fiction editor of a Big General Magazine extant who would have the guts to publish a story as profoundly Jewish as this one."[105] She remained amazed in 1975, when Lish expressed interest in another of her stories, "Bloodshed": "Yom Kippur stuff in *Esquire*? Queer! Strange! Weird! Impossible!"[106] Lish also advocated at *Esquire* on behalf of an incendiary political essay that Ozick wrote during Israel's 1973 Yom Kippur War, explaining that he was committed to it because of his own Jewishness, what he referred to as "an absolute personal imperative." Although he imagined that Ozick's essay might be dismissed by some of his colleagues as "chauvinism, mindlessness, screeching," Lish attested, "She is saying something I feel — every Jew REALLY feels — is undeniably true."[107] Ozick, in turn, gave Lish credit generously for her work, noting of the book manuscript she was sending to Robert Gottlieb at Knopf in June 1975 that "in every significant way it is a book of [Lish's] making."[108] Later, after Lish himself had moved to a job at Knopf, she said he deserved even more than his self-imposed title, "Captain Fiction": "Saint Fiction. Tsaddik Lish. Der Knopfer Rebbe."[109]

In an anthology of stories Lish culled from *Esquire,* called *All Our Secrets Are the Same* (1976), all of the contributing writers receive a standard author bio except for Ozick, whom Lish describes there as "a uniquely pitched voice in the general call made by those addressing themselves to readers of fiction that matters."[110] Finally, it is striking that Lish cared so much about Ozick's work that he sacrificed his job at *Esquire* out of loyalty to her. When the magazine's new owner, Clay Felker, demanded that Lish kill Ozick's story "Levitation" to make room in an upcoming issue for a piece of fiction by John Ehrlichman, a Nixon flunky who was sent to jail after Watergate as a perjurer, Lish threw a tantrum, involving a highly sarcastic telephone call to Arthur Miller, which prompted his firing.[111] That is how much Lish valued Ozick's work. The feeling was mutual, and for good reason, as Lish's advocacy on Ozick's behalf clearly made a major difference in her career: it was thanks to Lish that Ozick's writing found its way into a mass-market magazine for the first time, long before the *New Yorker* invited her to contribute and long before she won more first-place prizes in the O. Henry Short Story Awards than anyone else ever has (her first was for "Usurpation," which Lish published in *Esquire*).

To those who know Lish only as Carver's editor or as a single-minded patron of literary minimalism, it might seem odd that Lish would favor Ozick and Paley, as well as other Jewish writers like Brodkey, Elkin, Michaels, and Bloom and non-Jewish ones including Don DeLillo, as their literary styles, while varied, do not conform at all to a minimalist aesthetic and more often could be described as maximalist in one sense or another. What all of these writers have in common is that they privilege, above any other aspect of their fiction, the production of sinuous and beguiling and surprising sentences, which capture their readers' attention through a refusal to be conventional. It is the same quality that Lish labors to produce, through repetitions and ironies, in his own sentences, and it is the same quality he promoted in a great number of other American writers, including Amy Hempel, Raymond Carver, and Barry Hannah. What links Paley, Friedman, Elkin, Michaels, Ozick, Brodkey, and Lish himself is that the "new sounds" of *their* American fiction echo an old sound: the specific multilingual situation in which immigrant Yiddish cadences interfered with American English.[112] Not only were all of these writers published and promoted by Lish at *Esquire* or Knopf or the *Quarterly* during the 1970s, 1980s, and 1990s, but he also helped to ensure that their work would be read in creative-writing workshops and craft classes, both his own and an increasing number taught by his former students. Examples of these writers' work have therefore become important parts of what has come to be known as the "MFA canon."[113]

The prominence of these Jews among the cadre of Lish's favored writers is noteworthy because Lish's "school," so to speak, despite its fascination with the rhythms and patterns of speech, seems to have not been able to incorporate an

—

especially wide range of cultural difference. The novelist and critic Jess Row has remarked that "virtually every writer closely associated with Lish's teaching and editorial style is white."[114] Lish's editorial projects offered space to white Americans from small or unusual places — what Mark McGurl calls "Carver country," in general, and the Mennonite communities in Janet Kauffman's fictions, for two examples — but writers from recent immigrant, ethnic, and other minority communities are conspicuously rare in Lish's tables of contents and editorial lists.[115] One African American writer, Mitchell S. Jackson, wondered about this issue in an open letter to Lish in 2015, in which Jackson remarks on his own awareness of "what was not on [Lish's] grand list of scribes": "one of me" — a statement that ignores Lish's early support for Amiri Baraka and William Melvin Kelley but aligns with other evidence from Lish's publications and archives.[116] Of the twelve writers included in Lish's 1969 anthology *New Sounds in American Fiction,* Kelley is the only one who was not white, and as far as I can tell, there is not a single nonwhite author among the thirty writers published in Lish's 1976 anthology *All Our Secrets Are the Same.*[117] Moreover, among almost eight hundred writers whose manuscripts can be found in a subseries of Lish's papers at Indiana University — a list that includes virtually every writer ever mentioned in print as closely associated with Lish and hundreds of white writers from every corner of the U.S. — I could find only two who identified as African American, Ralph Ellison and James Alan McPherson.[118]

The magazine that Lish edited in the 1990s, the *Quarterly,* regularly published the Asian American poet Timothy Liu but not an enormous number of other writers of color.[119] One seeming exception to that pattern was a writer and artist named Yung Lung (or Ying Ling), but that may not have been an emerging Asian American writer and illustrator. Instead, it seems to have been a pseudonym under which the *Quarterly* published, on several occasions, writing and illustration that, in my opinion, bear a striking resemblance to the work of Lish's then-teenaged son, Atticus.[120] Atticus Lish has denied ever having shown his writing to his father, and as far as I am aware, no critics have mentioned "Yung Lung / Ying Ling," even during discussions of literary "yellowface" hoaxes.[121] As in those cases, though, if these writings and illustrations were indeed published under an invented Asian name (a name that one of Gordon Lish's correspondents referred to as "comic"), it would be difficult for me to understand except as reflecting a distressing disregard for Asian and Asian American writers and readers.[122]

The rarity of African American and Asian American writers on Lish's lists is especially striking given his interest in innovative, experimental prose. As scholars including Michael North and Joshua Miller have amply demonstrated, the linguistic innovations of U.S. modernism and postmodernism were often inspired and led by writers of color, and of course, many talented writers from such backgrounds were active and publishing during the decades that Lish developed his canon of avant-garde U.S. fiction.[123] Moreover, despite his having, on occasion, published some writers like A. B. Yehoshua, J. L. Borges, and Milan Kundera in translation in *Esquire* or elsewhere, Lish also stated explicitly that writing in translation did not interest him at all, which meant that he excluded from his serious consideration most writers from most of the world.[124] It could be argued that no literary editor can cover all the bases, and so these editors should be allowed to focus on whatever they want; but Lish's quite narrow interests matter, of course, because they suggest that he wielded his extraordinary literary influence in such a way that only a very select group of writers could benefit from it.

Put another way, it could be seen as justifying a concern about a so-called Jewish literary mafia that Lish, an extraordinarily influential American editor working at a series of nonsectarian publications and publishing houses, kept Jewish writers at the center of his editorial efforts, using his flair for promotion to win them exposure in venues that may have otherwise been unsympathetic to them, while excluding, if not by design, then in practice, writers from many other backgrounds.

Yet Lish was not in sync with, and did not garner much support from, other editors and institutions. He seems rather to have often alienated his peers at other magazines and publishing houses, including Jewish ones.[125] The writers on whom he bestowed his favor were not the ones who found widespread support elsewhere in the literary field. Of Lish's favored Jewish writers—Paley, Ozick, Brodkey, Elkin, and Michaels—the only one mentioned, in passing, as a beneficiary of a Jewish literary mafia in Kostelanetz's exhaustively detailed *The End of Intelligent Writing* (1974) is Michaels, and Lish himself is nowhere to be found there, despite his having been a few years into his celebrated run at *Esquire*

—

by the time Kostelanetz published the book and surely on Kostelanetz's radar. It would not make sense for Lish to appear there, though, because he did not align with the editors and critics whose putatively collusive behavior bothered Kostelanetz; on the contrary, Lish supported a distinct cadre of writers and had his own eccentric reasons for doing so, including an interest in inventive sentence-level prose and a vague but consistent and powerful commitment to Jewish solidarity.

What Jewish Editors Edit When They Edit Jews

Taken together, these cases of Knopf editors suggest that even when Jewish editors made decided efforts to publish Jewish writers, they had very specific ideas about what *kind* of Jewish literature they wanted to publish. Lish's case is also one example of a larger phenomenon, in which some Jewish editors relied on the Jewish writers on their lists, in one way or another, to help them think about their own relationships to literature or to Jewishness itself or to help them change the directions of their careers.

Similar examples are not difficult to find among other American editors in the postwar decades. At Simon & Schuster, Robert Gottlieb supported a "new wave of young Jewish writers" who "portrayed Jews as whining, complaining, neurotic, sex obsessed, and burdened with hellishly dominating mothers and weak fathers," but Gottlieb also especially appreciated Chaim Potok as his, and the United States', bestselling guide to a more knowledgeable, religious Judaism that Gottlieb felt he had missed growing up in a secular Jewish home.[126] The founder and publisher of Farrar, Straus & Giroux, Roger W. Straus Jr., and his wife, Dorothea, maintained relationships with Abraham Joshua Heschel and Isaac Bashevis Singer that far exceeded what was typical for authors and publishers: the Strauses attended Passover seders at Heschel's home and had Heschel officiate their son's bar mitzvah, while Singer helped Dorothea come to terms with her own Jewishness.[127] Ted Solotaroff's career as a literary critic and editor at *New American Review* and Harper & Row was never separable from his friendship with Philip Roth, whom he saw as a kindred spirit beginning in their graduate-student days in Chicago, in part because they were both Jews

from neighboring towns in New Jersey; Roth got Solotaroff the writing assign-
ment that led to his first editorial job, so in a very concrete sense, Solotaroff
owed his career to Roth.[128] While many editors did not leave oral histories or
memoirs that provide insights into their decision-making, intense relationships
based on ethnic solidarity are not unusual among those who did.

None of this substantiates claims about a Jewish literary mafia in U.S. publishing. Instead, it suggests that even as homophily operates for editors, it is
refracted, in each editor's case, through a particular and distinctive set of concerns and interests. Which makes perfect sense, because American Jews, in being
Jews, do not inevitably or invariably share any values, desires, or tastes.[129] Knowing that a particular editor is Jewish might make it likely that one will find some
Jewish writers on their lists but does not indicate what *kinds* of Jewish writers
they favor.

In other words, this chapter demonstrates two distinct but not contradictory
facts about the effects of Jews' prominence among literary gatekeepers in the
twentieth-century United States. The first fact is that it absolutely does matter
that Jews — unlike most other U.S. minority groups — had the opportunity to
occupy influential editorial roles on a regular basis. When one compares what
happens when Jews make a literary gatekeeping decision to what happens when
Protestants do so — as the history of National Book Award juries, and Ellison's
1953 award, allow us to do — it is starkly clear that Jews sometimes made
choices that had broad consequences for U.S. literary history overall. Such
choices were not inevitable because of Jews' Jewishness, of course, but it is not
difficult to divine the specific difference that Jewishness made in that case. When
we follow the career of an editor like Gordon Lish, we can see how not just
an individual or a group of writers but an entire aesthetic tendency — in his
case, one we can sometimes label as Jewish (if not exclusively so, then as one
Jewish possibility among many) — could attain publicity and institutional support through the efforts of a single committed gatekeeper.

The second fact, just as important, is that one cannot assume or predict *what*
difference Jewishness will make in an editorial or literary gatekeeping process.
We can examine that difference only *in retrospect*. Depending on the time, place,
and an individual's inclinations, a Jewish editor might be more or less likely to
publish this or that submission, and even if some historical cases suggest pat-

—

terns, it is irresponsible, racist, and just plain wrong to suppose that one can predict a person's literary tastes on the basis of their ethnic or religious identity. This last fact, more than anything else, undermines simplistic attacks on the Jewish literary mafia. It is not only, as those who reject such attacks often say, that New York literary intellectuals disagreed with one another more than they agreed; it is, more profoundly, that none of them, individually, sustained an ideology or program that articulated a set of principles about how to deploy the cultural power they had attained vis-à-vis Jewishness. Study any individual Jew's editorial career and you will find a complex and dynamic set of beliefs and impulses and both alignments with and rejections of various conventional aspects of Jewishness. That welter of possibilities does not make the work of gatekeeping simple or easy for a Jewish editor (they cannot, obviously, just fish all the Jewish names out of the slush pile and accept them), but it does give them considerably more power to influence what is published than someone from another demographic group who has been excluded from wielding editorial power on the basis of their identity, as has systematically been the case for many members of other minority groups in the U.S.

CHAPTER 2

TEACHERS AND STUDENTS

On Lionel Trilling's Blurbs

Jewish Professors and Jewish Students

It was a new possibility in the 1940s and 1950s that a Jewish college or graduate student, studying at the kind of elite university that often served as a training ground for a career in literature and publishing, could have, as one of their key mentors, a Jewish professor. Before then, and despite formal and informal quotas and other policies imposed by these institutions to limit the Jewish student population, there were *some* Jewish undergraduates at schools like Harvard, Yale, Princeton, and Columbia.[1] But if those Jewish students decided to study English and American literature, they would not have done so with professors who were Jewish, as there were virtually no Jews hired in that field until the 1940s.[2]

What happened when this changed? The key campus on which to answer this question is Columbia University, because for decades before the 1940s, a remarkable number of that school's graduates had already gone on to success in publishing, a pattern that owed to the geographic proximity between Columbia and the offices of New York–based publishers and that would continue into the postwar decades.[3] The key figure in a history of literary Jews at Columbia is, of course, Lionel Trilling, famously the first Jew tenured in the English department there and then, in his faculty role, both teacher and mentor to a vast number of the influential American literary professionals of the second half of

—

the twentieth century. Trilling himself had been a Jewish undergraduate at Columbia back in the 1920s and had studied with non-Jewish professors.[4] Because of this, Trilling understandably felt self-conscious about his own Jewishness when he began his teaching career, first during a stint at the University of Wisconsin: in a 1928 personal essay, "A Light to the Nations," he describes the reactions of two non-Jewish students there upon discovering that he, their teacher, was a Jew. More than their reactions, though, what is most striking about the essay is Trilling's forthright account of acting strategically in deciding whether to come out as Jewish to his students.[5]

When Trilling returned to Columbia to take up a teaching post, he encountered many Jewish students — and they, for the first time, had a celebrated professor of English literature who was Jewish, too. This shared Jewishness between Trilling and his students clearly mattered in the relationships that developed between them. In a 1951 *Commentary* symposium, Trilling was asked to reflect on whether Jewish college students had been changing in recent years and whether they had changed more or less than other American students. Trilling's response mostly argued against any specificity of the so-called Jewish student, past or present, though he also spoke out against practices that allowed for discrimination against them.[6] What is somewhat startling, though, is a stray observation: "Recently," he notes, "I have been struck by the number of well-heeled Jewish fathers, themselves without pretension to intellectual interests, who have expressed to me their perfect willingness and even their satisfaction that their sons should be drawn to academic careers."[7] This remark, aside from Trilling's actual point, raises a question: Why was Trilling talking regularly to the "Jewish fathers" of his students?

One way to answer that question is to say that while the Columbia student body was never close to entirely Jewish, and there were certainly always plenty of non-Jewish students in Trilling's classes, in the last three decades of his career, he seems to have maintained a particular rapport with, and a particular investment in, Jewish students specifically. In the case of one of them, Allen Ginsberg, that investment, including a relationship with Ginsberg's father, has been documented: Trilling met Ginsberg when the future poet was seventeen and enrolled as a freshman in Trilling's "Great Books" course, and for the next five years, he advised and advocated for Ginsberg, recommending him for jobs and helping Ginsberg's father, Louis, when Allen got into trouble with Columbia's administration and the police.[8] A long list of other Columbia students worked with Trilling over the years, and many of them have published accounts of their relationships with him. While not all of them were Jewish, Jews were certainly predominant among his protégés overall.[9] Surely, if Trilling had wanted to keep his distance from Jewish students and their families, he could have done so. Without assuming too much about the private motivations that determined many different relationships, it does not seem unfair to suggest that Trilling might be understood to have been expressing some kind of ethnic or cultural solidarity or affinity through these relationships — even if Trilling would probably have preferred not to describe the pattern in those terms. At least, such a suggestion aligns with the recollection of his wife, Diana Trilling, of how, at some point in the 1950s, when the English department at Columbia hired an instructor with a recognizably Jewish surname, Trilling came home with a noticeable "grin."[10]

As Trilling's reputation grew, he was well positioned to help his current and former students, from all backgrounds, who pursued literary careers, whether as scholars, editors, or writers. The means of that support were, increasingly in those decades, letters of recommendation or introduction and book blurbs. Though surely letters of recommendation and introduction, in one form or another, have existed as long as writing itself, such letters became increasingly formalized as a facet of U.S. literary dynamics in the postwar decades. This owed to the increasing degree to which American writers became members of academic communities, as Mark McGurl has influentially argued: as more American writers graduated from colleges and universities, enrolled in literature and creative-writing classes, sought residencies at artists' colonies, applied for and participated in MFA programs, and pursued jobs and tenure in academic institutions, more letters of recommendation piled up in the files of any individual writer or literary critic.[11] Meanwhile, for a variety of related reasons, book-jacket blurbs became increasingly plentiful on U.S. books of almost every kind in the same decades.[12]

For the most part, Trilling participated in this system with exemplary generosity. He vouched regularly for Columbia graduate students whose dissertations he had supervised, as one would expect, but also for undergraduates vying for fellowships. Often his interventions were decisive.[13] His letters regularly resulted in jobs being offered, fellowships being granted, and books being published. In a 1953 letter, acknowledging his record of success, Trilling made a joke suggesting he was just as good as an employment bureau: he wrote about one up-and-coming academic, "[He] got a job at Bard, I believe through my agency (The Trilling Cooperative Agency, I suppose)."[14] In pursuit of that effectiveness, Trilling was not above bending the truth if doing so would help a student he supported, though he would also pass the buck when he could appropriately do so, say, allowing someone else to reject writing he found weak.[15] But as generous as he was with letters of recommendation and introduction, both for his students and for colleagues and even for friends of his friends, it turned out in the 1950s that there was also a clear limit to what Trilling would do in support of other people's literary careers.

Trilling's Rule

Trilling's limit derived, it seems, from a shock he received at the breakfast table on the morning of September 23, 1953. Paging through that morning's *New York Times* over breakfast, Trilling came across an advertisement for Saul Bellow's new novel, *The Adventures of Augie March,* that contained an endorsement attributed to Trilling. The quotation came from a letter that Trilling had sent to the Viking Press editor Pat Covici in May of that year, with instructions that it could be read to Viking's salesmen at their conference but "not . . . used in any other connection." Trilling later recalled that he had even requested that the letter, full of extravagant praise, not be shown to Bellow himself.[16] It was not that Trilling was hesitant about his enthusiasm for Bellow's work; he had been praising the novelist energetically in private for years; for example, he and his wife, Diana, had called Bellow "the younger American novelist of most promise" at dinner with an officer of the Rockefeller Foundation two years earlier.[17] Still, the unauthorized exploitation of his words of praise for advertising purposes troubled Trilling.

As a result of that experience, Trilling explained repeatedly in the 1950s and

1960s, he "had to make a rule against giving statements for publication."[18] That this was a "rule" for him and not just a preference was a point he stressed, as in a 1960 letter: "I wish it were only a question of 'not liking to give quotes,' but the situation isn't that simple," he writes. He then describes three recent requests for blurbs. "If I say yes to all and my little words of praise all appear in the advertisements, I get to look silly and my praise comes to mean nothing. If I say yes to this or that one and no to that one or these ones, I am rude and unfriendly. So I must say nothing, which also makes me rude and unfriendly, but in a principled way."[19]

True to his word, Trilling often did "say nothing" for academic and professional colleagues and for friends; he also regularly rejected requests from former students.[20] It is worth emphasizing what Trilling understood as the danger of cavalier blurbing: not just that it would waste his time and not just that writing too many blurbs would make him "look silly." It is the danger that if too casually distributed, his praise would "mean nothing" – an idea that is both understandable (it accords with Gérard Genette's observation that because the blurb in the U.S. is "ritualistic" and "automatic," it is "deprive[d] of much of its power") and also not inevitably or obviously true.[21] After all, if all three books were truly praiseworthy and if Trilling praised them precisely and insightfully, why would this undermine anyone's faith in his judgment? Whether or not Trilling accurately apprehended the dynamics of what Mike McGuire calls the "literary blurb economy," Trilling's approach clearly reflects his desire to safeguard his influence, his symbolic capital.[22]

A reserve of capital, stockpiled and guarded jealously, will of course at some point be put to use, and Trilling was no exception. As he explained to an editor in 1963, "now and then," he could not "resist breaking" his rule about blurbs.[23] What Trilling did not say is that those rare instances in which his scruples were overcome bestowed the accumulated power of his reputation onto that exceptional book or writer. This makes it fascinating to consider the cases in which Trilling decided he could not resist. It turns out that Trilling broke his rule rarely and only for former Columbia students who could assimilate his own ideas about Jewishness and translate them into fiction and poetry in a way that Trilling himself could not.

—

Trilling's Jewishness

Trilling's ambivalence about Jewishness is a well-told tale. The son of Orthodox Jewish, unusually Anglophilic immigrants, he was born in 1905 and
grew up in Queens, matriculated at Columbia, and in his twenties began to
publish his writing in the *Menorah Journal,* a Jewish magazine. Then, in the
early 1930s, he turned decisively away from that journal and what it represented: without denying that he was Jewish, he sought less parochial venues
in which to explore questions about literature and politics and explicitly denied
that Jewishness influenced or inspired him.[24] Most famously, he wrote in a
symposium in 1944, "As the Jewish community now exists, it can give no sustenance to the American artist or intellectual who is born a Jew."[25] Meanwhile,
in the 1940s, he published a handful of short stories and a novel, *The Middle
of the Journey* (1947), and some reviews of the novel questioned why Trilling
had conspicuously avoided identifying any of its main characters as Jews.[26] He
did not publish any fiction after that but went on to produce increasingly widely
read essays and collections of criticism treating major touchstones of European
and U.S. culture, which included *The Liberal Imagination* (1950), *The Opposing
Self* (1955), *Beyond Culture* (1965), and *Sincerity and Authenticity* (1972). His
works came to serve as preeminent models for U.S. cultural criticism, and his
other professional activities — judging and writing for book clubs, teaching at
Columbia, editing a major textbook-cum-anthology, and discussing books on
radio and television — established him, in Irving Howe's phrase, as "the most
subtle and perhaps the most influential mind in the culture."[27] Depending on
who is telling it, this story carries distinct, if related, implications: about the
American intelligentsia, the ideological shift from communism to liberalism,
or the origins of neoconservatism, for example.[28]

Over the past two decades, scholars have also argued that Trilling was not
as distanced from Jewish issues as he himself claimed (even though they do not
deny the explicitness with which he asserted that distance). Trilling's dialectical
cast of mind, his refined prose style, his interest in Henry James, his references
to anti-Semitism and the Holocaust: all of these have been analyzed to suggest
the continued entanglement of his intellectual and literary drives, in the postwar
decades, with Jewishness.[29] Making such claims, critics tend to point out that

—

two of what Adam Kirsch calls Trilling's "most personal and suggestive essays," on Wordsworth (published in 1950) and Isaac Babel (in 1955), treat Jewish questions centrally.[30] Though some of Trilling's students recalled reacting, at that time, to his direct engagements with Jewishness with astonishment, suggesting how unusual they seemed, those essays, along with more obscure bits and pieces among Trilling's public and private writing, make it possible to read him as having always remained engaged, if always ambivalently, with Jewish culture.[31]

In attending to Trilling's recommendations and blurbs, this chapter reveals a heretofore unknown aspect of Trilling's role in the 1950s, as a mentor to Columbia students who became writers — specifically, the novelist Sam Astrachan, the poet Irving Feldman, and the short-story writer Ivan Gold — and brings into clearer focus his function as a node in the network of postwar U.S. literary production and circulation. Meanwhile, the chapter proposes a different way to think about Trilling's Jewishness. In a widely cited article, Mark Krupnick claims that "most of the important changes in [Trilling's] relation to his Jewishness, if we may judge from his writing, occurred between 1925 and 1950" and that, in the later years, "Trilling did not press the subject of his Jewishness."[32] But Krupnick's qualifying phrase is crucial, because if we judge *not* just from Trilling's published writing but also from the professional influence he wielded, quite a different picture emerges.

Sam Astrachan and the Jewish Family Saga

The first of three Jewish Columbia students to cause Trilling some anxiety about the application of his blurbing "rule" was Sam Astrachan, who did so, unintentionally, in the fall of 1955. On October 6 of that year, Trilling wrote to Robert Giroux, another one of his former students and a rising editorial star who had recently changed jobs, moving from the publishing house of Harcourt Brace to what was then called Farrar, Straus & Cudahy. Trilling was writing in anticipation of a problem that he expected would soon arise because Giroux had signed a contract to publish a first novel by Astrachan, a 1955 Columbia graduate whom Trilling had brought to Giroux's attention the previous month.

—

Trilling realized that in such a situation it might be expected for him to offer a blurb, and so he explained to Giroux, at length, his predicament and suggested an odd solution:

> I suppose that when you begin to promote the novel, you will want a statement from me to use in the advertising copy. I shall not, under the circumstances, very well be able to refuse it, but my giving it will be at some cost. For I have for some time made it a rule not to give pre-publication statements for promotion purposes. Reason is, of course, that I am very frequently asked for such statements. To say yes to some and not to others is an impossible situation for a man who has a great many book-writing friends and acquaintances. To say yes to all is to make one's name and opinion valueless. So I've established the rule to give no statements at all. I dislike having to do this, for publishers tell me that these statements really do have some use in selling a book. But I've never seen an alternative. Once an exception is made, the dyke is down—"You did it for X, why not for me?" I am, as I say, prepared to break the rule in Astrachan's case, and take the consequences, but I wonder if there is some way to get around my actually writing an opinion for publication? Could you, for instance, find a sentence in the letter I wrote you introducing Sam that might serve? Or summarizing the circumstance of my enthusiastic introduction? In sum: I will write a statement, if you want me to, but I'll be grateful if your ingenuity can find some way of indicating my strong support of the book without an *ad hoc* statement.[33]

In a more general form than in the letter quoted earlier, Trilling explains here why his rule is necessary and articulates in strikingly similar terms what worries him: his fear is that a wrong move could render his "name and opinion value-less." Was ever a writer more explicit about his covetousness of symbolic capital?

The "circumstances" that made it seem unavoidable, in Astrachan's case, "to break the rule" are simple enough to sketch: Trilling's recommendations of Astrachan's work had been instrumental in getting his work published. Astrachan, who was born in 1934 in the East Bronx, had graduated from Columbia a few months before Trilling wrote his letter. During Astrachan's undergraduate years, Trilling had gotten to know him, read his work in the *Columbia Review*, and liked him. Trilling's sympathy for Astrachan may have been bolstered by similarities in their family histories—Astrachan's uncles, like Trilling's father, had been eastern European Jewish immigrants to the U.S. who sold furs—or by the fact that Astrachan's parents died while he was a teenager. For those reasons and whatever other psychological, stylistic, or aesthetic affinities between the two men, Trilling felt very strongly about Astrachan, personally and profession-ally. In June 1955, he wrote to a mutual acquaintance, "I have the greatest re-spect for [Astrachan] as a person, as well as high admiration for his talent. I think I have never known anyone who had at so early an age so clear a moral and artistic direction."[34]

Acting on that respect and admiration, Trilling had orchestrated Astrachan's professional debut with remarkable efficacy. At the beginning of April 1955, looking ahead to Astrachan's graduation in June, Trilling had written to Eliza-beth Ames, the director of Yaddo, and requested a spot for the young man for the summer at the writers' colony, where he could complete the novel he had begun.[35] She agreed. When Astrachan returned to the city in August, Trilling introduced him to Giroux, noting how exceptional this was: "I almost never get myself involved with students who are devoted to creative writing, as it is called nowadays," Trilling wrote.[36] Giroux "read [the novel] in one sitting" and agreed to publish it. Both Giroux and his boss, Roger Straus Jr., wrote to Trilling en-thusiastically, praising Astrachan's novel, *An End to Dying,* and a few days later, Straus informed Trilling that the book had sold to the British publisher Victor Gollancz for "an advance of $1500, sight unseen, on the basis of [Trilling's] enthusiasm and the enthusiasm of Bob [Giroux] and [Straus himself]."[37]

It had been Straus's letter indicating the extraordinary power of Trilling's "enthusiasm"—a $1,500 advance on an unread manuscript by a debut author being quite a powerful effect—that occasioned Trilling's anxious letter to Giroux, invoking his blurb rule. His concern was not misplaced; Giroux had already written, in an internal memo, that the publisher "ought to take a lot of time and do a proper build-up, with advance quotes from people like Bellow, and Trilling . . . and [Alfred] Kazin."[38] Part of Trilling's anxiety may be explained by the fact that, at this point, he had not yet read Astrachan's complete manuscript and so could not be sure of what he would think about it as a whole. He had written to Giroux on September 13, "however strongly one recommends a new and young talent one always has a soft spot of diffidence about it and I feel relieved and gratified that your opinion of the whole book should confirm what I felt about the portion of it that I've read."[39] This may likewise explain why Trilling suggested that Giroux draw a statement of support out of one of his previous letters, rather than his writing a new statement expressly for promotion: the latter would have required him to read the "whole book."

Whether because Giroux could not or did not want to follow Trilling's suggestions, *An End to Dying* appeared without promotional blurbs from Trilling (or anyone else), though its paratexts were hardly subtle in emphasizing Astrachan's background. The book's front cover unusually proclaimed it "a first novel," while the back cover explained that "Mr. Astrachan wrote most of this book during his junior and senior years at college and completed it at Yaddo in the summer of 1955."[40] Astrachan, looking over the book jacket in advance of publication, objected not to the absence of a blurb or the presence of other biographical details but to the gloomy author photograph and to the claim — probably Giroux's — on the inside flap that "this is not another autobiographical novel of groping youth." Astrachan insisted that the book *was* autobiographical (and *Commentary*'s reviewer caught this, too, beginning her review with a roll of her eyes at the jacket copy; *Library Journal* called the book "obviously autobiographical").[41] None of the reviewers linked Astrachan with Trilling, mentioning Thomas Wolfe and Dostoyevsky as the relevant comparisons for Astrachan's style and for the novel's effects.

What *was* mentioned in almost every review — though strangely not in the *Springfield Republican*, which called the novel's Kagans and Cohens a "Russian family" — was the book's intense engagement with Jewishness. The review in *Booklist*, for example, praised it as a "strong, well-controlled story of people held together not only by love but also by their common heritage of Judaism."[42] What is remarkable about the novel, in retrospect, is not its execution — a point on which the mixed reviews agreed with the author himself, who, after looking over the galleys, called the book "very uneven" — but the ambition of its attempt to cover so much recent Jewish history, a project that one could by no means take for granted would appeal in the mid-1950s to Anglo-American critics or audiences.[43] Indeed, the British publisher, Gollancz, who reneged on his contract to publish Astrachan's novel once he got around to actually reading it, characterized its subject matter ("Russian background, immigration into America") as "positively repellent."[44]

Narrated by an autobiographical stand-in for the author—whose name, Sam Star, could suggest Astrachan's vision of himself as a celebrity waiting to be discovered—*An End to Dying* aspires to relate not just a young man's maturation but his complete family history, a project emphasized by the genealogy of "The Kagan-Cohen Family" that precedes the first chapter. The novel's first half focuses on Sam's uncle Jacob Kagan, the grandson of a nearly illiterate fur trader and son of a lumberyard foreman in Russia. Jacob vigorously contradicts the stereotype of the pale eastern European Jewish scholar: a giant, "the best wrestler in Nishkovitz," he "could lift a man over his head and throw him twenty feet" (31). Refusing to dodge the czar's draft in 1904, he is shot in the leg by his own anti-Semitic officer at the Japanese front. Upon his return to his village, he decides to seek wealth: "Not even the czar will spit at a millionaire" (49), he reasons. Übermensch that he is ("the truth of life is power," he remarks [113]), he is soon the richest Jew in Russia.

The novel's second half traces the degeneration of a hardy family of nature-loving Russian-Jewish lumbermen, the Kagans, into a tribe of slick American Jewish shysters, the Cohens. Like the Kagans, the Cohens earn vast fortunes; one of Sam's uncles is featured in *Fortune*, lauded as "a poor boy who now controlled millions of dollars" (200). Sam perceives this not as a happy example of American success but as a tremendous loss of vitality: "I hate West End Avenue Jews," he remarks. "They're all fakes" (187). As Suzanne Silberstein pointed out in her *Commentary* review, Sam personifies Hansen's Law, an immigration historian's well-known prediction that third-generation Americans will dismiss their assimilating parents as spiritually bankrupt and idolize their old-country ancestors.[45] "I cry," Sam proclaims, "for all the sons and daughters sucked into the watered-down version of their parents' watered-down new world existence" (221). Sam recognizes this emptiness seeping into literature, too: he admires a Yiddish storyteller, Shmyola Bernstein, who hangs around with his family in Russia and France, while he disdains Jess Kraut, an American Jewish writer who does not understand Yiddish and has not heard of Bernstein. For the ambitious and commercially inclined Kraut, "in business and art . . . it's the same thing," while for the sympathetic Bernstein, "a Jew must always work

—

with the knowledge that he is a Jew" (233). In the novel's effort to follow four generations of a Jewish family, it includes many vignettes and set pieces, inter-polating brief scenes set at Sam's bar mitzvah in 1946, as well as the Yiddish tales of Shmyola Bernstein. Everything in Astrachan's novel accentuates a stark contrast between the vivid, energetic Jews of eastern Europe and the unpleasant, contemptible Jews of contemporary New York.

Astrachan's embrace of an earthy Russian Jewish past and his rejection of the materialistic American Jewish present aligns precisely with Trilling's attitudes about Jews. In his essay on Isaac Babel, which was published in *Commentary* and as the introduction to Babel's *Collected Stories* in 1955, Trilling argued that Babel's fascination with two qualities "made his art": the brutal violence of the Cossacks and the soulfulness of poor Polish Jews. In Trilling's account, these qualities contrast with an intellectual effeteness that Babel associated with his father ("a shopkeeper, not well-to-do, a serious man, a failure") and the spiritual bankruptcy that he perceived in "the wealthy assimilated Jews of Petersburg."[46] As apt as this may have been as a description of Babel's inspiration, the essay, as Krupnick has noted, "reveals Trilling's knack for investing a literary-critical appreciation with his own wished-for way of being," and the critique of a bour-geois Jewish community clearly drew from Trilling's existing perspectives.[47] Trilling had been among the students opposing "Babbitry" on the staff of the *Columbia Morningside* as early as his undergraduate days, and much of the en-ergy of the *Menorah Journal* as a whole, during the time Trilling was associated with it, was devoted to critiques of middle-class Jewish small-mindedness.[48] More recently, in Trilling's often quoted "Under Forty" symposium comments, published in 1944, he had abjured precisely those assimilated, successful Amer-ican Jews, "the Jewish social group on its middle and wealthy levels," which was "one of the most self-indulgent and self-admiring groups it is possible to imag-ine." It was to that specific demographic subgroup that Trilling directed his remark that "as the Jewish community now exists it" — like the assimilating Odessa Jewish community in which Babel was raised — "can give no sustenance to the American artist or intellectual who is born a Jew."[49]

Astrachan's Jacob Kagan personifies the qualities that Trilling projected onto and admired in both Babel's Polish Jews and his Cossacks. This was not a co-incidence. Astrachan had read Trilling's essay on Babel during his summer at

Yaddo, and he wrote his professor an enthusiastic letter, pointing out the continuities: "Just today I read . . . your article on Isaac Babel. Certainly, if the Jew is to accept the heritage not simply of the ghetto and the concentration camps, but of the Old Testament, he must search out the primitive and appreciate that purity of action. In the first part of my book, Kagan must be seen as a man of natural force and abilities, to be contrasted in the second part with the new-type ghetto mediocrity of the family after arrival in New York City."[50] Whatever else *An End to Dying* was, and whether it succeeded or failed, it was an attempt to write a Jewish family chronicle, an updated version of Ludwig Lewisohn's *The Island Within* (1925) or Charles Reznikoff's *By the Rivers of Manhattan* (1930) that would align with the power and message of Babel's stories as Trilling had understood them. Astrachan explained this to Trilling two months *before* Trilling introduced him to Giroux, setting him on the road to publication — which means that Trilling championed a student who had explicitly understood himself to be assimilating the ideas about Jewishness that Trilling had expressed in a recent essay (and had, on some level, been formulating in symposia, speeches, fiction, and criticism since the 1920s) and transmuting them into fiction, which Trilling had been unable to do. That Trilling supported Astrachan because Astrachan was able to write what Trilling himself could not was obvious, at least to the younger man: Trilling's "support was that of a father," Astrachan recalled in an interview in 2008: "[He] let himself think that he himself might want to be living the life that I was living. Because he always wanted to be a writer, a fiction writer."[51]

Though Astrachan's career did not bring him as much critical acclaim as he or Trilling might have hoped for, its earliest phase demonstrates Trilling's extraordinary influence in the 1950s.[52] *An End to Dying* would certainly not have been completed or published as quickly without Trilling's letters on Astrachan's behalf. The novel also exemplifies the degree to which a student can serve, self-consciously and with both parties' knowledge, less as a disciple than as a proxy.

Irving Feldman and Jewish Languages

Irving Feldman (1928–) was a few years older than Astrachan, but he connected with Trilling in the same years. Having received his BA from City Col-

—

73

lege, he came to Columbia for a master's in the early 1950s, graduating in 1953. In the years that followed, while teaching at universities in Puerto Rico and France, Feldman began publishing poems in venues including the *Atlantic,* the *Nation, Poetry, Partisan Review,* and the *New Yorker.* His output increased in frequency throughout the decade, to a crescendo in 1960, during which single year he published poems in three separate issues of the *Carleton Miscellany,* four issues of *New World Writing,* and two issues of the *Atlantic Monthly,* as well as in *Kenyon Review, Portfolio and Art News Annual,* and *Commentary.* When his first book of poetry was published by Little, Brown, in the fall of 1961, its back cover featured two large blurbs. One came from John Crowe Ransom — who had helped to hire Feldman at Kenyon College in 1958 — and the other from Trilling:

> For some years now I have read Irving Feldman's verse with great pleasure and admiration — it makes for me the most interesting and satisfying body of work that any of the younger poets has yet produced. It has a remarkable lyric freshness and at the same time a quality of intellectual strength which does not in the least limit, rather enhances, the warmth and intensity of its feeling. It seems to me a more than usually large body of work for so young a man to have produced — Mr. Feldman writes freely and happily, and this seems to me to be in itself a virtue, the more so because the considerable size of the production allows for a notable variousness of theme and mood.[53]

Trilling's blurb for Feldman's collection followed years of steady correspondence, in which Feldman solicited Trilling's reactions to poems as he wrote them, exchanged ideas about art and culture, and asked, again and again and again, for Trilling's professional assistance. Trilling helped Feldman even more generously than he had helped Astrachan and much more often; he recommended him for fellowships and jobs tirelessly and advocated on his behalf with editors over and over. He recommended Feldman's collection to Giroux in 1954 and to Pat Covici in 1956. The editor who finally agreed to publish it, Seymour Lawrence, wrote to Trilling in 1960 to say, "Your candid and affirmative opinion of Irving Feldman's work . . . will be of immeasurable help to our board in reaching a final decision."[54] Trilling sent Feldman's work to W. H. Auden and to

—

Philip Rahv at *Partisan Review.*[55] He was responsible for Feldman's poems being published in *Commentary,* too: Feldman wrote in 1956, "Your command to [Norman] Podhoretz to print a poem of mine worked like a charm," explaining that "The Saint," which *Commentary* published in December of that year, had already been rejected by the magazine (probably, as Feldman assumed, because the editors had not even bothered to read it the first time he submitted it, without Trilling's backing).[56] These interactions reflect the extraordinary power of Trilling's recommendations.

Feldman frequently apologized for needing so much of Trilling's help (and wrote charmingly, at times, about the awkwardness of the requests), but he also suggested, at a few different moments, how central Trilling's support was to his own poetic vocation.[57] In the summer of 1954, Feldman wrote Trilling, "You know that I hate to trouble you for favor after favor — especially when I can offer in return no more than the writing of a good poem from time to time. But it is an important incentive to me to think that this is what you wish of me."[58] In other words, Trilling's willingness to support Feldman was, in and of itself, "incentive" to continue writing. Later that year, Feldman suggested that Trilling was playing an even more striking role. Distraught, Feldman remarked, "My poems are turned down with such regularity by editors that, believing in myself as I do, I begin to suspect my sanity. I know that my poems are good and real and sometimes even beautiful. If you don't mind playing alienist, let me know whether I am mad like your Tertan was."[59] Aside from the striking *chutzpah* of comparing himself to a character in Trilling's most famous short story, this comment also proposes, at least in jest, that Trilling's judgment of Feldman's work as worthwhile has the power to affirm Feldman's sanity. On a more practical level, because Feldman typically sent Trilling a few of his unpublished poems with every letter, he was not exaggerating when he described his first collection as follows: "Imagine all the poems I've been sending for the 3 or 4 years plus a number of other good poems."[60] The book published in 1961 as *Works and Days* was, in that sense, a direct product of their correspondence.

As in Astrachan's case, in Feldman's there was something slightly off-kilter between Trilling's engagement with Feldman's work and the enthusiasm (and effectiveness) with which Trilling advocated for Feldman. In July 1961, as publication neared, Feldman wrote to Trilling that he had just seen Trilling's blurb

—

75

for the first time, "quoted in the Little, Brown Catalog advertisement": "Naturally, I'm very pleased and flattered by your high praise – and it is, I think, the first time I've had your direct comment on my poems. . . . I think when you are able to see the book as a whole you will have no cause to regret what you say. Most important, your statement, if Atlantic uses it on the jacket and in its advertising, will go as far as anything possibly could to assure the poems a serious reading."[61] It was not precisely true that Trilling had not commented on Feldman's poems before. In their letters, Trilling would from time to time, if not consistently, respond to individual poems with precise suggestions – but Feldman was reacting to the blurb as the first time he had seen Trilling offer a broad assessment of his talents as a poet in general. Which is to say that despite the length of their correspondence and all the recommendations Trilling had written for Feldman, Trilling had not been especially effusive or specific about what it was in Feldman's poems that he felt merited his support. In fact, Trilling may simply have not felt especially confident about his judgment of the poems; thanking the editor Catharine Carver for a supportive rejection she sent Feldman in 1955, Trilling expressed his gratification that she found him "good": "I'm never quite sure of my judgment of unknown poets, especially if I know them personally (whether for good or for bad)."[62] Obviously, that uncertainty did not stop Trilling from writing letters for Feldman or from breaking his rule about blurbing in the case of *Works and Days.*

Trilling's blurb certainly did help "to assure the poems a serious reading," on the evidence of many reviews that mentioned it. The other facet of the collection that occasioned the most comment was the collection's exploration of Jewish questions and themes. In *Poetry,* Alan Dugan quipped that Feldman "has been called a religious poet fairly often" but that "to the extent that it is true, it should not be held against him."[63] In the *Times Literary Supplement,* a reviewer noted that of Feldman's autobiographical material, the poet "makes a great deal, particularly of his Jewishness."[64] In the *Saturday Review,* the reviewer called it "one of the most remarkable first books of poems in years," remarking that though "the Wandering Jew" is "explicitly the subject of only a few poems," the figure "is nevertheless the great presence who moves through these pages."[65] In *Commentary,* as one might expect, this aspect of Feldman's poetry was celebrated. The review remarked, "Mr. Feldman derives much of his strength as a

—

writer from his complex and intense struggle to define himself. His somber vision of existence . . . is that of a man who is at once religious and skeptical: the tormented Jew who is resigned to his inheritance and yet critical of it. . . . These poems are rooted in Feldman's commitment to a perspective which is peculiarly Jewish; one which is personal but is at the same time ancient and general."[66] Anthony Thwaite, writing for the *Spectator,* noticed that this distinguishing aspect of Feldman's work had gone unmentioned in his blurbs: "The jacket quotes glowing testimonials by John Crowe Ransom and Lionel Trilling; they speak of Mr. Feldman's versatility, passion and lyric freshness. All this he has, but more remarkable to me is his actual subject-matter. His poems cover the whole span of Jewish temper and experience, from mystical exultation to harsh incisive satire, from poems . . . which tremble on the edge of frivolous whimsy to others which brood long and hard on the problems of a race both chosen and rejected."[67] It is worth restating this striking critical judgment from a nonsectarian poet and reviewer of poetry, writing not in *Commentary* but in, of all things, a general-interest British magazine: Feldman's Jewish "subject-matter" is "more remarkable" than the fact that he writes with "versatility, passion, and lyric freshness."

Such a reaction suggests the changing status at that time of Jewishness in Anglo-American literature. As Leslie Fiedler pointed out in *Poetry* the previous summer, while "everywhere in the realm of prose Jewish writers have discovered their Jewishness to be an eminently marketable commodity, . . . Jewish poets have not prospered in a time of cultural philo-Semitism as have their opposite numbers."[68] So when Feldman's *Works and Days* appeared in 1961, there was reason to expect that such a poet, who demonstrated irreproachable Western culture credentials and a facility with traditional forms, would be greeted warmly for offering up a collection that explored "the whole span of Jewish temper and experience."

To manifest comfort in both areas was, without question, the project of *Works and Days.* The book proclaims Feldman's facility with Western culture by including monologues spoken by figures from the Western canon, Prometheus and Cato and Narcissus, and responses to the works of Herodotus, Goya, and Michelangelo. Other poems take similar approaches to Jewish figures and texts, with monologues for Abraham and Moses and a response to David Rousset's

L'univers concentrationnaire (1946). Meanwhile, Feldman's autobiographical poems in the collection playfully, sometimes nostalgically, evoke a Jewish New York childhood, including everything from biblical allusions (especially Psalm 137: "If I forget thee not, New York" [66]; "O Jerusalem, if I forget thee" [94]) to little rhyming jokes using Yinglish dialect spelling (rhyming "rich" with "Miami Bich" [98], à la Allan Sherman). Playful and comic as these poems often are, others treat religious commitment and the struggle to maintain faith with deep seriousness: one poem, "The Hand," strikingly offers a lyrical description of the festival of Simchat Torah (*Works and Days*, 73–75). The poems dealing with Jewish figures and religious practices resonate with Feldman's caustic review of Karl Shapiro's *Poems of a Jew* (1958), which was also criticized by Fiedler in *Poetry*. Feldman had noted in his review the absence of "out-and-out Jewish figures" and "Jewish holidays and ceremonies" in Shapiro's poems, at the same time that he was including such tropes and figures in his own.[69]

Meanwhile, *Works and Days* implies that its anticipated reader is not necessarily as well versed in Jewish languages as Feldman himself is. While the book offers no glosses for most of his allusions to Western culture – one exception is a note, on the poem titled "The Death of Vitellozzo Vitelli," that the title figure was "murdered by Cesare Borgia in 1502" (14) – Feldman presents explanatory notes at two key instances in which Jewish languages are invoked. In "To a Third-Generation Israeli Girl," the speaker expounds on an "irony" about how Jews who left Europe for Palestine in the first half of the twentieth century avoided, or were spared, the Holocaust. The poem ends with the rhyme, "Yet once Israel knew / How father Jacob labored for his Ewe," which is glossed with a note: "Jacob was also named Israel; 'Rachel' is the Hebrew for 'ewe'" (77). The note indicates an expectation that even if Feldman's anticipated reader knows the basic stories of Genesis, they probably will not know enough Hebrew to pick up on his wordplay with these characters' names.

The other example appears in the collection's final poem, "The Lost Language," making it, remarkably, the very last word of the book. The poem, which gathers snippets of language from Themistocles and Louis XV, *The Pirates of Penzance* and the American Transcendentalists, asks a question to which Feldman would return in a number of his most celebrated later works: What is left for a Jewish poet to say after the Holocaust? As Feldman's speaker phrases it here, "it's only disgrace, / At the very best, to outlive . . . / The saddest thing in the life of the race." The central problem that the poem confronts is that whereas words once had power (when words "were the things they named / And lay like manna in easy reach"), now they ring hollow: "I have eaten all my words, / And still I am not satisfied." Developing a conceit of words as food that has lost its nutritional value, the poem ends with a rhyming couplet: "One cup of Lethe and it's always too late. / Where are you, o *liebe breyt?*" The note that follows reads, "Yiddish for 'bread'" (120–21).

That note did not appear when the poem was first published in *Commentary,* in January 1960, which suggests it was added in the book to account for a different anticipated reader, who, unlike the presumed *Commentary* reader, knew no Yiddish.[70] Strangely, though, the note translates only the final Yiddish noun and not the preceding adjective (*liebe,* which in conventional Yiddish transliteration would be *libe,* meaning "dear"). The couplet, drawing together a reference to Greek mythology (Lethe, whose waters allow one to forget) and a culminating phrase that mixes an Anglophilic, early-modern "o" with a snippet of humble Yiddish, supplies a fitting ending for the collection, as it captures in miniature Feldman's efforts to demonstrate his fluency in the symbols and texts of the Western canon while also drawing on the textures of contemporary Jewish experience.

Treating many of the major issues of postwar Jewish life — the Holocaust, the State of Israel, the socioeconomic transformations experienced by Jews in the United States — and demonstrating facility in several different poetic modes, *Works and Days,* however uneven, should be understood as a landmark in American Jewish poetry. Indeed, it won the prize for the best work of 1961 Jewish poetry in English given by the Jewish Book Council, and Feldman, despite remaining not especially well-known, went on to receive many other awards, including a MacArthur Fellowship in 1992.[71] Trilling's generous encouragement of Feldman's career reflects his support for literary work that was frankly and unapologetically Jewish — though also, not incidentally, at the same time, invested in demonstrating a lack of parochialism, a wide frame of reference, and traditional formal skill. And, as in the case of Astrachan's work, perhaps it also points to what Trilling was simply not able to achieve in his own writing, as much as he might have liked to.

—

Specifically, Trilling's published statements suggest that his apparent lack of engagement with Jewish issues may have owed less to acts of will that he sometimes emphasized and more to a lack of ability that he acknowledged at other times. In the "Under Forty" symposium in which he denied that Jewishness influenced him, he remarked, "I can have no pride in seeing a long tradition, often great and heroic, reduced to this small status in me," a humble statement that speaks to Trilling's lack of familiarity and facility with Jewish sources: in Trilling, he himself acknowledges, there is simply not much of the Jewish textual and intellectual tradition left.[72]

In "Wordsworth and the Iron Time" (republished as "Wordsworth and the Rabbis"), Trilling begins his discussion of Wordsworth's putative "Judaic quality" with an admission about his own unsuitability to the task: "My own knowledge of Jewish tradition is, I fear, all too slight to permit me to hope that I can develop this new hypothesis in any very enlightening way."[73] He notes, later, that as a child he read *Pirkei Avot,* a famous chapter of the *Mishnah,* in English translation: "when I was supposed to be reading my prayers, very long and in the Hebrew language which I never mastered."[74] It is no disrespect to Trilling to point out that the prayer service is not especially long and that many children in Jewish schools, who are far from masters of the Hebrew language, manage to muddle their way through it on a regular basis. In a footnote to his essay, Trilling mentions that he has consulted two different translations and goes on to remark, "In my quotations I have drawn upon both versions. Sometimes, when it suited my point, I have combined two versions in a single quotation."[75] There is nothing wrong with that, but it seems likely that a critic who had the ability to read the text in its original language would also mention consulting that. Trilling did not; he never, in the essay, refers to the Hebrew text of *Pirkei Avot* to test or complicate the translations. As such, he offers another reminder of just how little Hebrew he knows. Which is perhaps to be expected, especially given his well-known family history: the story told about Trilling's father is that, as a boy in Bialystock, he was destined for a distinguished rabbinical career until he stumbled over the Hebrew of his bar mitzvah portion ("he forgot his lines," Diana Trilling supposes).[76] Trilling himself apparently did somewhat better at age thirteen but retained little Hebrew into adulthood.

—

Trilling also seems not to have known any Yiddish. Whatever his attitudes about the language might have been, his published work suggests he was ignorant of basic Yiddish vocabulary and grammar.[77] Edward Alexander points out that "the only time that Trilling uses a Yiddish word" in his essay on Babel, he "produces a howler: 'shtetln' instead of 'shtetlach' as the plural of 'shtetl.'"[78] As Jonathan Brent notes, discussing the same essay, Trilling also "cites approvingly Maurice Samuels' preposterous assertion 'that in the Yiddish vocabulary of the Jews of eastern Europe there are but two flower names (rose, violet) and no names for wild birds.'"[79] Of course, that Trilling did not speak Yiddish is not a strike against him; his parents were not Yiddish speakers, and he apparently did not hear the language at home as a child. Interestingly, though, Trilling was by no means uninterested in the language. At least, writing to Astrachan in May 1960, he reported his "long continuing desire to write a history of the last days of the Warsaw ghetto" ("really a history," as opposed to John Hersey's fictionalization in *The Wall*, which had "distressed" him), concluding, "if I could read Yiddish and Polish, I would really try it."[80]

In 1960, then, Trilling explicitly recognized what would in the following decade and a half become more and more obvious: that there were valuable, necessary American writing projects concerning the experiences of modern Jews—works treating, among other things, like Feldman's first book, the Holocaust, the foundation of the State of Israel, and the history of Jews in the United States—that required facility in Jewish languages that Trilling did not possess. But some of the students Trilling connected with at Columbia, like Feldman, *could* read or speak those languages to some greater or lesser degree, and some of them were talented, dedicated writers in English, dazzlingly well versed in the Western canon, too. Again, for reasons of temperament and experience, Trilling could not write what his students could: just as he had neither the family experience nor the novelistic skills to attempt the kind of multigenerational epic that Astrachan had produced, he could not have begun to craft the complex multilingual wordplay with which Feldman, at key moments, addresses modern Jewish experiences in *Works and Days*. But Trilling *could* offer extraordinary support to Feldman, making it possible for his work to be published and to receive critical attention.

—

Ivan Gold and Jews among Others

It was Trilling's former teacher and current colleague, Mark Van Doren, who first singled out a third Columbia undergraduate, Ivan Gold, as a promising writer in the early 1950s. According to the journalist Dan Wakefield's memoir, Van Doren interrupted one of his own classes to insist that his students read and respond to Gold's short story "A Change of Air," which had won a prize from a Columbia student magazine. Afterward, Van Doren submitted the story to the editors of *New World Writing,* where it was published after Gold's graduation, in 1953.[81] But Trilling's mentorship seems to have been more consequential than Van Doren's, at least according to Gold's novel-*cum*-memoir *Sams in a Dry Season* (1990). There, Gold reflects on his relationship to Trilling, recalling, for example, "the memorable occasion [when] the pair of them had taken a leak at the Columbia faculty club at adjacent urinals."[82] According to Wakefield's recollections, it was Trilling who had warned Gold away from further study in the spring of 1953, as graduation loomed: "If you want to write," the professor reportedly told Gold, "stay away from graduate school."[83] Following Trilling's advice, Gold was drafted, and as it turned out, three of the four new stories included in his debut collection, *Nickel Miseries* (1963), were inspired directly by his military service (the fifth was the one that had originally caught Van Doren's eye, a decade earlier). In that sense, at least, Trilling's advice had been decisive in providing Gold's literary career its direction.

Fittingly, then, it was a blurb from Trilling that helped to launch *Nickel Miseries.* Alone on the back cover of the book jacket, in a remarkably large font, and then again in an advertisement covering a sixth of a page in the *New York Times Book Review,* Trilling's name appeared alongside a statement in which he expressed his hopes for Gold's career:

> Some ten years ago, in *The Columbia Review,* the Columbia College literary
> magazine, I came on a story which startled me by its power and originality. I
> could scarcely believe that it had been written by an undergraduate, for it had a
> sureness of touch, a richness of detail, and a sense of performance such as are
> hardly ever to be seen in the writing of very young men. No less impressive than
> its brilliance of manner was the bold originality of its moral conception. Ivan

—

Gold's "A Change of Air" stayed in my memory as one of the most moving stories I had ever read. . . .

The stories that follow "A Change of Air" in *Nickel Miseries* make it plain that Mr. Gold had gone on as one would hope—masterly in themselves, they give promise of an even further development which will make Mr. Gold one of the commanding writers of our time.[84]

This was, obviously, another exception to what Trilling referred to as his "rule against giving statements for promotion purposes": "Now and then I can't resist breaking it, as in Ivan Gold's case," he wrote a few months later, in an attempt "to establish [the rule] again" by refusing to provide another such a statement for a biography of Keats.[85] As in the cases of Astrachan and Feldman, Trilling's support for Gold, which had also included recommendations to Yaddo and to the Guggenheim Foundation, was out of the ordinary for him, and as in those cases, it is not clear that he had carefully or recently read Gold's work.[86] (He did not remember the title of "A Change of Air" at the time when he agreed to blurb *Nickel Miseries*—he submitted his blurb with the title of the story left blank, expecting Gold's editor to fill in the proper title and dates to accord with his vague recollection.)[87] What was it about Gold's work, then, that earned him Trilling's support?

To answer this question, it is necessary to consider both the individual stories Gold had written and the project as a whole. Gold's literary imagination was fundamentally autobiographical; this became obvious with his two novels—*Sick Friends* (1969) and *Sams in a Dry Season* (1990)—which present a character named Jason Sams who shares Gold's biography.[88] *Nickel Miseries* at first blush seems much more varied in the backgrounds of its characters, a quality that reviewers noted and praised.[89] The first story, "A Change of Air," concerns a group of young men on the East Side of New York; the second is a monologue spoken by a Japanese sex worker; the third tells the story of a couple of African Americans in basic training; the fourth is set on a cargo ship off the coast of Spain; and the fifth is set among the personnel on a U.S. Army base in central Japan. Yet, for all the variety of these stories' settings, each reflects Gold's lived experiences, and they suggest the ways that Gold's perspective was informed by but also extended well beyond his experiences as a Jewish kid from New

—

York (like Trilling, Astrachan, and Feldman). In particular, Gold's fiction demonstrated his thoughtfulness about the relationship between Jews and other ethnic or racial groups, in the U.S. and outside it.

Gold's first published story, "A Change of Air," for example, is a moving story about the area of New York City that would come to be called the Lower East Side, with its unique legacy for American Jews and, during the years Gold was growing up there, already a gritty cosmopolitanism that brought Jews into contact with more recent immigrants.[90] Gold had been raised in the Colonial Hall building on East Third Street between Avenues A and B, by Orthodox Jewish parents.[91] "A Change of Air" centers on teenage boys from that neighborhood who met at high school.[92] In a sense, these are the same sort of tough city kids who had been the subjects of Irving Shulman's bestseller *The Amboy Dukes* (1947). Indeed, Gold's story begins by recalling one kind of event that Shulman had described as a typical, if highly distressing, practice of New York's youth gangs: the sexual sharing of women — sex workers or not, forcibly or not — by gang members.[93] The first section of "A Change of Air" describes a nineteen-year-old girl, Bobbie Bedmer, who "was taken, or rather had, one hundred and sixty times during seventy hours by a total of fifty-three persons (the entire membership of the Werewolves, their young brothers and friends) of all nationalities and sizes" (3).

Gold offers a strikingly calm recital of the kind of scandalous sexual practice that Shulman treated sensationally. The remark that the membership of this East Side gang encompasses "all nationalities" is, of course, a jokey exaggeration but not an incidental one. Contrary to what some reviewers implied, the story is not really about this attempt "to make East Side of New York (and possibly national) history" in the field of orgiastic sexuality (2) — it is about a night two years later, when a group of teenage boys cruising in a car run into Bedmer, who has recently returned from "Rehabilitation School," on the corner of First Avenue and Twenty-Sixth Street. Four of the guys are college students who know one another from high school, and the fifth is another friend. Two of them, Frank DeTorres and Joe Muñeco, are introduced explicitly as Puerto Ricans who had been members of the Werewolves at the time of Bedmer's incident; DeTorres, the narrator informs the reader, was "the first on line [with Bedmer], then . . . thirty-first, and again one hundred and sixth" (5). The other three men are given names that may or may not be Jewish but suggest that they are probably white ethnics of one sort or another: Phillip Zand, Jay Miller, and Benjamin Brock. The last of them to be introduced, Brock, is clearly Gold's fictional alter ego in the story: he is "the only one of them attending a college which it required money to attend" (Gold was, at the time he wrote the story, a Columbia under-graduate), and he is described as "writing all the time" (8).

Brock sets the story into motion by showing up one night with "the family car" (15) and offering to take his friends for a ride, during which they spot Bedmer on the street. The question motivating the story is whether Bedmer will be willing to have sex with one or more of the boys or whether she has been truly changed by therapy. Phil Zand is a virgin, and as Muñeco says, "This whole party is in Phil's honor" (22): in other words, they are especially eager for Bedmer to sleep with Zand, reprising the role she had with "the half-dozen or so twelve- to fifteen-year-old young men she devirginized" (2) during the incident with the Werewolves. Bedmer, for her part, turns out not to be inter-ested in Zand, but she does take a liking to Brock; he, having expressed his lack of interest in sleeping with a girl "who has already been on intimate terms with everyone in the neighborhood" (21), drives her home politely, and the story ends with Brock and Muñeco reflecting on how Bedmer has changed. Muñeco remarks that she must have been treated by "one hell of a psychiatrist," and Brock agrees, in the ironic, hifalutin language of a college boy making fun of his own pretentions: that therapist "wasn't an East Side boy," he says. "He performed a great disservice to an entire neighborhood. He dissolved the last trace of com-munal endeavor to which we could proudly point" (28).

One way to read "A Change of Air" is as a story about the way a group of Puerto Rican and Jewish teenagers talk and hang out on the Lower East Side in the 1940s — about, all jokes aside, the "communal endeavor" that unites "an entire neighborhood." This is not the way Van Doren asked his students to read it; in Wakefield's account, the class discussion focused on psychiatry as the "power of change behind this story." Gold found that convincing but recalled that originally he had "thought [the story] was about these guys pissing away their time."[94]

Taking Gold's original reading seriously does not at all lessen the story's interest: from that perspective, "A Change of Air" offers a remarkable, detailed

—

85

description of the way that the city brought Puerto Ricans and Jews together. It describes how in high school Muñeco "fell in love with and was loved by the editor of the high-school newspaper (a Jewish girl of orthodox parents who were destined to object to their daughter's keeping company with a Gentile, and with a Spanish Gentile, and with one who looked so typically and unhealthily Spanish)" (6–7). The other Puerto Rican teenager, DeTorres, is described as sitting down, at a chess club where the boys like to hang out, "to kibitz the game" (14). These small moments in the text reflect the connections made possible as public schools and city streets prompted Jews and more recently immigrated Puerto Ricans to connect.

But the story registers a significant amount of tension, too, between the Puerto Ricans and other young men in "A Change of Air." The story describes how Muñeco, who started out his teenage years as a troublemaker—an erstwhile mugger and pot smoker who had been "expelled from three high schools" (6)—discovers Thomas Wolfe and James Joyce and transforms himself into a literary intellectual. He is teased by his friends, the "cream of the intellectual crop," for being a "literate hoodlum," though, so he feels it necessary to prove to them, by memorizing and reciting reams of literature, that "whatever else he might also be," he is also "an intellectual" (9). Muñeco feels especially competitive with Brock, because while Muñeco had been "first-prize winner in a national short-story contest" in high school, he has not been writing lately, unlike Brock at his expensive college.

Taken together, these details reflect the fact that Jews growing up cheek by jowl with Puerto Ricans on the East Side in the 1940s and attending the same public schools faced many fewer obstacles between themselves and academic or literary success. Brock's family can afford tuition, and Zand and Miller, no matter how eccentric their scholarly interests, have no self-consciousness about themselves as intellectuals, while their two Puerto Rican friends, presented as just as intelligent as the others, feel a need to prove themselves. That tension notwithstanding, the picture presented is of a bunch of old friends on good terms, teasing one another. Even if the context for their camaraderie is homo-social bonding over the hope of coercing a young woman into having sex—which should not go unmentioned as disturbingly misogynist—it is worth emphasizing that the story's upshot is that these men ultimately leave Bedmer alone. Nothing happens in the diegetic present, except for some friends hanging out and getting along, despite their differences.

Even more clearly than "A Change of Air," the final story in Gold's *Nickel Miseries* unmistakably concerns Jews' interactions with non-Jews. The novella-length "Taub East" is set on and around a U.S. military base in central Japan in the 1950s. The titular character—whose training is not made entirely clear in the story, though it is reported that he was "chaplain's assistant in Georgia" and one soldier calls him, perhaps sarcastically, "rabbi" (203), while the narrator refers to him, twice, as "cantor" (175, 206)—struggles to gather Jews for a *minyan*, or quorum, for the prayer service he leads on Friday evenings on the base.

When the story begins, Taub has accepted that he will probably never gather the customary ten men, but gathering even seven or eight of them requires him to strike a bargain with Popkin, a forty-five-year-old alcoholic who has been in the army for more than two decades and has been court-martialed three times and has most recently been busted down to private first class after being away without leave. Taub, who is Popkin's room sergeant, proposes that if Popkin will attend Friday-night services regularly, Taub will in exchange cover him for one a.m. bed checks so that Popkin can sleep, off the base, in a shack he has set up with a local woman. Another of the Jews who turns up to Friday-night services reliably, Helver, is an army lawyer with his own spotty past and some unpleasant habits whom Taub nonetheless considers a friend. The plot turns on Popkin's stealing and wrecking a lieutenant's car. Helver covers for him and places the blame on another serviceman, but then, because Popkin and Helver do not show up to services that week, Taub spitefully takes action to exonerate the innocent man and get Popkin and Helver punished. In general, the story reads like a rewriting of Philip Roth's "Defender of the Faith" (1959), set on a base in Japan rather than Missouri but involving the same questions of whether an enlisted Jew should prioritize the putatively egalitarian regulations of the military or whether he should defend a Jewish peer.

This theme is elaborated, as it is in Roth's story, through characters who differ in their relations to Jewish tradition. Taub, though by no means Orthodox, is genuinely committed to the idea of holding religious services and seems to make a point of pride of not sleeping with the local sex workers; while Helver, the lawyer, is much less concerned about such issues. Popkin, meanwhile, when asked if he is Jewish, says, "On my father's side," and when Taub presses and asks, "Do you think of yourself as a Jew?" answers, "What's the angle?" (161), suggesting his insincerity and willingness to lie for advantages. He says he has never been inside a synagogue (161) and knows no Yiddish (162), and yet, so as to justify his addition to the *minyan,* Taub tells himself that Popkin must have been a victim of anti-Semitism (161). When Taub decides that he wants to help Popkin, he emphasizes Popkin's part-Jewishness as decisive (179). In other words, Gold's novella mordantly satirizes the well-documented and artificial attempt, in the postwar U.S., to shore up a sense of Jewish unity and community around religious practice — a target, likewise, of Roth's in early stories like "Defender of the Faith" and "Goodbye, Columbus."[95]

What distinguishes "Taub East" from other contemporary stories treating that same theme, like Roth's, is the story's focus on Japanese civilians, and especially sex workers, as third parties whose perceptions of Jews motivate, if obscurely, the protagonist's actions. Gold lived in Japan for several years and learned the language, and the novella contains quite a bit of untranslated Japanese, in a Western Honshu dialect, as well as specific details about local life.[96] Set pieces in the novella explore and riff on relationships between Jews and the Japanese whom they encounter through the U.S. military's presence in Japan. For one example, Taub tells a joke he says he "just received from a friend in the States" (152) — which would also be included, a few years later, in Roth's *Portnoy's Complaint* — about a Jewish soldier phoning his mother to tell her that he has married a Japanese girl, to which his mother responds with enthusiasm, saying there will be plenty of space at home for her son and his new bride, because as soon as she hangs up, she is going to kill herself (152–53).[97]

In another scene, Taub tries to convince Helver of the proposition that all non-Jews hate Jews by definition. Helver asks if this means that Taub considers the Japanese to be inevitably anti-Semitic, too, and Taub responds with his belief that the Japanese will quickly pick up anti-Semitism from Americans: "All prejudice is learned. . . . They already hate blacks, you know. . . . All they need to do is read a history of anti-Semitism in the West, they'll adapt quickly enough" (166). The novella follows up this idea when Taub's favorite among the Japanese sex workers, Akemi, tells Taub to "go to hell": "You a cheap stingy Jew" (174).

Later, she whispers something about him to an American GI that, the story implies, Taub imagines might also be an anti-Semitic slur (193). In Taub's imagination, at least, at stake in his own behavior and the behavior of Popkin and Helver is whether anti-Semitism will spread to Asia — and, in a larger sense, the story explores whether Japan has anything to offer Taub, as a space where Jewishness is not immediately recognizable and Jews like him are just, simply, white Americans.

The story's answers to these questions are profoundly ambivalent. In a final series of reflections, Taub declares to himself, "*We are all the same*" (eschewing parochialism in favor of universalism), and also says, "Bother the babel of the non-Jewish world." He concludes on a note that forthrightly acknowledges his ambivalence: "He's been right from the start, right both ways. Nothing of the tortuous dialectic need be disclaimed" (208–9). As such, Taub espouses, vis-à-vis the question of Jewish particularism or cosmopolitan universalism, a specifically Trillingesque ambivalence: as Mark Krupnick observes, "Trilling decided that he preferred the continued existence of oppositions to any program for resolving them."[98] At the same time, these reflections of Taub's are followed by a very definite moment of violence, not unlike the climaxes typical of Flannery O'Connor's stories: the trolley on which Taub is having these thoughts runs over and crushes the right foot of Popkin, who has fallen asleep, drunk, on the tracks. Even if there are hints of Taub as an autobiographical character (it is implied that he has, unlike his military peers, "breathed four years running the heady involuted air of the highest-priced college in New York" [165] and studied the Japanese language seriously, as Gold did), it seems sensible to read Taub's dialectical internal monologue about Jews and Japan not as Gold's sincere thoughts on the matter but through the scrim of irony and distance we bring to O'Connor's stories (and not only because Gold admired O'Connor's work so much that he once went to visit her at home, uninvited).[99] That Taub's actions lead directly to a man's body being mutilated suggests that his instincts and ideas probably should not be trusted entirely and maybe not at all.

One suspects that if Gold's later career had been more productive, he might have continued to be thought of as "one of the commanding writers of our time," as Trilling's blurb projected. Gold's work has some of the humor and violent intensity of Roth's, O'Connor's, Mailer's, and Joseph Heller's; Trilling's support

—

of Gold suggests sympathy with that kind of antic, violent postwar realism, which a reductive vision of Trilling, one that too glibly buys into his donnish persona, tends to array him against. In Gold—both in the characters who populate his fictions and also in the alcoholism that undermined his career—there is plenty of the "wickedness," "the chutzpah and mishagass [sic]" that Trilling, in his notebooks, assumed were necessary for creativity.[100] Since Gold's subject in Nickel Miseries was, in part, how Jewishness might or might not remain relevant in a widening, transnational United States in which Jews, Hispanics, and Asians became more and more entangled, the book pushes some of Trilling's oldest concerns further into the world of the multiethnic, globalizing 1960s than Trilling himself could.

Indeed, on one occasion—the same year that Gold's "A Change of Air" was published in New World Writing—Trilling expressed, in a letter to a student in England, his feelings toward New York's growing Puerto Rican population in terms that strike a contemporary reader as appallingly racist. Generalizing about a "huge influx of Puerto Ricans," Trilling claimed that their "level of culture is quite low" and that "it will take many generations before they are a part of the central culture." Notably, his concern centered on the consequences of this wave of immigration on New York's public schools: "In my boyhood only the very rich or the very snobbish sent their children to any but the public schools, which were, on the whole, fairly good; now it is virtually impossible to expect a child to get any sort of real schooling in them because the Puerto Ricans, scarcely speaking English, have invaded so many neighborhoods."[101] Whatever critiques one may reasonably make of Gold's representation of DeTorres and Muñeco, the story understands them as intellectual equals of their Jewish high school peers and as having been prevented from fulfilling their potential because of their exclusion from universities like Columbia. As for Japanese people, whom Gold represents in substantial detail in two of his stories, Trilling does not seem ever to have had much to say about them for better or worse, which makes sense: he never traveled to Asia and probably had not met many Asian Americans at Columbia.[102] Gold was not necessarily a paragon of antiracism, but by the time he published Nickel Miseries, he had traveled to more places and spent time with a wider variety of people than Trilling ever did.[103] A major part of Gold's literary project was to imagine the relationships between New York Jews like himself

—

and people from other ethnic, racial, and national groups, which involved at least taking them seriously as interlocutors. This can be understood as extending Trilling's liberalism in a direction Trilling himself could not.

Trilling's Students and Everybody Else's

Some of Trilling's slightly younger colleagues in the field of cultural criticism, like Alfred Kazin and Irving Howe, began their careers writing generally about Anglo-American literature, and then, participating in a transformation of U.S. culture, they turned decisively in the 1950s and 1960s to projects that dealt in sustained and intensive ways with Jewish history and culture, succeeding both commercially and critically by doing so.[104] Though Trilling transformed himself politically from the 1930s to the 1950s, he does not seem to have had the option of changing himself into the kind of writer that could contribute to a growing interest in Jewishness; unlike Howe and Kazin, he did not have the background, knowledge, or inclination to produce books like *A Walker in the City, The World of Our Fathers, A Treasury of Yiddish Stories,* or *New York Jew.* He was emphatic, in fact, about his own inability to speak intelligently about Jewish issues; in a letter from 1959, declining an invitation to address a group of Jewish students at Columbia, he insisted — and can be taken at his word — "It is my respect for the Jewish tradition that has dictated my refusals of your invitations. I am not learned in that tradition and there is nothing that I might say about it that would conceivably be worth hearing."[105]

Trilling could not suddenly become proficient in Jewish languages or an expert in Jewish literature or history, but what he could do was signal his acceptance of a new moment in U.S. culture by supporting a few students who would act as his literary proxies, writing the literary works he himself could not. We can speculate that he was especially primed to accept Columbia students in this role, because he had once been a student there himself and so much of his thinking was shaped by that institution.[106] In any case, appreciating Trilling's role in these three writers' careers should change the way we think about him. It might have already done so if these students had achieved more literary success or notoriety, as many of Trilling's other, unblurbed students did. Still, they demonstrate how Trilling linked disparate literary institutions – Columbia, Yaddo, *Partisan Review, Commentary,* and Farrar, Straus & Cudahy, among others – helping them to coordinate, and, in so doing, privileged Jewish students who were interested in writing about Jewishness. As such, Trilling deserves credit as one of the forces that helped to bring Jews to the center of U.S. literary and culture life in the 1950s and 1960s, even if his support for the writers who are most famously associated with that moment (Bellow, Malamud, Roth, Paley) was less pronounced or decisive.[107]

Trilling does, in fact, receive such credit in Richard Kostelanetz's critique of nepotism and cronyism in postwar U.S. publishing, *The End of Intelligent Writing,* where he is called "the closest semblance of a chief" that the "disparate tribe" of New York Intellectuals had and, quoting Norman Podhoretz's *Making It,* "the family's single most influential member in the 1950's."[108] Moreover, Kostelanetz correctly characterizes the form that Trilling's influence took, noting that he wielded a "kind of power-behind-power . . . over the policies of several young editors in the fifties."[109] This prompts a more general ethical question, for which Trilling is a fitting case study: Was Trilling's consequential support of Astrachan, Feldman, and Gold or of the other students and colleagues he recommended for opportunities with extraordinary success and influence somehow ethically dubious?

On the one hand, with the benefit of hindsight, it is worth considering how the investment of such power in a university professor like Trilling, in that place and time, narrowed the range of who could benefit from his support. Columbia was, in the 1940s, 1950s, and 1960s, an institution open to many young Jewish men but not, of course, to everyone. Among the students it excluded, until several decades later, were, of course, women.[110] Trilling had very few female students and was not in a position to promote their work in the way he could for male writers or critics. The writer, translator, and editor Marion Magid, who was a Barnard student in the 1950s, recalled, "You never questioned that Trilling was for the boys and you were a girl, so you had to make do."[111] Carolyn Heilbrun, who was first a graduate student at Columbia and then a colleague of Trilling's in the English department there, was sure that Trilling "didn't know [she] existed" and said, "he never once talked to me, except in the most routine way of politeness."[112] Trilling did occasionally write recommendations for

—

women, but those letters reflect rather than subvert this pattern of institutional exclusion: rather than praising one candidate for her undergraduate work, as he did for Gold and others, Trilling remarked, "[She] has not been a student of mine. But I know her well . . . because for a summer she lived in my family as a companion to my little boy."[113] It is hard to see how that fact could be relevant to a student's application to graduate school in English literature, and it shows how a system depending on letters of recommendation could be much more difficult on candidates who were denied access to potential recommenders.

A powerful example is that of the novelist and critic Cynthia Ozick, who enrolled in a seminar with Trilling at Columbia in 1951 and remembered the experience later as "a disappointment," with Trilling having among the students "one or two favorites, whom he would praise profusely" while remaining "sarcastic or indifferent to others," including her.[114] She recounts that Trilling once confused her with the one other female student in the seminar: "because we were a connected blur of Woman, the Famous Critic, master of ultimate distinctions, couldn't tell us apart."[115] Two decades later, Trilling read an essay of Ozick's and praised it, and the two reconciled — sensibly enough, because Ozick more than any other American writer has gone on to accomplish what Trilling aspired to, publishing many acclaimed novels and fictions and an extraordinary number of learned essays on topics both Jewish and not. But the disappointment of their early interactions reflects how Trilling's positioning at Columbia in the 1950s made it unlikely that he could serve as a woman's mentor, no matter how deserving she might be.

There were, of course, also other kinds of people who were not generally welcomed into the Columbia College community during Trilling's tenure there — even a historian of Columbia who is sympathetic to the institution cannot gainsay the "negligible numbers" of "blacks or Puerto Ricans" enrolled as late as the early 1960s — and if we might hope that Trilling would have been supportive of students and writers from those backgrounds who pursued literary careers, it is more than likely that they would also have been disappointed if they, like Ozick, had succeeded in joining one of his seminars against the institutional odds.[116]

All that said, Trilling cannot really be blamed for the misogynist and racist practices of the Columbia admissions office and administration, and whatever

—

93

Kostelanetz says, it was not an ethical problem that Trilling helped Astrachan, Feldman, and Gold, as well as dozens of other Jewish students and a good number of non-Jewish ones, find their way to the careers as writers, scholars, and editors that they desired. There *can* of course be cases where a professor's solicitude on behalf of a student crosses an ethical line, as in the examples discussed within the field of U.S. poetry in the middle of the first decade of the twenty-first century, when poets were accused of awarding prizes to their own students without giving reasonable consideration to the applications of other poets who had paid entry fees in order to have their work considered.[117] But Trilling simply used the power he had earned to promote the work of some young writers he liked. He did what teachers always try to do, what they are expected to do, which is to extend their influence in the world through the achievements of their best students. And, in a historically specific way, it is worth emphasizing that the effect of Trilling's influence was to create opportunities for a particular group of people – American Jews – who were still subject to exclusion and marginalization in U.S. literary culture at the very time he was doing so (as Gollancz's responses to Astrachan's novel make clear). Trilling's efforts on behalf of these three particular writers helped to make it more possible for Jewish students, in general, to imagine themselves pursuing careers in the field of American literature, in a time and place in which that possibility could not by any means be taken for granted.

Trilling was a uniquely influential figure and a pioneer, but as a Jew hired to teach English literature and mentor to aspiring literary professionals, he was less an exception to a rule than a harbinger of things to come. In the years that would follow, and with increasing rapidity in the late 1950s and 1960s, more Jews would be hired by English literature departments at elite universities – notably, Harry Levin (who began teaching at Harvard in 1939), M. H. Abrams (Cornell, 1945), Charles Feidelson (Yale, 1947), and Charles Muscatine (UC Berkeley, 1948) – until, by the mid-1970s, by one assessment, Jews represented 13 percent of the faculty of English departments at "the better universities."[118] These scholars' letters of recommendation and blurbs for their students may have carried somewhat less weight than Trilling's did at the peak of his influence, but surely, like Trilling, each of them allowed many Jewish students on their campuses who dreamed of careers in literature and who were sensitive

—

to their teacher's and their own Jewishness to see it as genuinely possible for them to pursue literature as a profession. And, along with Trilling, these professors must have affected, in this way, the relationship between American Jews and American literature, by making it easier for Jewish students, in particular, to imagine themselves into literary futures.

—

CHAPTER 3

WOMEN AND SHITTY MEDIA MEN

Whisper Novels, 1958–1984

Women, the Postwar U.S. Literary Field,
and Gendered Myths of Editorial Autonomy

The experiences of women like Marion Magid, Carolyn Heilbrun, and Cynthia Ozick with Lionel Trilling, mentioned at the end of chapter 2, reflect the degree to which gender was a major factor in literary access in the mid-twentieth-century U.S. Indeed, the enfranchisement of Jews in the U.S. literary field has its parallel in the literary enfranchisement of women, who over the course of the twentieth and twenty-first centuries went from being a marginalized and exploited segment of the publishing industry to leading the field and constituting a demographic majority within it. For Jewish women, in particular, opportunities to take on leadership roles became available largely in the postwar decades, and during those transitional decades, it turned out that few women could succeed if they did not have male spouses who were celebrated in the same field. This chapter explores the consequences of that dynamic and the questions raised by collaborations between men and women in publishing and literary culture during a time when professional and personal relationships could not be disentangled.

In the nineteenth and early twentieth centuries, women had played important roles, as authors, readers, and in some cases as editors of periodicals, in U.S. literary culture.[1] But many influential positions within the field, particularly in book publishing and literary studies, remained barred to women then and continued to exclude them until the second half of the twentieth century. According to the publishing historian John Tebbel, while some women held editorial positions in New York in the late nineteenth century, book publishing "began, reluctantly, to open its doors to women" only in the years immediately before World War I. At first women were hired largely as stenographers and secretaries.[2] Jews like Blanche Knopf and Adele Seltzer and non-Jews like Ellen Knowles Harcourt (née Eayres), who were married to the chief executives of publishing companies, exerted substantial influence on the activities of those firms, and by midcentury, women had found roles as editors at specialty and university presses and at children's book imprints inside major publishing houses.[3] Still, the editor Michael Korda, reflecting on the period during which he joined the field, at the end of the 1950s, notes that "while there were more women executives in book publishing than in most other business, real power remained in the hands of men"; "even though much of the useful work in it was done by women," he reflects, "it was still thought of as a man's world."[4]

There had been important exceptions—Frances Phillips, for one, had been the editor in chief at William Morrow from 1931 to 1957—but Tebbel's general assessment is that "it was, in fact, not until the 1960s that women began to make real headway in book publishing," at the same time that second-wave feminist activism was bringing about systemic transformations of women's opportunities in a wide variety of U.S. industries and institutions, including feminist publishing interventions like the founding of the Feminist Press (1970) and *Ms.* magazine (1971).[5] In book publishing, much of the opening of new opportunities to women resulted from women's successes in areas of the field, such as subsidiary rights, that had not commanded much prestige in the past but came to take on increasing centrality in the postwar decades. Still, in the early 1980s, a group of sociologists who surveyed the history and contemporary state of women's experiences in U.S. book publishing concluded that it was still fair to say that "book publishers are characterized by a kind of paternalism at all levels."[6]

That paternalism took a specific form during the transitional postwar decades, roughly from the 1950s to the 1980s, in which women's opportunities in publishing changed steadily. In the first decades after World War II, it was still the case that most women who worked in book publishing started out in secretarial or assistant roles.[7] So even while the number of women who rose from such roles to more influential editorial and executive ones began to increase in the 1950s and 1960s, an industry in which a relatively small number of empowered men presided over large staffs of relatively disempowered women and wielded the power to determine which women could and could not advance in the field presented a variety of problems. Writing in the 1980s, sociologists observed the dynamics that were then typical in publishing, "especially older men dealing with younger women," who start out as assistants and secretaries, noting that "such relationships . . . are inherently ambiguous." In what sense, precisely, these relationships were "ambiguous" was not elaborated on, but the authors did quote "one male colleague of a well-known subsidiary rights director" who, in explaining her success in the field, remarked that "having long eyelashes doesn't hurt."[8]

We can be less coy than this, now, in describing the challenges that faced women who aspired to careers in publishing. In those transitional decades, these challenges included the perception, suggested by the remark just quoted, that a woman's appearance or sexual appeal explained her success; this was one way that the intelligence and effectiveness of a woman could be cast into doubt as she rose in the profession. Women also struggled against a narrative that cast doubts on their motivations, by questioning whether they had joined the business aspiring to positions of editorial or executive leadership or whether they were just there to meet their husbands. If they were married, another common narrative suggested that they were simply advancing their husbands' interests rather than pursuing their own goals. Finally and, in retrospect, somewhat obviously – though this has remarkably not been broached with specificity or explicitness by sociological or journalistic observers of publishing, then or now, by historians of the field, or even for the most part by memoirists – women, under this system in transition, regularly experienced what we would now call sexual harassment and abuse.

During those transitional decades, it was of course not all women who even had the opportunity to face those kinds of challenges and vie for positions of influence in U.S. publishing. The field of book publishing remained closed, for the most part, to women of color until at least the 1980s. In many cases, though, the women who joined the field in the transitional postwar decades were Jewish.

White women from Protestant and Catholic backgrounds were prominent among the female exceptions who had risen to positions of prominence in U.S. book publishing in the 1930s and 1940s, including Frances Phillips at William Morrow and Catherine Heald at Crowell-Collier, and also among the group of women who began to rise as literary editors in the 1950s and 1960s, like Judith Jones at Knopf, Catharine Carver at Viking (and other houses), and Nan Talese at Random House.[9] At the same time, the list of rising female Jewish editorial stars was growing, too, and it increased continually in the ensuing decades (though many of these pioneering editors have been barely mentioned in histories of U.S. publishing). They include Evelyn Shrifte at Vanguard, Betty Prashker at Doubleday, Leona Nevler at Fawcett, Helen Honig Meyer at Dell, and Charlotte Mayerson at Random House, among many others.[10] Other women who pioneered as editors in different areas of literary culture during those postwar decades were also Jewish, including Barbara Epstein, who was a founding coeditor of the *New York Review of Books* in 1963; Midge Decter, who was hired as a senior editor of *Harper's* in the late 1960s; Florence Howe, who was a pioneering academic and founded the Feminist Press in 1970; and a number of the founding editors of *Ms.* magazine in 1971. While many of these female editors, like many of their male colleagues, did not emphasize their own Jewishness, clearly women did benefit from the field's openness to Jews at a time when other minority groups remained largely excluded.[11]

One major response to the narratives that circulated about women in literary culture, undermining their professional aims, has been to buy into, and promulgate, a specifically gendered version of the myth of editorial autonomy and literary objectivity that, as discussed in the introduction, is regularly invoked by editors as well as literary scholars, prize judges, and others. Accusations of women's lack of editorial autonomy mostly circulated privately, in conversation, and were not published or recorded, but a fascinating case in which they were made in a public forum took place in the late 1960s, in the pages of the *New York Review of Books*. Christopher Ricks, reviewing a book by Gertrude Himmelfarb in 1968, claimed that "there are two Miss Himmelfarbs": "The first is Miss Himmelfarb, a first-rate intellectual historian," and the second is "Mrs. Irving Kristol," a less sympathetic figure who "can't stop intoning" "slogans and stock responses" and "is interested only in her *idée fixe*." Ricks suggested, in other

—

words, that Himmelfarb's scholarship and writing had been substantially and perniciously "influenced by the politics of" her husband, "Mr. Kristol," and could not be judged independently.[12] Midge Decter, who had recently been hired as senior editor at *Harper's*, responded with a letter rejecting Ricks's claim, and in reply Ricks doubled down, addressing a similar critique to Decter herself. Ricks wondered, "If *Commentary* were to publish an ill-considered article by Midge Decter, would nobody be allowed to mention the fact that she is married to the editor? Or put another hypothetical case: if Midge Decter were to write to *The New York Review* protesting, say, about its recent review of *Making It*, would nobody be allowed to mention that she is Mrs. Norman Podhoretz?"[13] Given Decter's own prominent editorial position and her marriage to a well-known editor, she had good reason to be concerned about a claim that a married woman could not be perceived as editorially independent from her husband. In fact, a few years later, a letter to the editor of the *New York Times Book Review* critical of Decter's book *The Liberated Woman* wondered, "Why doesn't she identify herself as Mrs. Norman Podhoretz, her married name?"[14] Decter responded, indignantly, that it was "in time-honored fashion" that she had "retained the name under which [she had] always written."[15] (No one mentioned the back cover of the original dust jacket for *The Liberated Woman*, which notes that Decter "is married to Norman Podhoretz, editor of *Commentary*.")[16] Decter's objection notwithstanding, a few years later the same publication published a review mentioning Podhoretz again and also listing the names of Decter's children, in the context of assessing Decter's book *Liberal Parents, Radical Children*. Decter and a number of her friends wrote to complain about that; Marion Magid, who worked at *Commentary*, in her letter wondered, incredulously, whether the reviewer had been "suggesting—with all those cozy innuendoes about Midge Decter's private life—that a woman writer's ideas cannot be discussed except in the context of her domestic arrangements?"[17] Nonetheless, critics would continue to refer to Decter as "Mrs. Norman Podhoretz," often as a way to undermine or attack her, for decades to come.[18]

At the same time, the coeditor of the *New York Review*, where the original exchange of letters appeared, Barbara Epstein, would have also been invested in this debate (notwithstanding that Epstein, Decter, and Himmelfarb, who all socialized with one another, are remembered now as ideological opponents).

—

Epstein was also married to a prominent editor, and as it happened, she would soon be the subject of the most detailed, quantitative, and emphatic critique of a spousal conflict of interest in U.S. letters. In a number of venues over several years, Harry Smith, Philip Nobile, and Richard Kostelanetz asserted that her marriage to Jason Epstein, a vice president of Random House, was one of the drivers of a "collusive," "bias[ed]" relationship between the *Review* and the publisher.[19] That Decter, Epstein, and Himmelfarb were married to other leading editors and intellectuals was not at all atypical: of 144 writers and editors Kostelanetz mentioned by name, in 1973, as constituting the "New York Literary Mob," only 19 were female (or 13 percent), and virtually all of these women were married to men in the same circles.[20] To be precise, of the ten women in Kostelanetz's top three tiers of literary influence, seven were married, or had at one point been married, to men whose names appear on the same list, and two more on the list—Marion Magid and Susan Sontag—were, or had been, married to men (Edward Hoagland and Philip Rieff) who were also writers and intellectuals, though not quite prominent enough to catch Kostelanetz's attention.[21] This suggests that it was entirely typical for a prominent female literary editor or writer of this generation to have married a prominent male literary intellectual.

The harm that accusations of nonindependence, like the ones made by Ricks, could cause for women in U.S. literary culture was analogous to the harm that had been caused to women in U.S. academia by antinepotism rules (which prohibited the hiring of women who were married to men employed by a university). Decter's response was, somewhat understandably, a flat denial that married men and women influence each other at all. She called Ricks's claim "one of the more blatant violations . . . in recent memory" of "current standards of literary, intellectual, and political discussion in America" and asserted that while he was "entitled . . . to find and expose in [Himmelfarb's book] whatever political bias he does so find and does so expose, . . . to have attempted to reinforce the impact of his analysis by identifying the author's husband—with the implied insulting, breezy, cozy assurance that everyone knows what *that* means—is just plain beyond the pale."[22] In later years, Decter would claim that she and her husband did not generally read drafts of, let alone influence, each other's work.[23] An even clearer statement of the principle of spousal noninfluence behind Decter's statement was made a few years later by Jason Epstein, in response to accusations that he and his wife might have a conflict of interest because of their leadership positions at two major literary institutions. He regarded as ridiculous and offensive the theory that since he is "married to one of the editors" of the *Review,* their "thoughts are alike."[24]

Such denials of spousal influence may be quite understandable and even politically sympathetic—especially because of the harm that was being done to women by claims of spousal nepotism and collusion during this period of women's increasing opportunities in publishing—but they are not very convincing. In these specific cases, Himmelfarb published regularly in publications where her husband worked on the editorial staff; Podhoretz published Decter's writing in *Commentary,* and some scholars argue that they influenced each other's writing in clear and unmistakable ways; and the Epsteins shared enthusiasms and reinforced each other's aims and projects.[25] That they did so is consistent with sociological literature on how spouses typically influence each other, in general, and such influences should not necessarily be cause for any embarrassment.[26] But like the broader claims of editorial autonomy that have circulated as a response to claims about literary nepotism generally or a Jewish literary mafia in specific, the myths of objectivity are less compelling responses to unjust attacks on female editors, in retrospect, than a detailed and insightful accounting of what it meant to be a woman who sought out an editorial role during this transitional period.

Whisper Novels: Romans à Clef about Publishing by Women

Perhaps our best source for an accounting of the challenges facing women in midcentury U.S. publishing is in a series of studiously neglected or misread postwar fictions written by women who had experiences in or near positions of U.S. editorial influence and who used the form of the novel in subtle, complex ways to report on what they observed. I propose that we call these "whisper novels," alluding to the "whisper networks" that women use to communicate about men's abusive behavior within industries and encoding ironies about the ways these fictions, like the information shared in those networks, have circulated

—

and communicated. Including works as stylistically distinct as Rona Jaffe's *The Best of Everything* (1958), Ann Birstein's *Dickie's List* (1973), and T. Gertler's *Elbowing the Seducer* (1984), these novels can be understood as a particular subspecies of the roman à clef—a genre of fiction set in the world of the people writing it, with fictional characters that many (though not all) of the work's contemporary readers could understand as based on, or as reflecting the personalities and behaviors of, specific real-life people. In these whisper fictions, the roman à clef's self-reflexive subject is the publishing system through which the fiction itself has come to exist and find its way into the reader's hands and, crucially, the misogyny and sexual misconduct of powerful men within that system.

Such novels continue a tradition of the roman à clef that played a major role in the rise of the novel in the eighteenth century and, according to Sean Latham, in the development of modernist fiction in the twentieth.[27] Often written by women, early romans à clef sometimes reflected overtly on the gendered imbalance of power operating in and around literary culture, as when Caroline Lamb's foreword to *Glenarvon* (1816), her roman à clef about Lord Byron, noted that "those who have been cruelly attacked will use the means of resistance which are within their reach."[28] Surveying this history, Lauren McCoy notes that "the *roman à clef* allows discounted voices . . . a space to tell their stories, challenging more established narratives."[29] Concentrating on the first half of the twentieth century, Latham remarks on the many "women writers [who] found themselves in a position similar to [Virginia] Woolf's: subject to sexual abuse and manipulation, uncertain about how to access the public sphere with the same freedom and confidence as the men around them, and yet eager to claim a room of their own" (157). The form of the roman à clef, Latham suggests, was one way in which they attempted to do so.

Specifically, Latham reads Jean Rhys's novel *Quartet* (1927) as revealing "the ways women writers struggled to access a public sphere in which free speech was starkly delimited by gender" (166), and he credits the book as "an innovative and largely successful act of social and economic revenge" (165) against Ford Madox Ford, whom the novel, when read as a roman à clef, indicts for "misogyny, snobbery, and hypocrisy" (164). Strangely, though, Latham's study highlights one of the confounding aspects of the roman à clef, undermining his own remark about Rhys's book as "successful . . . revenge," when he details, over the course of three pages, how "reviewers and scholars" from the 1960s to the 1990s consistently invoked "literary autonomy, the intentional fallacy, and narrative impersonality so that *Quartet* [could] be preserved as a highbrow modernist masterpiece" (160), not as a work of gossip, let alone testimony, about Ford's abusive behavior (or not, as one might hope, as *both* a modernist masterpiece *and* a testimonial work). What Latham could have done in his excellent study of the roman à clef, but does not do, is examine how "successful" Rhys's book has been in affecting Ford's reputation: to put the matter simply, if it is true that one of Rhys's primary goals in *Quartet,* as Latham convincingly argues, was to make her readers see Ford as, first and foremost, a contemptible misogynist and hypocrite, one could presumably measure the success of Rhys's project by consulting encyclopedia entries and biographies of Ford and checking to see whether Ford's misogyny and hypocrisy have been emphasized in them. As far as I can tell, the answer is clearly that they are not: what tends to be emphasized about Ford is that he was the masterful modernist author of *The Good Soldier,* and any mention of his affair with Rhys is minimal at most.[30]

As Latham's study makes clear, then, no matter how flimsy or "conditional" it may be, what is both fascinating and troubling about the fictional framing of the roman à clef is that it allows factual content embedded in these narratives to circulate widely and reach a large audience but also not to be taken *too* seriously. Very disturbing stories about abuse and misbehavior, which might seem to require a legal or ethical response if reported by other means, can circulate within this genre of text without triggering any legal or institutional consequences — neither the restorative consequences we might hope for nor the punitive consequences that Leigh Gilmore shows are often meted out to the women who testify against abusers through both formal and informal means.[31] Novelists who represent real-life characters and events too directly can, like those testifying more formally in courts, be punished or constrained by libel law (or castigated according to ethical standards for "literary identity theft"), but the idea that a roman à clef would function as what Gilmore calls "literary witness" — that is, that an abuse or crime recorded in fictionalized form in a roman à clef would be counted in a legal setting, be investigated by the police, or be punished by private institutions—runs up against a laboriously produced consensus, chronicled by Latham, that insists on novels as autonomous and fictional.[32] This quality of romans à clef is clearly a double-edged sword: as we will see, it means that, in general, there have not been consequences for the real-life men whose deeply upsetting sexual behavior has been described in these fictions. But at the same time, as the creator of the "Shitty Media Men" spreadsheet, Moira Donegan, has insightfully observed, there can be substantial "value" in a venue for women's expression that has "no enforcement mechanisms," no "legal authority or professional power," intended "not to inflict consequences," especially in shielding the women who express themselves therein from the all-too-typical, discrediting, and often violent attacks chronicled by Gilmore.[33]

This chapter reads whisper fictions as thoughtfully and complexly engaging with all of these considerations and as bracing acts of resistance against the conditions of their own production. While not acceding to women's being barred from the opportunities or credit they deserve as editors, writers, and literary intellectuals, these fictions refuse to accept that the price of such opportunity be a false objectivity that pretends that married people do not influence each other or that people's sexual and romantic attractions to one another would never influence their tastes and professional behavior. Instead, these novels acknowledge and describe sexual nepotism not as a simple binary operation but as a complex playing out of power in all its various psychological and institutional complexities. The novels do so as a strategy to carve out space for women in publishing and in literary culture more generally, in large part by undermining false myths about editorial autonomy and especially the intellectual authority of men. But like Rhys's *Quartet,* measured by a standard of whether they transformed the reputations of the specific abusive men whose alleged misdeeds they chronicle—measured by the standards of "literary witness"—these works have largely not achieved their aims, at least until now. Possibly for the reasons discussed by Rita Felski in *Beyond Feminist Aesthetics*—they are largely realistic, rather than formally experimental, novels—they have not been included in histories of postwar feminist literature, either.[34] This chapter is written in the hope that these books might be more widely and sympathetically read and that they can contribute to efforts to rewrite and rethink literary and cultural history through the perspectives of #MeToo.[35]

—

105

Women in Publishing and Rona Jaffe's *The Best of Everything*

The first of these novels was a major bestseller that has unfortunately not tended to be taken very seriously by literary scholars or cultural historians. Rona Jaffe's novel *The Best of Everything* (1958) tells the stories of several young women employed at a New York publishing house and indexes the changes that were under way for women in book publishing in those years. Some of the novel's characters go on to pursue other professional or personal paths, but the book's protagonist, Caroline Bender, rises from an assistant role to that of an editor at Fabian Books, a publisher of original paperbacks modeled on Fawcett's Gold Medal Books, where Jaffe herself worked after graduating from Radcliffe College in 1953.

Among the novel's other virtues, it describes how a highly educated, independent woman like Caroline had to struggle, in the 1950s, against the presumption that she could not possibly have meaningful professional aspirations. The operating assumption within the novel is that any woman who marries will necessarily stop working immediately upon doing so; a married woman who continues to work is more or less unimaginable in Jaffe's fictional world. This, of course, undermines the seriousness with which any woman's work could be regarded. A man Caroline has been dating, Paul Landis, says as much to her, late in the novel:

> Where is it all going to lead you? It's one thing to enjoy your job, every girl should have something to do until she's married, but you live with it every minute of the day. You take work home, you worry about office politics, you let [her senior colleague] Miss Farrow get you down. . . . You're much too ambitious, and the worst of it is, you're fighting with windmills. . . . You're knocking yourself out for that third-rate publishing company. . . . Do you honestly think you're doing a job that some other girl couldn't step in and do just as well five minutes after you've left?[36]

For Paul, Caroline's professionalism is quixotic both because the company she works for is "third-rate" and because there is not anything unique about her contribution to it. Caroline eventually rejects this line of reasoning, and the man offering it, but the novel generally sides with Paul: other than Caroline, every other woman in the novel seeks marriage above all, and even "Miss Farrow," the unpleasant "bitch" who has fought her way up the ranks at Fabian Books and is the only woman senior to Caroline there, turns out to be willing to abandon her job for a marriage proposal. Aside from dreams of celebrity and wealth, none of the women have any professional ambitions to speak of. In the world of the novel, Carolyn stands out as pioneering and possibly even a little fool-hardy in believing that, as a woman, she can or should succeed as a literary professional at all—but while the novel has been recently read as "show[ing] that love and marriage, not a career, were best for women," one can also read Caroline's refusal to submit to this regime as an attempt, by Jaffe, to open up a small avenue of resistance.[37]

Indeed, *The Best of Everything*'s representation of the imposition of marriage and male control on women's professional trajectories reflects not only the book's historical moment but also the way Jaffe's novel came to be written and published. While Jaffe had begun to publish short stories while working at Fawcett, it was only because of her Radcliffe roommate, Phyllis Levy, who had become secretary to Simon & Schuster's editor in chief, Jack Goodman, that she met the man who would make her first novel possible. That man was Jerry Wald, a Hollywood producer who came up with the idea of paying fledgling writers to create novels matching film treatments that Wald had concocted that would then be adapted into films in what turned out to be a commercially successful cross-media marketing scheme.[38] Two Jewish men, Goodman and Wald, who had risen to power in New York publishing and Hollywood, respectively, were the authorities who green-lit *The Best of Everything,* even if Jewish women like Jaffe and Levy, still fighting for their positions in the publishing industry, were necessary in the process of its production. And just as Paul suggests that "some other girl" could "step in and do just as well" as Caroline, the arrangement with Wald stripped the traditional prerogatives of authorship—first and fore-most, independent choice about what subject matter should be the focus of a particular novel—from Jaffe and transformed her into a cog, if a highly rewarded one, in Wald's powerful content-production machine. These men eroded, in other words, Jaffe's autonomy, and the young author was treated like an emerg-ing Hollywood starlet: an astonishing prepublication media blitz that Wald funded on behalf of the novel emphasized Jaffe's appearance. Unusually, photographs of the author appeared on the *front* of the novel's dust jacket, as well as in many wire-service stories that circulated in dozens of newspapers in the run-up to the novel's publication.[39] While this fascination with her might seem to suggest that Jaffe was empowered by her success, as in the Hollywood system, the creation of a star by a publicity machine often renders an individual less, rather than more, powerful.[40] The coverage was by no means universally respectful; a review in the *Shreveport Times* captioned a photo of Jaffe, "Authors are getting prettier all the time," and the *Evening Review* of East Liverpool, Ohio, noted, vis-à-vis Jaffe's success, "It makes you wonder how a chick so young knows so much so fully."[41]

While bearing in mind the degree to which the novel came into being as part of a publicity system that could be said to have exploited Jaffe at least as much as it empowered her, it is worthwhile to consider what the novel wanted to convey to its readers about the gender politics of New York publishing. The book drew on Jaffe's experience and on those of her friends, like Levy, as well as of other women in the business whom she interviewed. One of the novel's interventions is to offer up a portrait of Mr. Shalimar, the editor in chief of Fabian's Derby Books (who was modeled on William Lengel, the editor in chief of Fawcett's Gold Medal Books), that emphasizes how the authority of a previous generation of abusive publishing men had declined.[42] The novel first mentions him as a "tall, older man with a grayish face and strongly hewn features" — "he looked a little like a Greek shipping magnate, or some kind of Near East tycoon" (27), one of his young employees thinks, linking him to power and wealth — and emphasizes that he "had known Eugene O'Neill" (21). Early on, he also gives grandiose speeches about the democratic potential of the paperback book, but Jaffe does not waste time in pointing to his desuetude and, eventually, pathetic ridiculousness. The first time one of the book's characters meets him, he is sleeping at his desk (21–22), and before the end of the second chapter, he has tried and failed to seduce — or, one could more precisely if anachronistically say, he has sexually harassed — a woman serving as his temporary secretary, his mouth "hot and violent and *authoritative*" (32–33, my emphasis) as he presses himself onto her. At a Christmas party, Shalimar gets sloppily drunk and harasses another woman who works at the firm, kissing her and then "lower[ing] himself to the floor on all fours and [creeping] under the table" to inspect her legs (168), then, upon being rebuffed, calls her a "little bitch" and tells her she is fired (169). Despite his position at the company, though, this incident reveals how little power he has — Caroline tells the woman, "Don't you worry. . . . He hasn't any authority to fire you" (169) — and Caroline and everyone else see that he is "nothing more than a foolish old lecher" (167) and a "dirty old man" (169). Within a few months, Caroline reflects that "he looked smaller, *less authoritative,* less frightening," and that "no one in the office . . . was afraid of Mr. Shalimar anymore, they all thought of him as a rather pathetic, lecherous old man," partly because, joining the crucial, long-standing tradition of women's whisper networks, "every girl who had been pinched or kissed by Mr. Shalimar had come forth . . . to add her story to the office gossip" (297, my emphasis). Finally, Caroline reflects that "she would never again be awed and frightened by a Mr. Shalimar" (327), generalizing, through the insertion of an indefinite article, "a," from the one individual to his whole type. Indeed, when, after this realization, Shalimar attempts to reduce Caroline's editorial responsibilities, she stands up for herself ("if you take away any of my authors I'm going to leave" [333]) and prevails over him. For Caroline, the reign of Shalimar and the old male guard of the 1920s was over — whether this was Jaffe's sense of the situation when she wrote the novel or her hope for the future is difficult to say.

Still, consistent with Michael Korda's recollection of publishing as still a "man's world" in the late 1950s, the novel could not imagine a more progressive publishing industry that would be more comfortable for women. Appropriately enough, given the novel's inception as a Hollywood project, at the end of Jaffe's novel Caroline heads toward Hollywood — flying to Las Vegas with a famous comedian who is also one of her authors and being photographed for a tabloid — though it is not clear where she is ultimately headed: whether, like Jaffe, out of publishing and into a Hollywood-supported, lifelong career as a novelist or, like Jaffe's friend Levy, into a long string of editorial jobs.[43] If *The Best of Everything,* true to its flatly ironic title, is committed to dispelling illusions — illusions of marital bliss, of editorial work, of young love — it cannot envision the reality that would arrive just a few decades later, in which women like Caroline would come to dominate the publishing industry demographically (even while vestiges of male authority at the executive level would stubbornly persist).[44]

—

Nor did Jaffe's novel explicitly address how many of the women on the front lines of this transformation would be, like Jaffe and Levy themselves, Jewish. This might be considered an example of a preemptory erasure of Jewishness that was not unusual in U.S. popular culture of the time, what Harry Popkin called "the vanishing Jew of our popular culture": in several cases in the 1940s and early 1950s, hardcover novels with explicitly Jewish characters became paperback novels or movies with ethnically unmarked characters.[45] It seems likely that Jaffe avoids explicitly identifying Caroline as Jewish (while avoiding identifying her as Christian, either) so as to eliminate this problem in anticipation of the novel's preordained mass-market circulation and Hollywood adaptation.[46] The Jewishness of the men and women involved, and the conflicts that arose once increasing numbers of women had the opportunity simultaneously to marry and to work professionally in the publishing industry, would be treated much more explicitly in later romans à clef that updated Jaffe's project for the 1970s and 1980s.

Women and the New York Literary Establishment: Ann Birstein's *Dickie's List*

Ann Birstein was a precocious novelist who married the critic Alfred Kazin, himself prominent on Kostelanetz's list, in 1952. Through her marriage to Kazin, Birstein gained an entrée to the New York intellectual community, but her feelings about her peers were complicated by her unusual background: because her father was a charismatic, media-savvy rabbi, she had grown up among Hollywood and Broadway celebrities, and she achieved success early as a writer, publishing her first book at the age of twenty-three after winning a literary prize while still in college.[47] Often addressed as "Mrs. Alfred Kazin" after her wedding, Birstein was her husband's first reader during the period he wrote the classic memoir *A Walker in the City*, and despite a growing animus between them—in their memoirs, they would eventually depict each other unkindly—the two sent loving, if somewhat narcissistic, notes back and forth throughout the 1950s, 1960s, and 1970s. Birstein benefited from her marriage to Kazin—in 1959, a note in the files of Yaddo, the artist colony, suggested, "perhaps . . . we

should pay deference to Alfred . . . by giving her" the residency she requested —
and during this period, she was deeply connected to other Jewish female intellectuals of her generation and specifically to Decter, Himmelfarb, and Barbara
Epstein, who, as discussed earlier, were concerned about claims of spousal nepotism and conflict of interest; these women all socialized together, attending
one another's parties and visiting one another's homes.[48]

As close as Birstein was to the center of this New York literary demimonde,
she never felt entirely comfortable in it, largely because she objected to its gender
dynamics. She saw herself as a well-educated, confident, and attractive woman,
who, by the time she met the intellectuals in Kazin's circles, had already accomplished what many of the men in those circles either secretly or openly aspired
to do but never could (publish a novel) — though she never felt she got the respect she deserved for all this.[49] She noted, in retrospect, that many of these
intellectual men had married "dim" women, "relegated to the background," who
"seemed to support their husbands financially," and she related that dynamic to
the patriarchal aspects of traditional eastern European Jewish life: "I was amazed
to see shtetl conditions prevail in a group so intellectually advanced."[50] Moreover, Birstein realized that these men were inclined to ignore or belittle the
writing of women like her.[51] While not the most consistently active feminist,
she participated enthusiastically in what was then called the women's movement
and described that involvement, in 1972, as "one of the most heartening things
that's ever happened in my whole life."[52] With all this in mind, and having
steadily written and published novels throughout her marriage to Kazin — *The
Troublemaker* (1955), *The Sweet Birds of Gorham* (1966), and *Summer Situations*
(1971) — at some point in the mid-1960s, Birstein began to draft a novel to
which she gave a working title of "The Ladies."

From the outset of the project, Birstein knew the novel would focus on a
group of New York intellectuals and that it would have, as its protagonist, a
Jewish woman married to a respected literary editor. Many small details shifted
and changed as her drafts progressed, but most of the novel's key scenes — the
party with which it begins, for example — remained consistent. The version that
was finally published in 1973 was titled not "The Ladies" or, as Birstein once
scrawled in her notes, "The Yachnas" (from Yiddish, meaning "the gossipy
women") but *Dickie's List*, a title that somewhat obscures the novel's deliberate

—

centering of women's perspectives (although in its potentially playful connotations, it introduces a variety of other interpretive possibilities, including misogyny and phallocentrism). While Birstein might have chosen to name Sandra's husband Richard/Dick for any number of reasons, it is suggestive that it was the same name she used casually for her friend the historian Richard Hofstadter, a Columbia professor who died in 1970 and whose *New York Times* obituary included a number of quotations from an essay by none other than Kostelanetz, who had profiled Hofstadter in his 1969 book *Master Minds*. Writing to Hofstadter's widow, Bede, in 1972, Birstein complained about "this Kostelanetz jerk," describing him as "only a kind of gimmick man" and lamenting that he had painted false "pictures of [Bede] and Dick running a kind of superior book factory."[53] Though Birstein's novel takes as its primary models not the Hofstadters but Jason and Barbara Epstein and Birstein herself and Kazin, it offers a detailed, sympathetic, but unflinching description of a husband and wife whose efforts overlap and intertwine in the production of "superior book[s]."

The novel is not especially subtle about itself as a roman à clef, announcing on its first page that its action takes place among "what everybody denied was the New York literary establishment."[54] Later, the protagonist, Sandra Wolfe Baxter, flips through the *New York Times Magazine* and finds an "exposé of the New York literary mafia" (163) that includes a picture of Dickie, her husband, who is an editor at a respected New York publishing house called Gaskell Press. The press is clearly modeled on Alfred A. Knopf, Inc., a correspondence made especially clear late in the novel with a reference to "Felicity Gaskell and her borzoi" (246), the borzoi being a famous emblem of Knopf particularly favored by Blanche Knopf. Many characters who appear in the novel have obvious real-world parallels, like Gertrude Dienst, who is clearly modeled on Susan Sontag. For convenience's sake, Birstein makes Gaskell the publisher of many writers who were not Knopf authors, like "Erika Hauptman, the Gaskell Press expert on Auschwitz," modeled on Hannah Arendt, who published with Viking and Harcourt Brace, and "Hershel Meyers," modeled on Saul Bellow, who published with Vanguard and Viking.

Readers and reviewers recognized that the novel was a roman à clef about the New York publishing scene. The *New York Times,* for example, referred to it as "a literary who's who," and a review in the *Waco News-Tribune* was titled

—

112

"Literary 'Mafia' Gets Knife."[55] The flamboyant publisher Roger W. Straus Jr. wrote to Birstein jokingly, "I was told I was a minor character, and you and I both know I couldn't be a minor character in anybody's book."[56] Birstein's unpublished notes make some of the real-life correspondences clearer, as when she describes Sandra and Dickie as being "like Barbara and Jason at time when NY Review was started" or when, considering what kind of an apartment she should give to the fictional couple, she wonders, "Should they live in a duplex like the Epsteins?"[57] Birstein sometimes mixes and conflates characteristics of real people in her characters; in another note for the novel, she describes Dickie's physical appearance as "sort of like Pete LeMay" (who took the role of publicity director at Knopf in 1958 and went on to become a vice president of the company, as well as a writer for television).[58] This suggests that notwithstanding Birstein's insistence that "it's not meant to be 'in' or a roman a clef or anything of that kind" and Bel Kaufman's remark, in a blurb submitted for promotional purposes, that she hoped "readers [would] not treat [the novel] as a guessing game of who's who in the publishing world," the correspondences with real-life figures mattered in Birstein's writing process.[59] Indeed, in one draft, she seems to have slipped, writing "Saul" instead of "Hershel" (or "Neil," which is used in other drafts) for the character based on Bellow.[60]

Recognizing that the correspondence of Birstein's characters to real people is a deliberate aspect of her project makes funnier a knowing joke that she includes in her first chapter. At the party that opens the novel, Birstein has a few of her characters banter about the "legal business" as it relates to literary types like themselves: "There is no obscenity anymore," a lawyer among them says, "only plagiarism and libel," meaning that since the late 1960s, there is no longer any danger of obscenity prosecutions of literature and also no longer any opportunity to gain notoriety and press coverage through such prosecutions. "Okay," says Hershel, the novelist character based on Bellow, "we'll try for libel" (20), suggesting, comically, that literary descriptions of real people might now be the best way to stir up interest and controversy in the postobscenity era.[61] Another writer, not incidentally a woman, chimes in at this point, "But what would be the point aesthetically?" Hershel dodges that question with a semi-ironic, crudely misogynist joke — "I leave it to you chicks to worry about my aesthetics" (20) — and the novel passes on to other characters and topics; but the whole exchange amounts to Birstein's self-conscious wink about her book's goals. That question—What "would be the point" of a novel, like this one, that flirts with libel in describing the milieu of its own production?—is the one *Dickie's List* proceeds to explore.

Part of the answer is that by representing secondary characters who resemble Birstein's real-life friends and acquaintances, but making Sandra and Dickie at least superficially distinct from herself and Kazin, Birstein could explore some of her own most intense feelings about her opportunities as a woman within her intellectual milieu without writing openly about her difficult, abusive marriage. Though the novel is less plotted than gently exploratory, it often focuses on tensions between Sandra and Dickie around questions about her professional opportunities and his professional competency. During the opening scene, for example, Sandra is asked by an unfamiliar party guest what she does. She first pauses to think that it is noteworthy that the person asking her "had not understood that she was married to Dickie"—as if to say that it is generally understood by most of the people whom she encounters at such events that the primary thing she does is be her husband's wife—before explaining that she has published a "few translations for the Press. From the French. Though there are always these silly questions of nepotism" (14).

As the novel fleshes out Sandra's life, it backs up to explain that she first met Dickie when she was a year out of college at Barnard, "selling books at Doubleday's, at night," when "blond smiling Dickie appeared and took her over to Gaskell Press, where suddenly the whole world opened up" (164). Despite the fact that it is Dickie who introduced her to the press, Sandra recalls that soon they "were young and in love and working at Gaskell Press together" (27), and in retrospect, Sandra considers that as a moment in their lives when they "really had been equals" (41). Sandra's experience resembles not only that of Barbara Epstein, who began her career alongside Jason Epstein at Doubleday, but also Decter, whose literary-intellectual career began when her first husband began contributing to *Commentary,* which led to her own contributions and eventually a secretarial job.[62] Unlike Epstein and Decter, Sandra has by the novel's present foregone her full-time editorial job, for a reason that Epstein and Decter also had to consider. When she mentions that she would like to come back to work as an editor at the press alongside Dickie, he does not encourage her: "Do you think that's such a good idea?" he asks. "I can't believe that anybody worries anymore about nepotism, do they?" (232), she responds, suggesting that the appearance of spousal conflict of interest—the same accusation leveled at Decter and Epstein in the late 1960s—may be exactly the reason that Dickie thinks it is not a good idea for Sandra to return to such a position.

Dickie's List invites its readers to sympathize with Sandra, a woman with literary interests and experience for whom it is not at all taken for granted that she is as entitled to a job in publishing as a similarly interested and experienced man would be. Sharpening that sense, Sandra is aware of a different kind of woman from herself—"a type of female who was always madly attracted to famous intellectuals, . . . the chicks, secretaries, assistant publicity girls, buzzing like honeybees around" novelists and editors (40) and, recalling Jaffe's *The Best of Everything,* the "secretaries [who] had been gigglingly eager, first for the chance to break into publishing and then for the chance to break out of it and get married" (87). These latter are especially loathsome to Sandra because in their lack of commitment to the editorial work she values, they make suspect the desire to "break into publishing" in the first place. Sandra, clearly not one of *those* females, is not exactly miserable in the position she finds herself, but she is somewhat stymied by her proximity to a literary community of which she is not fully a member and specifically in her relationship with her successful husband. She imagines telling her therapist "about it being not so easy to act independently" (152) and asks Dickie, "Don't you ever feel that we really don't do as well by each other as we should?" (153).

One of the novel's narrative threads offers Sandra an opportunity to participate in the kind of editorial deliberation that she has been missing out on lately because she lacks a position at the press. This plot point concerns a manuscript that an old friend of Sandra and Dickie's, the Bellow stand-in Hershel Meyers, has shared with Dickie, expecting that Gaskell Press will publish it. Like Bellow and Birstein, Hershel and Sandra have always shared a mutual attraction but have never dated.[63] Dickie convinces Hershel to share the manuscript of his novel. When Sandra asks Dickie about it, he lets her know in not so many words that he is not enthusiastic (151), and when she reads it herself, she has to agree: "It was such a mess, an even worse mess than she had expected. Not a novel at all, just page after page of infantile pornography, adolescent political satire, page

—

after incoherent page of masturbating Presidents, Berrigan brothers ejaculating simultaneously on gallows, sodomy, rape, lesbian Cabinet wives, endless descriptions of sphincters, genitalia" (167). Writing this in the early 1970s, it seems that Birstein was probably thinking less of Bellow's recent novels and more of Philip Roth's *Portnoy's Complaint* (1969), *Our Gang* (1971), and *The Breast* (1972). "Must you publish it?" Sandra has already asked Dickie (151), but then at a party on Cape Cod, she learns from another editor at the press that Hershel "says he's going to insist on an advance of two hundred and fifty thousand bucks": "Didn't Dickie tell you?" Moreover, Sandra is told, the press will actually pay this extraordinary sum, feeling "they can't afford not to" (196). Later, Sandra and Dickie argue about Hershel's novel, with Sandra saying that Hershel has "sold out" and Dickie offering an insincere defense: "I happen to think it's a very interesting experiment. . . . Very good of its kind" (235).

At the same time, another novelist, Sophie Katz, who has been hoping Dickie might publish her novel—and whom he "pit[ies]" as a "wet-eyed, eager, middle-aged, probably glandular" person with a "slightly rancid odor" (47–48), not at all stylish and dashing like the novel's Sontag stand-in—is told by a magazine editor, Ralph Gorella, that he has no interest in publishing an excerpt of it: "Even the switchboard girl thought it stank. . . . What are you trying to do in that thing, anyway? . . . Make fun of the intellectuals?" Dickie, hearing this, says nothing, even though he admires the novel and sent it to Gorella in the hopes of building up buzz for it (205).

Through these events, the novel demonstrates how Dickie, despite his prominence as an editor, cannot oppose the worst excesses of the publishing system, which, in Sandra's view, lavishes absurd sums of money on terrible books so as not to threaten the tenuous friendships of vain men, while at the same time disadvantaging deserving female novelists. Perhaps because Sandra is more rooted in Jewish family life than Dickie is and less invested in the concerns of commercial publishing, she, even though she harbors romantic feelings for Hershel, is able to judge both literature and people much more clearly. But, as should not be surprising in a novel by a feminist, it turns out to be Dick, and not she, who gets to decide.

When Birstein published a memoir, *What I Saw at the Fair*, in 2003, a couple of reviewers noted that it described Kazin as emotionally and physically abusive

—

and that it presented a feminist perspective on Birstein's experiences.[64] With the benefit of hindsight, and after Kazin's death, Birstein was able to recognize how consistently she had been disrespected and marginalized by the literati with whom she socialized and how that kind of professional disrespect was echoed, in her intimate life, by physical and verbal abuse that Kazin directed toward her: in public, Kazin's friends would speak condescendingly to her, and he would not object; in private, Birstein recalls, Kazin would rage and sometimes hit her.[65] Like many survivors of abuse, Birstein reflects on the question of why she did not leave Kazin earlier, but she never mentions *Dickie's List* in her memoir or seems to recall that while still married to Kazin and still, however uncomfortably, a member of the literary circles in which Kazin was prominent, she had written and published a novel that openly exposed the pettiness of the figures in that system and many, if not all, of their excesses. Among other revelations, she had demonstrated in the novel how hollow were the claims of male editors and literary critics, including Kazin (and some female ones, too) to literary and moral authority, how partial or partisan such claims must be, and how much they are based on the aggressive exclusion of others from opportunities to speak and assert authority.

In the same years that Birstein was finishing and publishing the novel, Kazin's letters and journals make clear how little respect he had for his wife as a professional. As Joseph Epstein puts it, "Kazin could have helped gain attention for [Birstein's novels] but didn't in the least bestir himself to do so."[66] In 1971, as Kazin worked on a chapter for *The Bright Book of Life,* on "lady novelists," he explained to an editor at Little, Brown that he was writing about Katherine Anne Porter, Jane Bowles, Sontag, Grace Paley, Joan Didion, and Joyce Carol Oates, but that "it's a difficult because *thin* chapter so far." He asked for suggestions. The editor, Esther Yntema, replied mentioning Jean Stafford, Hortense Calisher, Shirley Ann Grau, and Kay Boyle. Neither of them mentioned Birstein, and Kazin did not agonize over a potential conflict of interest in writing about contemporary women writers while being married to one. He simply seems to have pretended that his wife's work did not exist; his book's dedication thanks her "for more than twenty years of conversation about the novel and her fellow novelists," as if her own work just never came up as a subject.[67] In Kazin's memoir *New York Jew* (1978), he refers to Ann not by her name

—

117

but as "Beth" and notes her anger at "the indifference to fiction, and especially woman's fiction, by the literary Establishment," but he does not acknowledge there – as he does in his journals – how much she directed her ire specifically at him for *his* indifference to her fiction.[68] In a journal entry on July 16, 1973, Kazin spelled this out, noting that Ann claimed that he "joined the Pulitzer Prize committee to keep her from winning the Prize."[69] As ridiculous an accusation as that might seem, Kazin's role on such a committee would indeed have disqualified Birstein's books from consideration (as he also excluded her from his *Bright Book of Life*). Kazin could be excited about Birstein's success: he noted in his journal that it was "one of those 'lucky days'" when "everything worked" on June 23, 1971, because "Ann has a publisher for her book" (probably, given the timing, this book was *Dickie's List* itself).[70] But the sense of competition and of Kazin's professional stature hurting, not helping, Birstein's career seems to have haunted the marriage and grown in intensity in the wake of the publication of *Dickie's List*. In an undated, unpublished manuscript, in a folder labeled "Ann 1950–1978," Kazin wrote about a stay in Stanford, California, in 1977–78, remarking, "[Ann's] bitterness against me is more deeply engrained here than ever. She will simply not let me, as a scholar, enjoy any honor, any place, that as a novelist she has not achieved for herself."[71] The two often fought, and Kazin's journals from the early 1970s are filled with anguished entries about Ann. All of this suggests how much Birstein's concerns about the ways that Kazin, in particular, failed to support her were expressed in the strained professional relations between Sandra and Dickie in *Dickie's List*.

Of course, there were other real-life circumstances, involving men other than Birstein's husband, that also inspired her novel. In one particularly concrete example, the novel describes how a magazine editor modeled on Philip Rahv (1908–73), who cofounded and edited *Partisan Review*, gropes and disrespects Sandra: the character, Gorella, who has a "famous gravelly, gangster's voice" and is a "repulsive" "beefy ape" (18, 19), moves his hand "up and down [Sandra's] smooth thigh, still in search of that erotically titillating bump of a garter" (210). This description is echoed in detail in Birstein's memoir, four decades later, where Birstein describes Rahv as "a gravel-voice gorilla" "groping at [her] thigh in the region of [her] garter." It was Rahv, too, who according to Birstein's memoir, asked whether in her fiction she was trying to "make fun of the intellectuals" when she showed him her story "Love in the Dunes."[72] Rahv died only a few months after *Dickie's List* was published, but he was alive and very much active as an editor throughout the decade that Birstein had been drafting it and circulating drafts to fellowship committees, agents, editors, and almost certainly Kazin, too.[73] It was brave enough that Birstein, in her late memoir, risked the ire of everyone for whom Rahv still at that point represented a towering cultural figure, but it is nothing short of astonishing to consider that she had already done so much earlier, as early as the 1960s, when, if someone had cared, they might have brought Rahv's conduct to the attention of his literary and intellectual peers and to his superiors at Brandeis, where he was a professor. As of this writing, I have not found a single discussion of Rahv, in any source, that mentions his portrayal in *Dickie's List* or in Birstein's memoir or, more generally, considers that he may have used his editorial and academic positions to prey on younger female writers.[74]

One complimentary letter that Birstein received after *Dickie's List* was published, from the novelist Johanna Davis, praised the book—"Nasty, touching, really wildly vivid, it snagged me hopelessly and would not let me go"—and noted something about the novel's achievement that recalls to mind Birstein's joke, at the book's start, about libel: "and oh Ann how close you come to so many truths, and with such dexterity."[75] This might seem an odd or backhanded compliment for one novelist to give another: Is it not the fiction writer's job to present truths direct and unvarnished? But what Davis's letter suggests is that it would not have been possible for someone like Birstein to tell "truths" about powerful men in publishing in 1973; at best, she could, with skillful "dexterity," *come close* to those truths—intimate them, make them felt, but without stating them explicitly. In fact, a year or so before *Dickie's List* was published, Birstein participated vigorously in a symposium, "Women on Women," which was hosted by the *American Scholar* and moderated by Lillian Hellman and which included a group of successful female writers and intellectuals (Nancy Wilson Ross, Norma Rosen, Renata Adler, Carolyn Heilbrun, Alice Walker, Elizabeth Janeway). Even in that forum, neither Birstein nor any of the other women felt they could say, explicitly, that they were being physically and emotionally abused by men in their professional circles; instead they dwelled on issues like whether men or women should take out the garbage.[76]

—

In *Dickie's List,* at least, Birstein did make the case – obvious to everyone except those who are motivated to believe otherwise for professional reasons – that the male intellectuals who energetically propped themselves up as the moral and aesthetic authorities of the twentieth-century U.S. turned out very often to be broken people who behaved terribly and exhibited deplorable judgment.

The Whisper Novel in the 1980s:
T. Gertler's *Elbowing the Seducer*

Although influential female editors and publishing executives had become increasingly common in the U.S. publishing industry by the 1980s, some men within the literary system of course still held the kinds of powerful positions that allowed them to exploit younger women who were eager to gain entrance to the field. Writers continued to turn to the roman à clef as a response, and one of the most complex and compelling examples of such a project is T. Gertler's novel *Elbowing the Seducer* (1984). Its author, Trudy Gertler, was born in New York in 1946 and raised in Miami Beach, where she attended a Jewish day school and began winning writing contests as a teenager.[77] She was married at the age of nineteen and got divorced twelve years later, and at that point, she began to find her voice, and more success, as a writer. She wrote the screenplay for a 1978 film, *Convention Girls,* that despite more serious intentions on the part of its writer and director wound up being marketed successfully as an exploitation film and reportedly grossing $4 million domestically.[78] Though an article about that film's release, in 1978, noted that Gertler "had published a number of short stories," profiles of the author that appeared in the wake of her novel's publication remarked that screenplays she had worked on previously "were never made into films" and that "her first published short story" was one that had appeared in *Esquire* in 1979 (and in *The Best American Short Stories of 1980*).[79] When the novel *Elbowing the Seducer* appeared, it attracted quite a bit of press attention and was optioned for film, and eventually it became something of a cult classic – out of print but recalled recently by a critic as "almost certainly the best [literary-world roman à clef] of the last four decades."[80]

The novel centers on a young female writer, Dina Reeve, hoping to be pub-

—

lished by a dynamic, influential male editor, Howard Ritchie. Gertler makes clear how high the stakes are for this writer, who feels that if Ritchie's magazine "published her story, then she'd be better than real, she'd be justified"; her sense of self is on the line.[81] At the same time, she is aware of how her gender complicates her literary aspirations and signs the story she submits to Ritchie's magazine "D. Reeve": "The initial was supposed to defeminize her, to prevent obscene phone calls and a reader's conscious or unconscious prejudice against writers who happened to be female through no fault of their own" (31). She understands, in other words, before even publishing her first story, that to appear female to editors and readers would make her the subject of sexual abuse ("obscene phone calls," at least) and "prejudice" — and while she recognizes these as problems in the literary scene she hopes to enter, they do not deter her from pursuing writing. She is willing to "defeminize" herself as a defensive measure, despite the fact that the reason literature appeals to her in the first place is its promise of "justif[ying]" her, of making her inclinations and eccentricities seem reasonable or valuable.

Meanwhile, the novel presents the editor, Ritchie, as relying on sex for compensations not too different from what Reeve wants literature to provide: "At least once a week and usually twice a week he lay naked, bone on bone, with one woman or another. Or with two women, because he liked playing ringmaster"; and he feels that these "lunchtime affairs made his life tolerable. Without them . . . he wouldn't survive in the structure he had built for himself" (14). Moreover, "he preferred literate sex" (16), meaning sex with women knowledgeable about literature. Given that portrait of Ritchie, it is not surprising — notwithstanding that "he didn't want writing to crawl to him, hat in hand" (49) — that he does not waste time in transforming Reeve's literary aspirations into sexual vulnerability.

When Reeve and Ritchie meet for the first time, he says, "What are you, nineteen?" and then, when she tells him "apologetically" that she is twenty-eight, he says, "Don't ever tell anybody else. It's much more . . ." and breaks off, suggesting at least the possibility of something lewd or unmentionable (60). From the start, he undermines her perception of reality, introduces the vague possibility of sex, and aggressively projects youthful vulnerability onto her. Soon, he is telling her that she "reminds" him of "the first girlfriend [he] ever had"

—

(62). He also establishes a connection between them through their shared Jewishness: he uses a Yinglish vulgarism ("*shtupping* . . . It's slang, Yiddish for
screwing"), and when she, in response, mentions that she attended "Hebrew
school once a week till [she] was eleven," he notes — as if to illustrate how editors
seek out similarity with their writers — "with enjoyment," "We're both Jewish"
(63). In a second meeting, as he offers her editorial feedback on the story she
has sent him and explaining that he will not publish it, Ritchie indulges in
"wonderful obscene visions" (88), sexual fantasies that combine sexual manipulation with line editing, when he imagines his hand "kneading a nipple between the E and the A" on Reeve's *Grateful Dead* T-shirt (89).

Reeve and Ritchie go on to have a sexual affair, and she reflects that "he'd
given her life a purpose: him" (123). Then she writes another short story, titled
"An Affair, I Guess," and sends it to him; he says he will publish it, but he also
breaks off their affair. She thinks, "If he didn't want her anymore, she would
die," and more tellingly, she worries that "if he didn't want her anymore, he
might not publish her story" (190). Though it is a sad joke that Reeve is unsure
which would be the worse fate, what this underscores is the degree to which
she has understood their sexual relationship as inseparable from his offer to
publish her work. Reeve's estranged husband tries to get the editor fired from
his teaching position by informing his university superiors that he "seduces
under the name of literature" (200), and that description, however awkwardly
expressed, does accurately describe Ritchie's approach to Reeve.

Reeve then has an affair with one of Ritchie's friends, a literary critic named
Newman Sykes, and begins to write fiction about the two men. Reading some
of it, Sykes tells her, "It's marvelous how you've captured Howard," and he
suggests that it is quite possible to infer real-world events from the fiction: "It's
clear from what you've written here that you've been lovers" (251). Reporting
back to Ritchie, Sykes explains that Reeve is "writing a book" about him: "anybody who knows you or knows about you, everybody who counts, is going to
know it's you" (261). Reeve uses some of the classic tactics and defensive for-
mulae of the author of the roman à clef — "I wasn't writing about you," "I made
it all up" (251), "It's fiction" (264) — but the stakes for the men are high: "You
can't publish it this way," Sykes tells Reeve. "Howard has a family and a job to
keep." Ritchie himself threatens Reeve with both legal action and violence: "I'll

—

sue you. I'll get you" (261). Even more so than the other novels discussed in this chapter, which all have a self-referential quality, the latter sections of *Elbowing the Seducer* read as the roman à clef meets *mise en abyme,* and it playfully anticipates, or perhaps simply describes, the reactions to the fiction of the real-life figures on whom the characters in the novel have, at least in part, been based.

Unsurprisingly, Gertler was careful to intone, in interviews, the same suspiciously pat pieties about fiction being fiction that she had already parodied in the novel: "It's fiction!" she exclaimed to one reporter; "I made it up," she told another. A *Boston Globe* profile noted that Gertler "swears all the characters are totally imaginary."[82] For the *Washington Post,* meanwhile, Gertler went further, striking a pose of weary protest: "The notion that people are attaching real people to characters I made up is distressing. It's invasive – as well as preposterous": "I find it appalling for someone to mistake fictional characters for real life. . . . The first time it happened . . . I was very insulted, as though someone had called me a vampire living off someone's blood or something. People read a book and associate it with the author. If there's a heroine with an initial it must be slapped right down from life."[83] The book itself begins with a standard-issue indemnifying statement: "This is fiction. The characters don't have counterparts in real life. No reference to any person, living or dead, is intended or should be inferred" (v). But, as a short piece in the *Boston Globe* put it, "Any time a novel bears [such a] disclaimer . . . you know it's time to count the silverware and check the Yellow Pages listings under 'Lawyers, Libel.'"[84] And prior to the disclaimer, the novel, perhaps tipping its hat, includes as an epigraph a line credited to David Letterman: "Accept the premise, and you'll enjoy the bit" (iv) – as if to say that the suspension of disbelief necessary here is, specifically, that these characters *are not* recognizable figures. Journalists suggested that Gertler was being playfully ambivalent about the relation of her characters to real people; one reviewer suggested that Gertler had "exercised considerable ingenuity in deflecting (or perhaps supporting) any suspicions that some people from New York City might possibly have that [her characters] can be glimpsed in real life at literary cocktail parties."[85] That she could at the same time be "deflecting" (and not denying) while simultaneously "supporting" these suspicions does suggest quite a bit of ingenuity, not distinct from the ingenuity with which the novel itself predicts and lampoons all of these reactions and discussions.

—

This whole, playful approach to the question of truth in Gertler's fiction was reflected, to a point, in the novel's reception. Some reviewers characterized the book as "doing some roman a clef teasing" or noted that it is "full of characters said to be based on current, well-known critics and editors who make up Manhattan's literati."[86] Other reviews did not mention that the novel's characters have real-life analogues, but a few played along with the game by declaring that people were "riffl[ing the book's] pages in search of clues to [Ritchie's] identity" without ever mentioning the names of the likely real-life models of the characters.[87] This approach is taken furthest in a *Washington Post* profile by Paula Span:

> An actual case study, confirmed by participants, of New York's response to "Elbowing the Seducer": Editor A, at *Esquire* (where T.'s first published story appeared), has to order review copies from Random House four times because intrigued colleagues keep swiping them. At the office and at Elaine's, Editor A and associates believe they've figured out precisely which fiction editor and which newspaper critic Howard and Newman represent. Editor A calls Writer B, who sits up nights reading the book. B passes her inside information along over dinner with Agent C, who has already heard all the dirt at lunch with another editor.[88]

While this "case study" offers a detailed account of how gossip circulates in literary New York, what is most striking about it is its anonymization of its subjects. Span could just have easily given the names of A and B and C, without any serious danger of a libel prosecution (as none of the behaviors discussed in this passage are criminal or unpleasant, and these are all presumably public figures in the publishing industry). She chose not to do so, probably because once one has named "Editor A," who "believe[s] they've figured out" the key to the novel, it would seem only reasonable then to report that editor's belief. And that is what virtually none of the book's reviewers or Gertler's profilers or even literary scholars who have written about the book more recently have been willing to do.[89]

In fact, the only name that seems to have been mentioned in the initial reception of the novel was that of Jonathan Galassi, Gertler's editor at Random House. *Book World* noted that "the description of the youthful editor who buys her character's first novel fits Jonathan Galassi . . . down to the cowlick and bow

—

tie" (see Gertler, *Elbowing the Seducer,* 232–33).[90] Which is true enough, but that minor character appears for only a couple of pages. It would not be until two years after the novel's first publication, in 1986, that in a profile of Gordon Lish in *Spy* magazine, Mimi Kramer would note that Gertler's book features "a charismatic editor and professor who dresses well, tells jokes incessantly, is a compulsive womanizer and fond of talking dirty in Yiddish": "People say he is based on Gordon Lish. I wouldn't know. I've never met Gordon Lish. I have read him and heard him speak. I've talked to people who have studied with him. But Lish didn't want to be interviewed for this article."[91] Kramer does not return to the question, as if to suggest it is an unanswerable mystery for the ages. A decade later, a paragraph in *New York* magazine noted parenthetically that "some suggest that a portion of novice novelist Trudy Gertler's *Elbowing the Seducer* might be about Lish, although he denies it and she will not say" — again, leaving the question open as if it were unknowable.[92]

These refusals to make a definitive claim strike me as deeply disingenuous. It does not take a private detective to demonstrate, on the basis of the contents of *Elbowing the Seducer* itself and information freely available in 1984, that Howard Ritchie was at least partly modeled on Lish. Aside from Ritchie's Yinglish *shtik* and obsession with Jewish jokes, which had already become a recognizable part of Lish's published oeuvre by 1984, and many other clear correspondences, there is one unmistakable detail. Meeting with Reeve about one of her stories, Ritchie points out to her, "You have a character here named Ritchyoffsky. That used to be my father's name" (62). Gertler's short story "In Case of Survival," first published in *Esquire* in 1979 and then in *Prize Stories 1980: The O. Henry Awards,* includes a character named "Lishinsky." It should not need to be spelled out: Ritchie is to Ritchyoffsky as Lish is to Lishinsky. Without more evidence, one cannot know whether Lish and Gertler ever slept together or whether any other details of Reeve and Ritchie's relationship have any truth to them or whether some of Ritchie's characteristics were drawn from other real-life people in Gertler's life or invented. Certainly some of the plot of *Elbowing the Seducer* seems unlikely to have been drawn from reality, like Reeve's setting fire to the bookstore over which the critic Newman owns an apartment in which she first had sex with Ritchie. Ritchie is a fictional character, and it would be erroneous to conclude that Ritchie somehow *is* Lish or that Ritchie is identical in every

—

way to Lish. (That is not how literary characters work.) But it is also not credible to deny that Gertler modeled at least some of Ritchie's traits and behaviors on Lish's — all of Gertler's playful denials notwithstanding.[93]

It is valuable to read Gertler's novel for what it tells us about the gender dynamics of New York publishing in the 1980s, in general. It is a culture in which a writer might want to use only her first initial, to "defeminize" herself and "prevent obscene phone calls" and "prejudice" (31), and in which she might have to accept as an "obligatory nod to [her] gender" (160), a male writer's invitation to have a drink with him, and the likelihood that an editor giving her feedback on her story might be mentally undressing her. Furthermore, it is a culture in which a woman writer would understand that it might be necessary or at least effective to have sex with an editor in order for him to publish her work and use his connections to help her professionally. Reading the novel, and the others discussed in this chapter, that way is especially important for creating industry-wide policies and standards to safeguard against abuse and more generally to transform the culture of publishing, eradicating the "paternalism" once observed as ubiquitous in it — a goal that seems especially pressing given that such abusive practices continued long after the heyday of "Howard Ritchie." But another way to read the novel would be for information about particular real-life men whose conduct created those conditions, especially when many of those men continued to have careers, in which they continued to create similar conditions for several successive generations of women, more than three decades after these novels' publications.[94]

What to Do with the Whisper Novel

Of all the many reviewers, profile writers, biographers, and scholars who discussed *The Best of Everything* in 1958 and *Dickie's List* in 1973 and *Elbowing the Seducer* in 1984 and in the years afterward, virtually none have said what, after the #MeToo eruptions of 2017, seems obvious: Maybe someone should *do* something about this?[95] About sleazy or abusive editors, in some general sense — the "shitty media men" of earlier historical eras — yes, but specifically about the individual sleazy or abusive editors whom the women who wrote these novels had worked with and described. Lengel lived eight years after *The Best of Everything* was published and Rahv about six months after the publication of *Dickie's List,* and nothing about the way they were portrayed in these fictions — as lecherous exploiters of young women — was mentioned in their obituaries; and only in Lengel's case has his "reputation . . . for groping young women" since then become a facet of how he is remembered.[96] It may seem naïve to imagine that someone might have investigated these men and even removed them from positions of power and responsibility while they still held them (during a historical era in which so much other sexual abuse went on, unchecked, in other industries), but perhaps it is not too much to imagine that scholars and historians writing about these men since, say, the 1990s might have at least noted their alleged misconduct. They have not.

It is easier to be explicit now about what these men were accused of doing not only because of the models of reporting practices provided during the first years after #MeToo but also, more specifically, because there no longer seems to be a threat of reprisal from these particular men, as there may well have been while they were still alive or in their prime. For similar reasons, many other cases of abuse and inequality from these years have already begun to be reconsidered. For example, the nature of Susan Sontag's professional and marital relationship with Philip Rieff, especially with regard to the authorship of his book *Freud: Mind of the Moralist* (1959), has been the subject of a spirited debate in a recent biography and in critical responses to it (though no one has yet noted that Birstein, in *Dickie's List,* almost fifty years ago, described her Sontag stand-in as "unknown, except that she had just been divorced from a famous husband whose pseudo-Freudian interpretation of history she was reputed to have written" [47]).[97] Interestingly, writers continue to turn to the roman à clef form to tell such stories.[98]

But questions remain about how we should read and think about fiction that may be describing, using tactics of the roman à clef, the abusive or unethical behavior of real people. In earlier periods, scholars have shown that women writers often had sociopolitical goals in mind in their fiction; Clare Virginia Eby, for example, demonstrates how Progressive-era writers used their novels, often based on their own romantic and marital relationships, to argue for marriage reform.[99] Readers have had no trouble treating books like Jaffe's, Birstein's, and

—

Gertler's as salacious and sometimes enjoyable gossip but have not seen them as grounds for action. Latham notes that the roman à clef places itself in "an ambiguous critical space by seeming to insist on itself as fiction while encoding scandalous and often disturbing facts about real people and events" (13). A whisper novel "insist[s] on itself as fiction," in part, to protect from reprisals against women or other vulnerable people speaking against abuse, but it would seem wrong to read such fictions for the sake of enjoyment or edification without taking seriously the claims an author could be making about the real people on whom her characters are based.

What these whisper fictions show us as we look back at literary history, in particular, is that the real threat to men posed by women's rise in the literary system was not that the women would benefit unfairly from nepotism but that they would shift the balance of power. They might hold accountable perpetrators and enablers of abuse and also reveal as fictional the myths of authority that had helped to prop up men's careers, enabling abuse along the way. It could be one of the more lasting contributions of the work of writers like Jaffe, Birstein, and Gertler if they could be understood and appreciated as complementing the unsung efforts that have gone on in a thousand publishing and literary offices in New York and beyond, in which, in less public ways, women have chipped away at the edifice of patriarchy within U.S. literary culture — a thousand lost stories of shitty media men and their incompetence and venality, shared through whisper networks if at all or hidden behind nondisclosure agreements and mostly irretrievable by historians (though a few women of that generation continue to tell their stories, whether or not doing so has any effect on the men who abused them).[100] Of course, recognizing the history of abuse and exploitation is not a magic cure for anything; even after women became demographically dominant in publishing, conditions promoting or allowing the exploitation of vulnerability, including the vulnerability of women, certainly did not disappear, and they persist today.[101] This makes it all the more evident that when a writer publishes a novel or a story — even one presented resolutely and consistently as pure, invented fiction — in which a man abuses his professional power to prey on women, it might be prudent at least to take a close look at the men with whom that writer has associated to see how similar the details are; to see if any other women might have stories about those men; and, if they do, to see whether

—

there is any hope of changing those conditions. That would seem the least we owe to Jaffe, Birstein, and Gertler, who did what they could to tell us about the injustices of the system in which they toiled, and to a whole generation of women in publishing and literary culture for whom marriages, affairs, and harassment were a painful part of their professional experiences.

CHAPTER 4

PARENTS AND CHILDREN

Literary Inheritances and Nepotism, 1959–2012

We have a little girl now who is three and a half,
but luckily she hasn't written anything yet. I'm sure that when she does
she too will be bothering you about coming up to Yaddo.

—ANN KAZIN [BIRSTEIN] to Elizabeth Ames,
Executive Director of Yaddo, January 30, 1959

Jews and the Novelty of Literary Inheritance

In addition to everything else that the Jewish men and women who entered
the U.S. literary field between the 1910s and 1960s accomplished, often succeeding wildly within it, they placed their children in unprecedented positions
for people like them: positions of privileged literary access and inherited cultural
capital.

Before then, in the eighteenth and nineteenth centuries, whether in Europe,
the Americas, or elsewhere in the Diaspora, literature was not something Jewish
people tended to inherit. On the contrary, the pursuit of a literary vocation for
a young Jewish man or woman typically involved that young person cutting
themselves off in a more or less concrete way from their parents. As far back as
the Haskalah, or Jewish Enlightenment, Jews who wrote or published secular
literature in European languages or even reform-minded works in Jewish lan-

—

guages understood that in doing so, they were alienating themselves at least partially from their families of origin. The scholar Alan Mintz titles his study of Hebrew autobiography in the nineteenth and early twentieth centuries *"Banished from Their Father's Table,"* quoting that phrase from a Talmudic parable that "was used self-consciously in the literary criticism and journalism of the period as a tag for the generation as a whole and its condition."[1] The novelist and Yiddish journalist Abraham Cahan remembered, in his autobiography, "sever[ing] relations" with his father as he became involved in secular politics and enduring his mother's suspicions about the "reading matter" that she felt would "bring misfortune on [his] head."[2] Anzia Yezierska captured this sense of generational divide in the subtitle of her 1925 novel *Bread Givers: A Struggle between a Father of the Old World and a Daughter of the New,* and one critic, retrospectively surveying Yiddish-, Hebrew-, and English-language fiction written by Jews in the U.S. in the first half of the twentieth century, calls the "widening distance between generations" one of the major themes of that literature.[3] This was true even of those who were born in the New World, a generation younger than Cahan and Yezierska: Saul Bellow's biographer remarks that it was in his "temperament" and disinterest in entrepreneurship that the author-to-be "diverged from the family line," and while his brothers fulfilled their father's aspirations of financial success, Saul, "even as a child . . . claimed, he was different from his brothers, marked out for a more exalted destiny."[4] As Norman Podhoretz looked back at his Brooklyn childhood in the 1930s, he noted that because he had "literary ambitions even as a small boy," he developed "a distaste for the surroundings in which [he] was bred, and ultimately . . . even for many of the people [he] loved," including his mother, of whom he discovered he was "ashamed" and "ready to betray."[5] No one's feelings about their parents are simple, of course, but as Jews in the U.S. became the first members of their families to attend colleges and graduate schools and to pursue literary vocations and professions, they often found their parents at worst dismissive and uncomprehending of their literary aspirations and at best vaguely supportive, cheering them on from the sidelines without, however, being able to offer any concrete help, a model to emulate, or a leg up on the competition.[6]

Many non-Jewish, Anglo-American writers and literary professionals, at the end of the nineteenth century and in the first half of the twentieth, found themselves in quite different situations. Many of the most successful writers of those decades — and especially the most successful white, Protestant, male ones — had family members and ancestors whom they could look to as models, whether of failure or of success, in the field of literature. F. Scott Fitzgerald was named for an ancestor, Francis Scott Key, who wrote "The Star-Spangled Banner"; T. S. Eliot's mother published poetry; John Steinbeck learned his love of literature from his mother; Robert Lowell's ancestors included the poets Amy Lowell and James Russell Lowell; John Updike was inspired by his mother's literary aspirations.[7] American Jews who became writers sometimes traced their descent from rabbis and religious leaders, and occasionally, as in the case of Cynthia Ozick, they might count a Hebrew or Yiddish author among their older relations.[8] Until the middle of the twentieth century, though, it was very unlikely that an American Jew's parents would have successfully pursued a career in literature, publishing, or literary scholarship.[9]

In the postwar decades, though, this all changed rapidly and thoroughly. Many of the American Jews who founded literary publishing houses in the 1910s and 1920s and the Jewish writers who had published novels and poems to increasing acclaim in the 1920s and 1930s and after and the Jews who became tenured professors of literature in the 1940s and 1950s and after had children. Those children grew to adulthood in the 1950s, 1960s, 1970s, and 1980s, and if they had literary inclinations of their own, these young men and women found themselves in a position to benefit from their parents' literary achievements, to take possession of the symbolic capital their parents had accrued, and, in some cases, to inherit directly the valuable companies and intellectual properties that their parents had created. For a few publishing families, the financial stakes of these inheritances grew very large, as family businesses had expanded into companies worth tens of millions of dollars. The question of inheritance thus became a central one in postwar U.S. literary culture and in publishing especially. Al Silverman notes, in *The Time of Their Lives* (2008), his extensive, breezy survey of postwar publishing, "I hadn't expected . . . to give so much attention to the relationships between fathers and sons."[10] This despite the fact that a 1979 article in the *Washington Post* about literary children of literary parents had noted that Silverman, an executive at the Book of the Month Club, had a son, Brian, who was conspicuously also in the business as an editor at Berkley Books.[11]

These generational dynamics meant that a new and pressing question faced many Jewish editors and writers, the same question that has often faced those who inherit great stores of cultural, symbolic, or financial capital: How can one benefit from one's inheritance while also proving—to others and to oneself— that one's successes are not simply a matter of inherited privilege and without sacrificing one's sense of self-worth and professional and personal autonomy?[12] Answers to this question varied from individual to individual, of course, but this chapter explores the ways in which a series of these individuals responded to this problem. The first three examples—the publisher Pat Knopf and the novelists Stephen Millhauser and Jacob Epstein—did so with powerful ambivalence in the 1960s and 1970s.

Atheneum: "By Whose Decree Am I Called Jew?"

One crucial, representative case of awkward generational transmission took place at the prestigious U.S. publishing house discussed in chapter 1, Knopf. Most of the major U.S. publishing houses that had been established in the 1910s and 1920s experienced generational shifts, predictably enough, in the late 1950s and 1960s, as their founders reached retirement age or died. One unusually smooth family transition took place at Viking Press, where Tom Guinzburg took over as president when his father, Harold Guinzburg, died in 1961; the younger Guinzburg, who had come to work for the family business after founding the *Paris Review,* shepherded the company until its sale, for an estimated $12 million, in 1975, and beyond. A more typical case was that of Christopher Cerf, who worked for a few years at Random House, the firm his father, Bennett Cerf, had founded, but then left, on amicable terms, to pursue other opportunities more suited to him. When it was time for the elder Cerf to retire, he left the company in the hands not of a family member but of Robert Bernstein, whom he had hired out of the blue, some ten years earlier, based on the younger man's reputation as an editor at Simon & Schuster. There were other successful passings of

—

the reins from father to son—as in the cases of Arthur Thornhill Sr. and Arthur Thornhill Jr. at Little, Brown in Boston and of Cass Canfield and Cass Canfield Jr. at the venerable house of Harper's in New York—but it was the Knopfs' failed family transition that received the most attention.[13]

The story was reported on the front page of the *New York Times* on March 15, 1959. Alfred Knopf Jr., who was called Pat, had worked for his family's business for many years and had expected to take over when his parents retired. But then Pat proposed that the company hire a successful editor, Mike Bessie, whose competencies overlapped with those of Pat's mother, Blanche Knopf, and the elder Knopfs demurred. Pat, Bessie, and a third partner, the editor Hiram Haydn, left their positions at three major publishing houses, secured financial backing, and founded their own company, Atheneum. As one industry source told the *Times,* it was "as if 'the presidents of General Motors, Chrysler and Ford left their jobs to start an automobile company.'"[14] That, in doing so, Pat was seeking autonomy or, more precisely, to get out from under the thumb of his influential parents could not be clearer. Haydn, who recalled being "sick of the way the senior Knopfs . . . treated Pat," as "a boy or a chattel" rather than a "man," described the foundation of the new company as Pat Knopf's "assertion of man-hood, of freedom from the tyrannical father."[15] Meanwhile, Bessie—at least according to Haydn's recollection—was only half joking when he suggested that the new publishing house might be called "Chutzpah House," and Haydn also registered the Jewishness of the firm's two other founders (and of the publishing business more generally, by this point in its history) when he described himself as the firm's "Golden Goy."[16]

As Haydn's recollections suggest, one of the ways in which Pat and his col-laborators seem to have distinguished their company from that of Alfred and Blanche Knopf was through a different, more comfortable, jokey, and embracing attitude toward Jewishness, both on their staff and in the books they published. The earliest Atheneum lists are noteworthy for the degree to which, a step or two ahead of their times, they set no limit on the number of books of Jewish interest they published and for how open-minded they were about the kinds of literary Jewishness they imagined might appeal to their readers.

A brief introduction to Mike Bessie's biography and career seems called for, because if Alfred and Blanche Knopf had been willing to hire Bessie, there is

—

every reason to believe Atheneum would not have been founded: instead, Pat and Bessie would have become the new generation of editorial and business leaders at Alfred A. Knopf, Inc. In that sense, at least, the raison d'être of Atheneum was, first and foremost, to provide Bessie with the support Pat wanted him to have to publish the kinds of books that interested him.

A younger cousin of the writer Alvah Bessie, who was well-known as one of the Hollywood Ten, Simon Michael Bessie was born in 1916 in New York City and raised in Washington Heights. His mother had been born in Riga, Latvia, and immigrated to New York as a child, while Bessie's father, a doctor, was the son of a Civil War brigadier whose ongoing military service led to his being based in North Dakota, where the Bessie family had been "probably the only Jews" in the town of Wahpeton.[17] Even in New York's Washington Heights during his own childhood, Bessie recalled, his was "the only Jewish family" on an Irish block (7). The family did not practice any religion at all, and Bessie recalled that he "wasn't aware . . . of being Jewish until maybe the second maybe the third grade in elementary school," when a teacher asked him why he was in class on a Jewish holiday (47). Bessie attended DeWitt Clinton High School and then Harvard in the mid-1930s, where he became more aware of his own Jewishness: "Since 1933, since Hitler came to power," he later recalled, "I of course have been thoroughly conscious of being Jewish" (49–50).

Bessie experienced some anti-Semitism at Harvard. He recalled, "It was quite clear to me that I was not going to be invited to join things like Hasty Pudding or a final club" – prestigious Harvard social organizations – "because I was Jewish" (50). Bessie nonetheless became an editor of the school newspaper, the *Harvard Crimson*, and prospered academically; he wrote an undergraduate thesis about tabloid journalism that he later developed into a book, *Jazz Journalism* (1938). When the sale of that book earned him enough money to do so, he moved to France and wrote freelance pieces for magazines and newspapers, taking translation jobs when he could, traveling to Morocco and Algeria, and witnessing firsthand what he called "the terrible spectacle of Hitlerism in Germany" (16–17). He recalled, "I can remember frequently finding it necessary early in a conversation with French people to make it clear that I was Jewish because many of them were overtly anti-Semitic and it seemed to me easier to come right on with it than to wait for something to happen" (50). He also re-

—

membered being aware of the unfolding events in nearby areas under German control: "I think one knew about the concentration camps whether one talked about it or not. Certainly after the pogroms [of 1939]" (17). Bessie was living in the South of France, near Grasse, at the start of the war and recalled that he decided to return to the U.S. then because he felt "depressed and discouraged by the atmosphere in France" and specifically what he perceived as an increase among the French of "fairly openly anti-Semitic talk" (19–20). After returning to the U.S., he took a job with *Look* magazine in Des Moines, Iowa, and then a commission from the Office of War Information (OWI) that brought him back to Algiers in 1943. He remained abroad until 1946, leading news operations for the OWI in North Africa, meanwhile accepting an offer from Cass Canfield Sr. of an editorial position at Harper's, which he began upon his return to New York after the war. When he started at Harper's, he had no experience whatsoever in book publishing, but he quickly found his way: he edited books by John Cheever and Tallulah Bankhead and pursued interests he had honed while abroad in European, and specifically French, literature, publishing writers like Marcel Aymé and Ignazio Silone.

As Bessie understood it, Pat approached him about joining Knopf almost explicitly as a replacement for his own parents: "Pat perceived that there was no strong future editorial presence in the house, that his parents were aging, . . . and he thought that the day might come when they might not be able to contribute as they had, and what would take their place?" (178). When the elder Knopfs refused to hire Bessie, and Pat Knopf, Bessie, and Haydn founded Atheneum, it was not only desirable but also necessary for the founders to pursue and discover new writers, because a new publishing company, by its nature, cannot rely on its backlist, which presents a major challenge.[18]

Appropriately, the firm's first major bestseller was an unlikely success: a debut novel in translation by an unknown writer. Bessie recalled that in 1959, his friend Paul Flamand, the head of Editions du Seuil in Paris, tipped him off to a forthcoming book of Seuil's and sent a set of the French proofs to Bessie, who read them "in one night" and convinced his partners the following day to make an offer on the U.S. rights (195). The book, Andre Schwarz-Bart's *Le dernier des Justes,* was subsequently published by Seuil and awarded the prestigious Prix Goncourt, and it sold hundreds of thousands of copies in France. As

—

Bessie explained, it was by no means a simple book to translate, as it was "written in French by a then young writer whose first language was Yiddish" (196). Bessie sent it to an American novelist he had published at Harper's a few years earlier, Stephen Becker, and explained that he thought Becker could be "the ideal translator" for Schwarz-Bart's novel because he was "Jewish in background, with a knowledge of Hebrew and Yiddish and of Jewish tradition" (197). Bessie, who had been self-conscious about anti-Semitism in France, purchased rights to a massive novel of Jewish history and myth, beginning with medieval pogroms and ending, notoriously, in the gas chambers of Auschwitz, and arranged its translation by a writer whom he trusted to appreciate its Jewish linguistic and cultural complexities.[19] The book, *The Last of the Just*, went on to become a number-one *New York Times* bestseller, a major success for a newly established publisher's first list.

Schwarz-Bart's novel was, in many ways, unusual—it was virtually unprecedented for a French novel in translation to be the number-one bestseller in the U.S., and in 1960, it was not yet quite expected for a book about the Holocaust to become a commercial smash in the United States. There is also an uncanny irony in the novel's attention to generational issues and to inheritance, given Atheneum's history as a company formed because of a conflict in the generational transmission of a family business.

Schwarz-Bart's novel begins with a myth of divinely guaranteed inheritance. Starting with the son of a rabbi named Yom Tov Levy in twelfth-century England, every generation of the family inherits the mantle of the *lamed-vovniks*, the thirty-six righteous men of Jewish mythology: while other sources emphasize that the thirty-six unknown righteous men can be anyone, from any background, in Schwarz-Bart's recasting of the myth, the title of *lamed-vovnik* becomes a Levy family inheritance, descending "to all his line, and for all the centuries."[20] The book proceeds on that basis to chronicle the successive generations of the Levys as they move from place to place in Europe and experience a sampling of the oppressions of Jewish history. It is a legacy that begins with a profound act of religious martyrdom and ends with the titular "last" of the family line, Ernie Levy, dying in the gas chamber at Auschwitz. The novel's premise, then, is a fantasy about a Jewish inheritance so powerful that no amount of human capriciousness can interrupt it. Successive Levy boys are, among other

—

things, burned in an auto-da-fé, sold as a slave, raised in a convent and converted to Christianity, broken on a rack, drowned in a river, and murdered by
Cossacks, until, inevitably, the Nazi genocide ends the story—but none of this
prevents their inheriting their special family status. It is not difficult to understand why such a premise succeeded in France, where Jews had lived for many
centuries before facing the radical trauma of the Holocaust. Even in the U.S.,
there were many people, like Bessie, for whom Jewishness may not have im-
pacted their daily experience very much during their childhoods but who had
been reminded by the scope and proximity of the European genocide that their
own Jewishness came down to them from generation after generation of ancestors who had safeguarded it in difficult circumstances and passed it down as an
inheritance that now, in the face of genocidal persecution, had accrued renewed
spiritual salience.

Pat Knopf did not leave a memoir or oral history, so it is difficult to know
what all of this, and his own family's history of Jewishness and assimilation,
meant to him personally. But Bessie makes clear that he was not just open to
Jewish literature but eager for it. That eagerness played out in his new firm's
enthusiasm in its first five years of operation not just for Schwarz-Bart's novel
but also for a variety of other books of Jewish interest. First, and somewhat
expectedly given the success of *The Last of the Just*, Atheneum published more
European fiction, much of it in translation, about the Holocaust, including
works by Ilse Aichinger, Jacob Klein-Haparash, George Steiner, and Elie Wiesel,
and biographies of European Jewish figures like the Rothschilds and Chaim
Weizmann.[21] All of this was in line with the kind of European-oriented Jewish-
interest titles that Knopf might have published around midcentury (and it is
worth noting that Blanche Knopf reportedly felt aggrieved that Bessie had stolen
Schwarz-Bart's manuscript out from under her). More unusual and pioneering
was the small specialty that the new house developed in Hebrew literature in
English translation, as it published multiple works by the humorist Ephraim
Kishon and the first novel of Yoram Kaniuk, *The Acrophile* (1961), even before
it had appeared in Hebrew—which made Atheneum a significant pioneer in the
publishing of Israeli literature in the U.S.[22]

Meanwhile, like *The Last of the Just*, one novel that the firm published during
its first years that addressed aspects of American Jewish life, Samuel Yellen's *The*

—

Wedding Band (1961), also focused squarely on inheritance. In fact, its first line reads, "When Mama died, I got her gold wedding band."[23] The short, moving novel that follows uses this inherited ring as a central image as it explores the lives of the narrator's parents, Meyer Davidov, a Jewish immigrant, and Eleanor Harper, an orphaned Ohioan non-Jewish woman. The narrator, Alexandra, thinking about herself and her two siblings, muses on the eccentricities of phenotypic inheritance: while "not one minim of [their father's] germ plasm made its way into" her sister, Christina (12), and while her brother, Aldous, has taken steps to eliminate his paternal inheritance, through plastic surgery on the "unmistakable huge, hooked Jewish nose" he received from Meyer, as well as changing his name from "Davidov to Danton" (14), Alexandra notes, "There is no question whatsoever about me. I am Meyer Davidov's daughter" (16), in appearance at least. "Papa had stamped his likeness on me" (18), she explains, and the connection goes back at least one more generation, to Alexandra's Polish Jewish grandmother, Bubbeh, whose "genes," passed down first to Meyer and then onward to his daughter, had "doggedly reproduce[d] the physical pattern" (98) in her.

The novel's plot climaxes with Alexandra's recounting of a set of incidents from her childhood, when Eleanor, lonely and miserable as a young mother, was seduced by a con man and tricked into selling the family's house and liquidating their savings, plunging the middle-class and upwardly mobile Davidovs into crippling poverty. The book's interest in telling this sad story, and telling it from Alexandra's perspective, is in exploring how an adult child comes to understand and accept the weaknesses and vulnerabilities of her parents: Alexandra recognizes that her parents were mismatched, that her father made her mother feel miserable, desperate, and trapped, and that this was what allowed Eleanor to be exploited, putting the whole family in a terrible position. The novel complicates the issue of culpability, though, because it makes clear that Meyer and Eleanor married only because Eleanor had gotten pregnant (at a time when abortion was illegal) with Alexandra; so, in one sense, the person responsible for these two mismatched people marrying in the first place was Alexandra, the narrator herself.[24] Still, the novel registers with pathos Alexandra's understanding that as their child, she cannot change her parents' behavior; when, at fifteen, she realizes her mother has been gambling away small but significant

—

amounts of money in poker games with her friends, she tries to suggest a program for saving: "Mama, Papa, why don't you let me put aside just ten dollars
a week? You won't miss it. And at the end of a year we'll have five hundred
dollars in the bank. . . . Or even *five* dollars a week to start with." Her father's
response is to "[slap her] across the cheek as hard as he could," the "only time in
[her] life Papa struck [her]" (123–24). At the time, Alexandra does not realize
that this has provoked her father because it stirs up memories of her mother's
infidelity and betrayal (which she learns of only later), but her father's violence
makes clear to her that her father refuses to have his child tell him how to manage
his money or relate to his wife. In a quite different—American Jewish—context,
however, what *The Wedding Band* has to say about inheritance is not too different from what *The Last of the Just* understands about it: if Alexandra's inheritance
from her Jewish father is not exactly the Levys' inheritances of noble, saintly
suffering, it is no less inevitable or pathetic in its effects on her.

The questions raised about Jewish inheritance in these novels is nicely captured by one of the poets whose work Atheneum published in its early years.
The firm's notable program in publishing contemporary U.S. poetry included,
in its first years, collections by a number of American Jewish poets, including
Hyam Plutzik and John Hollander.[25] In 1964, the house published Donald Finkel's *Simeon,* a varied and well-reviewed collection, which included one poem that
again takes up the question of a Jewish inheritance. The poem, "Note in Lieu
of a Suicide," resonates forcefully with *The Last of the Just, The Wedding Band,*
and Bessie's experiences, beginning with its speaker asking, "By whose decree
am I called Jew?" The poem continues with a series of possible answers it considers and rejects, one by one:

> By my grandfather's who observed the passover?
> They have sent word back it was not they.
> By my father's who knows a few yiddish jokes?
> I shake my fist at the sky and there is no lightning.
> By the local rabbi's who has recognized my name?
> I have just looked in the ark and found a stone.
> Yet since when have I not been a Jew?
> Since the day I heard God was dead?

—

The blood is on me, I am not clean.

Since the day I became a Unitarian?

Like a woman in her time I am not clean.

Since the day I first discovered that in these

perilous times every man jack is circumcised?

Like a dog that has rolled in dogshit I am not clean.[26]

Musing here from a perspective that shifts from the ancient world to the contemporary one, Finkel's speaker riffs on the question of the moment: What kind of inheritance was Jewishness in the early 1960s United States? Did it descend from one's "grandfather" and "father" and their ritual ("passover") and cultural ("yiddish") commitments? If so, why does so little of that resonate for the speaker now? There is "no lightning," and all that is left in the synagogue's ark, which conventionally holds the sacred book of Judaism, is a "stone." And "Yet," it remains difficult, perhaps impossible, for the speaker to become "clean" of that inheritance, whether by asserting "God was dead," converting to another religion ("I became a Unitarian"), or remarking that what has traditionally set Jewish men apart ("circumcision") no longer, in "these perilous times," distinguishes them.

For Schwarz-Bart, the answer to the question that Finkel's speaker poses, "By whose decree am I called Jew?" is simply: Auschwitz. In *The Last of the Just*, what ensures the continuity between a twelfth-century Jew and his twentieth-century descendant is the endurance of anti-Semitic persecution. For Yellen's Alexandra, it is her eastern European Jewish genes, "doggedly reproducing the physical pattern." For Finkel, spared by the accident of his U.S. birth in 1929 a direct confrontation with the Nazi genocide, the answer seems less clear, and for the speaker of his poem, a Jewish inheritance feels like a stain, the kind left by blood or feces. In other words, one more Atheneum author makes the point that Jewish inheritances, ambivalent as they are, have shown themselves after World War II to be powerful and impossible to ignore. For those who lived through World War II as children, like Schwarz-Bart and Finkel, the question of what, exactly, their Jewish ancestors had passed on to them, however they answered it, was a particularly salient question, as it was for the men a decade their senior, like Pat Knopf (born 1918) and Bessie (born 1916), who saw the

—

war up close in their early twenties. Whatever their parents had not given Knopf and Bessie – awareness of themselves as Jews, control of the family business – mattered less, as for Finkel's speaker, than the inheritances that they could not get clean of. Luckily for them, that situation was one they shared with many readers in the postwar U.S., and Atheneum's openness to texts treating Jewish inheritances helped to make its first years a success.

Scholar/Father, Writer/Son, Mullhouse/Millhauser

While Jewish editors explored their ambivalent feelings about their inheritances through the books that they accepted for publication, writers worked to develop innovative means of exploiting while constraining their inheritances from parents who had achieved positions of influence in American literature. A striking example is Steven Millhauser, a Pulitzer Prize–winning novelist and admired short-story writer whose work began to appear, to much acclaim, in the mid-1970s. Millhauser's father, Milton Millhauser, was a pioneering Jewish professor of English literature who received a PhD from Columbia University and then served in a brief instructorship at the City College of New York before taking a position as assistant professor of English at the University of Bridgeport, Connecticut, in 1947.[27] His son, Steven, who was born in 1943, at first seemed to be following in his father's footsteps when he enrolled after college in the doctoral program in English literature at Brown University, but he then turned to writing fiction.

How does it affect a developing novelist to know that his own father is a knowledgeable scholar and literary critic? If this was not a new problem in general in Western culture, it was, as explained earlier, a relatively new and suddenly widespread one for American Jews; as discussed in chapter 2, between Lionel Trilling's receiving tenure in English at Columbia in 1940 and the 1970s, hundreds of Jewish men (and a smaller number of Jewish women) became professors of literary studies in hundreds of colleges and universities. Eventually, many of their children would find their way into literature – whether thanks to their parents' connections or despite them – and Millhauser was at the vanguard of this wave, coming of age as a Jew in the 1950s and 1960s, in the home of a tenured scholar of English literature.

This childhood experience inspired Millhauser's first novel, *Edwin Mullhouse: The Life and Death of an American Writer 1943–1954 by Jeffrey Cartwright*, which was published by Knopf in 1972. The *Washington Post*'s reviewer, capturing a general sentiment, called it "an extraordinarily good novel" by a "dazzlingly successful writer."[28] Translated into French, the novel won the prestigious Prix Médicis étranger for 1975, the second book by a U.S. citizen ever to do so. Beginning with the earliest journalistic reviews and continuing with more recent scholarly appraisals, critical responses to the novel have praised Millhauser's parody of the genre of literary biography, characterizing it as a "mock" or an "apocryphal" biography and citing Leon Edel and Richard Ellmann — along with James Boswell, who is mentioned within the novel's own metaparatextual preface — as the primary targets of Millhauser's satire, while also rightly naming Vladimir Nabokov and Jorge Luis Borges as the models for Millhauser's generically playful project.[29] These reviewers and scholars summarize the novel diligently, explaining that it takes the form of an exhaustive and pretentious literary biography written by the twelve-year-old Jeffrey Cartwright about his neighbor Edwin Mullhouse, who wrote a novel called *Cartoons* and died on his eleventh birthday.

What journalistic and scholarly responses to the novel missed is the extent to which the novel describes and instantiates a Jewish inheritance drama. In representing the relationship between a writer son and a critic father, one obviously modeled on Steven Millhauser's relationship with his father, Milton, the novel subtly conveys the son's awareness of the Jewish family history that his father has given up in the process of what Jonathan Freedman has called "assimilation by culture."[30] Millhauser's novel is fascinating for its engagement with literary criticism and theory, for its highly textured representation of a 1950s Connecticut childhood, and for its oddly obtuse reception (which did not recognize the Mullhouses as Jews), but for the purposes of this chapter, what bears emphasis is what Millhauser conveys about the situation of a writer with a critic father.[31] In the novel, Edwin's father, Dr. Mullhouse, has pursued the classic kind of literary academic career of his generation, transforming himself in the

—

process from a Jew into an American. He has eliminated any telltale signs of Jewishness from his speech, directly evoking Jewishness only in occasional puns.[32] ("One Saturday," having driven the children "to a distant picnic ground" amid "tall evergreen trees," he makes what Jeffrey describes as "obscure jokes about pine Cohens and evergreen Levis" [182]; for these Connecticut children, New England foliage has replaced the Cohens and Levis—that is, the hereditary Priests and Levites who are honored first and second during the Torah-reading service on Saturday mornings in Orthodox Jewish prayer services—who presumably figured in his own New York City upbringing.) An assistant professor of English literature at Newfield College in Connecticut, Dr. Mullhouse teaches courses titled "Survey of English Literature from Beowulf to Joyce" and "Victorian Fiction," and, as if to emphasize how his literary affinities have come to substitute for traditional religious and/or ethnic commitments, he escorts his children to the public library "every Saturday" morning, rather than to a synagogue (116). In the novel's portrait of Dr. Mullhouse, it dramatizes Freedman's insight that an extraordinary zeal for fluency in the English language and mastery over canonical English and U.S. literary texts could express an academic Jew's grappling with genteel anti-Semitism and ambivalence about ethnicity in the mid-twentieth century.

Most of the novel's focus, however, is on Dr. Mullhouse's son, Edwin. Though Edwin's experiences are conveyed by a deeply unreliable narrator/biographer, Jeffrey Cartwright—who, in fact, finally murders the subject of his biography in a nearly explicit nod to Roland Barthes's "The Death of the Author"—the book does offer a few glimpses of Edwin's awareness of the Jewish inheritance that he has not quite received from his father. Given that Edwin is a third-generation American, it is not surprising that, as Hansen's Law would predict, he might reject his parents' assimilationism and embrace the ethnic heritage of his grandparents; the novel notes that "Edwin would long to talk to" his grandfather, "a man whose blood flowed in his veins and who had escaped to America from the Czar of Russia" (193).[33] The narrator also conveys the schoolyard rumor that "Edwin said he was a Jew" (174), dismissing it as malicious. Most striking is one of Edwin's jokes, which suggests his precocious awareness of the self-abnegation implicit in assimilation-by-culture as practiced by his father and aped by his own literary biographer. The novel describes how

—

144

Edwin, "extracting from the mahogany bookcase a fat volume which he said was written in Hebrew, . . . would open the first page and begin reading very slowly in a voice as solemn and deep as possible: *Tiurf eht dna ecneidebosid tsrif snam fo / Etsat latrom esohw eert neddibrof taht fo. / Eow—*" (18). This would be a truly remarkable joke for a child to make: he reads the opening lines of *Paradise Lost* from right to left, as if reciting the Hebrew text that inspired Milton's project, despite their having been composed by Milton in English. In addition to sounding very silly, Edwin's reading recalls that one of the paragons of the English literary culture that Dr. Mullhouse reveres and teaches (presumably Milton receives his due in Dr. Mullhouse's "Survey of English Literature from Beowulf to Joyce") found his inspiration in the Jewish poetry of antiquity and was a more competent Hebraist than the majority of American Jews of Edwin's, or of any other, generation.[34]

It is a joke, too, that resonates with Steven Millhauser's real-life experience. His father, Milton, resented his own bar mitzvah to the point that he refused to impose the ritual on his son, and his sense of his own identity is reflected in his response to a biographical survey, in which he describes his religion as "humanist" rather than, say, "Jewish."[35] Milton Millhauser's perspective on Hebrew, furthermore, seems to resonate with the attitude lampooned in Edwin's reading of Milton from right to left. In an article titled "Advice to My Son, or the Linguistics of Suburbia," published in the *English Journal* in 1959, Milton Millhauser wondered, in public, about which second language he should advise his son, Steven, to study during high school, mentioning Latin, Greek, French, German, and Spanish as the possibilities. He conspicuously does not mention Hebrew as a possibility. On the contrary, while Milton Millhauser had, some years earlier, enrolled Steven in a supplementary Jewish educational program on Sunday mornings that was followed by a course in Hebrew language, he deliberately exempted the boy from the language instruction. "All the other kids—there were no exceptions—stayed for Hebrew class," Steven Millhauser has recalled. "My father was against Hebrew class, or rather, specifically, against requiring me to go to Hebrew class."[36] Can Edwin's joke about the Milton who wrote *Paradise Lost* (whose name conspicuously overlaps with the real-life elder Millhauser's) therefore be understood as Steven Millhauser's critique of his father's preference for Latin and Greek, or French and German, over Hebrew?

—

As tricky as such biographical speculations may seem — especially when dealing with a novelist inspired by Nabokov and Borges, Barthes and Foucault, in equal measure, to play games with ideas of authorship — in this case, it is not so difficult to draw lines between literature and life. After I asked Millhauser about his father and raised these questions about *Edwin Mullhouse* in 2009, he wrote and published a story in the *New Yorker*, in the fall of 2012, that answers them with fiction. Titled "A Voice in the Night," the story describes, in part, a seven-year-old boy in Stratford, Connecticut, in 1950 (the age and place correspond to Millhauser's own biography) who attends a "Sunday-school class at the Jewish Community Centre" and whose "father says God is a story that people made up to explain things they don't understand." Another section focuses on an "Author," "sixty-eight years old," who "thinks of the boy a lot these days" and remembers his "God-scorning father driving him to Sunday school but taking him home when the others went to Hebrew class."[37] The story goes on to offer a detailed, thoughtful meditation on the subject of Millhauser's Jewishness: what it has meant to him at different points in his life and what he gained and lost by being introduced to religion by an atheist father.

The story makes explicit what critics missed, or misunderstood, forty years earlier, about *Edwin Mullhouse:* that the drama of becoming the novelist son of a critic father was, for Steven Millhauser, also the drama of developing his own relationship to Jewishness. The story explains that, for the younger Millhauser, his literary aspirations developed along with a feeling about the intensity and magic of Hebrew scripture. Building to its climax, "A Voice in the Night" suggests that something profound connects the seven-year-old boy moved by Bible stories in 1950s Connecticut and the adult Author. It proposes the story of 1 Samuel 3, which the Author remembers shaking him in his childhood, as the answer to the cliché questions asked at every post-author-reading Q&A session: "The boy listening for his name, the man waiting for the rush of inspiration. Where do you get your ideas? A voice in the night. When did you decide to become a writer? Three thousand years ago, in the temple of Shiloh."[38] Whether Steven Millhauser really believes this or not — that his path to his career as a fiction writer can be traced back to a Bible story he was taught at a Jewish Community Center and, in a broader sense, to a vocation he inherited, as a Jew, from the Hebrew prophets — "A Voice in the Night" suggests how fully he has em-

—

braced a literary, secular inheritance from his father and how much he has complicated it. In so doing, the story makes explicit what was already implicit in Millhauser's extraordinary first novel, *Edwin Mullhouse*, which manages impressively to be both a loving portrait of Millhauser's literature-infused childhood and, at the same time, a grim parody of the heavy burden a literary scholar father imposed on a child who would grow up to write fiction.

Inheritance as Burden: Jacob Epstein's *Wild Oats*

Possibly the most notorious case of a child of influential Jewish literary professionals in the postwar U.S. who went on to write fiction was that of Jacob Epstein, the son of the Random House editor Jason Epstein and *New York Review of Books* editor Barbara Epstein. (I will refer to all the Epsteins by their first names in what follows, for clarity's sake.) Jacob plagiarized dozens of phrases and descriptions from Martin Amis, himself the son of a celebrated novelist, in his debut novel, *Wild Oats* (1979). The story of Jacob's plagiarism has been told often and at some length, first in newspaper and magazine articles, some gleeful in their schadenfreude, and then in a long, central chapter of Thomas Mallon's study of plagiarism, *Stolen Words* (1989). Mallon can only guess at the motivation for Jacob's act, but newly discovered material in Jason and Barbara's archives provides support for the idea that *Wild Oats,* plagiarism and all, was an act of revenge on literary parents, specifically parents who offered their child too much help.

As mentioned in chapter 3, in the 1970s, Harry Smith, Richard Kostelanetz, and Philip Nobile discussed what these critics considered a spousal conflict of interest between Jason and Barbara Epstein. Like many people who worked in publishing, the Epsteins also engaged in behavior that could arguably be construed as a collusive trading of favors. It was not out of character for Jason, in 1960, to write a glowing review of a book that he himself was editing and publishing and offer the review to a magazine, only to be told by the editor there that "it would seem like log rolling, wouldn't it?" and that the editor "cannot publish it," if only for the sake of "good form and appearances."[39] Unbowed, Jason apparently tried the same thing three years later and succeeded: Nobile

—

reports that in 1963, Jason placed in *Partisan Review* a review he wrote of a book of W. H. Auden's essays that he himself had been involved in publishing at Random House.[40]

Notwithstanding these acts, Jason had given considerable thought to conspiracies and nepotism. While it is not clear whether he ever connected his writing on these issues to his own behavior, he wrote in his 1970 book *The Great Conspiracy Trial* about the ways that collusion could harm businesses and how politicians offering help to their family members signaled corruption.[41] Out of concerns around these issues, Jason and Barbara regularly reminded people, as mentioned in chapter 3, that Jason did not influence the editorial practices at the *New York Review of Books*, despite his being married to one of its editors; in a letter to the *New York Times* in 1972, for example, he protested the suggestion that the journal was under his influence: "That I could, even if I chose, advise these people how to run their magazine is untrue."[42] This was not just a pose for public consumption, either. When a writer addressed a query to "Mr. Jason Epstein, Editor, New York Review of Books" in 1964, Barbara wrote back calmly, "Jason Epstein doesn't work here," and when, a decade later, an author suggested a reviewer for his book and further suggested to Jason, "Perhaps you would be good enough to mention this matter to Mrs. Epstein," Jason replied, simply and professionally, "I'm careful to avoid suggesting books for review to the people at *The New York Review,* but I see no reason why you shouldn't write to Mrs. Epstein directly."[43]

When it came to the literary aspirations of Jason and Barbara's son, they exercised considerably less circumspection. In the summer of 1974, Barbara wrote to John Gross, the editor of the *Times Literary Supplement* in London, noting that Jacob was "about to turn eighteen" and had just graduated high school and that while he was "supposed to be going to Yale this fall to study English and become a writer, . . . he thought he might want to work for a year in London instead." She acknowledged the challenges ("the working-papers problem and scarcity of jobs, as well as his age") but expressed the hope that Gross might be able to help: "as a Jewish mother, I'd be very grateful for anything." (Gross replied to say he would be happy to help, though it does not seem that a job at the *TLS* was actually forthcoming for Jacob.)[44] What is most striking about the exchange is the nonchalant confidence with which Barbara described her teenage son's literary ambitions: while many professional editors would regard a seventeen-year-old's desire to "become a writer" with some healthy, supportive skepticism, she does not express anything but confidence in Jacob's plans, and she went so far as to ask a respected colleague to offer the teenager a job, on this basis, at one of the most prestigious publications in England.

A few years later, a letter drafted by Jason suggests how he was able, and may have been willing, to help out with Jacob's budding literary career. On October 26, 1978, Jason wrote a letter to Robert E. Ginna, the editor at Little, Brown who was publishing Jacob's *Wild Oats*, enclosing a Random House marketing list as an example of what Random House would "use for a novel like Jacob's." In addition to what would be a surprising sharing of marketing materials with one of Random House's chief competitors (though it should be noted that it is not clear whether the letter was ever actually sent to Ginna), Jason goes on to list Elizabeth Hardwick, Lillian Hellman, Gore Vidal, and Jane Kramer as having "all read [Jacob's] manuscript and lik[ed] it very much" and noting Francine du Plessix Gray, Pete Hamill, Peter Mathiessen, William Styron, Renata Adler, and Philip Roth as "friends of Jacob's" who might help promote the novel.[45] Unsurprisingly, many of these celebrated authors had written for the *New York Review of Books* or had had books published by Random House; a few years earlier, for example, Roth dedicated his 1974 novel *My Life as a Man* to Jason, his Random House editor. Moreover, these writers were all substantially older than Jacob, who was then twenty-two (their ages ranged; Adler and Kramer were in their early forties, while Hellman was seventy-three). If there is any doubt about what Jason meant when he wrote that his son, a recent college graduate, counted some of the country's most prominent middle-aged and elderly writers and intellectuals among his "friends," it may help to know that Jacob inscribed the copy of *Wild Oats* that he sent to Vidal, "To Gore, my mother's friend and mine!"[46]

In short, this network of writers and intellectuals — who, of course, may have genuinely adored Jacob and earnestly believed in the value of his novel — was unquestionably Jason and Barbara's network. And there can be no doubt, either, that some people allowed their reading of *Wild Oats* to be colored by the way they felt about how their friends' son had been shaping up as a young man. Ginna,

—

the book's editor, said so explicitly when he described the novel's protagonist, in a letter he shared with Jason, as "a refreshing idealist among somewhat feckless peers, reflecting not a little of Jacob's own character, wry, tolerant, and wise."[47] Hellman's blurb on the novel's dust jacket, meanwhile, goes even further: "Once in a while a young writer sees himself, his friends and his parents with a remarkable good-natured brilliance."[48] Here Hellman strikingly describes *Wild Oats* less as a novel than as a memoir, suggesting that its achievement is, at least in part, that it represents not only Jacob and his friends but also "his parents."

The novel does begin with a collect call from its protagonist, a college student named Billy, to his mother, and it ends with Billy on the phone with his father; in between, it represents these adults satirically, as selfish and out of touch. To whatever degree these characters might have been drawn from life, though, they cannot be understood, *pace* Hellman, as nonfictional portraits of Jason and Barbara; Billy's father, in the novel, is a former "assistant professor of creative writing at New York University" (80) who "has long since moved away to the West Coast" (16) and has already been separated from Billy's mother long enough to remarry and have a child with his new partner. (In actuality, Jason and Barbara did not divorce until after the novel was published, in 1980.) Yet Hellman's blurb suggests just how easy it was to read *Wild Oats* as a window into Jason and Barbara's lives.

Reviewers did often mention the novel's focus on Billy's parents. Writing in the *New York Times Book Review,* Anne Tyler noted that Billy is "burdened . . . by a family that seems to have gone askew in nearly every way imaginable," and *Time*'s critic said Jacob was "at his best with fresh comic perceptions of growing up absurd in a multiparent home." Remarkably, though, none of the initial reviews published in the U.S. in the summer of 1979 — in publications including the *Boston Globe*, the *New York Times, Time, Newsweek, Harper's,* the *New Republic,* and *Saturday Review,* among others — mentioned that Jacob was the son of Jason and Barbara.[49] Following the novel's flap copy, which described Jacob as a 1978 graduate of Yale not once but twice, these reviewers regularly mentioned Epstein's college degree, and one remarked that "part of the charm of the novel comes from the fact that its author doesn't have to remember . . . what being an undergraduate is like."[50] Jacob's youth attracted attention — a photo of him, accompanying one review, was captioned "Boy Wonder" — and, according to

—

one report, the novel was remarkably successful, selling twenty thousand copies in hard cover.[51]

The fact that Jacob was the child of two of the most prominent literary eminences in the U.S. was not raised in the novel's reception until Amis mentioned it in his account of Jacob's plagiarism more than a year after the novel's initial publication, in October 1980.[52] Even then, Jason does not seem to have been shy about publicly advocating for his son: an account of the plagiarism controversy in the *Boston Globe* remarked that Jason "wasted no time coming to the rescue . . . fielding much of the flack and saying that Jacob should be allowed a certain amount of 'professional naivete.'"[53] In other words, rather than Jason distancing himself from the mess that Jacob had made or letting Jacob deal with the fallout himself, he seems to have been more than willing to serve as his son's press representative. Barbara did not, as far as I can tell, speak publicly about *Wild Oats*. In 1996, asked about her son and what he does, she said simply (and consistently with the way she had described his aspirations twenty years earlier), "he's a writer and does some producing in Hollywood"—but a critic has observed that in the wake of this controversy, "the [*New York*] *Review* [*of Books*], which had applauded Amis's first novel, thereafter ignored all his subsequent work, shunning him for more than 30 years—until Barbara Epstein's death in 2006," suggesting that Barbara's response to her son's act of plagiarism was, at least in part, to shun its victim.[54]

All of this increases one's sense that Jacob's act of plagiarism might be understood specifically in the context of his parents' roles in literary culture. Before the plagiarism came to light, one of *Wild Oats*'s initial reviewers remarked that it "is a story not about growing up, but about refusing to—or at least refusing to turn into the kind of person most of the adults in the book . . . are," and as Mallon perceptively phrases it, through plagiarism Jacob achieved this result metatextually: "If your parents are important editors in New York, what, after all, is the worst possible thing you can be caught doing?"[55] After the plagiarism came to light, Jacob pursued a successful career writing for television, for shows including *Hill Street Blues* and *L.A. Law*. He noted in 1996 the irony that, growing up, his had been "one of the last families . . . to own a TV" and that his "parents were scornful of 'junk culture,'" which suggests that his second profession may have functioned as a rejection of his parents' influence.[56]

—

While Amis called "the psychology of plagiarism . . . fascinatingly perverse," as "it risks, or invites, a deep shame, and there must be something of the death-wish in it," Mallon hypothesizes that the target of Jacob's animus might have been not himself but his celebrated parents: by plagiarizing, Jacob could "accomplish a sort of Oedipal slaying."[57] Since both of the parents in this case were his putative victims, the slaying seems less strictly Oedipal than more generally parricidal, aimed at both the literary eminences who had done so much – by introducing him to their famous friends and colleagues, writing letters on his behalf, and maybe smoothing his path in other ways not visible in the archive – to make it possible for him to publish a novel at a precociously young age. Consistent with, but more than, the satirical portraits of Billy's parents within the novel, the act of plagiarism could be understood to have served as Jacob's filial revenge, a potent means of eschewing the symbolic capital that he did not stand to inherit passively but that his parents had been actively foisting onto him.

Normalizing Literary Inheritances since the 1990s

The cases of Pat Knopf and Atheneum, Steven Millhauser, and Jacob Epstein each suggest, in their own way, how awkward and fraught the transfer of symbolic capital from one generation of a Jewish family to another could be in the 1960s and 1970s and how much resistance there was to such transfers on the part of the people who stood to benefit from them. To some degree, that awkwardness can be understood as specific to the personalities and aspirations of the individuals involved, and in part it may have owed to this having been the first period during which Jews, in the U.S., had dealt with this particular set of challenges. The Jewish community may not have had opportunities to develop the strategies that existed in some non-Jewish American and European families for dealing with the contingencies of such transfers of capital from one generation to another. In part, the awkwardness must also have been strengthened by the general ethos of that specific moment in U.S. history, in which generational conflicts were taken as given and foundational; rejecting whatever one's parents had to offer was, after all, a key element of 1960s and 1970s U.S. youth culture (a dynamic marked, linguistically, by the popularization of the term "generation gap").[58]

In the ensuing decades, as many more people found themselves in positions parallel to those of Pat Knopf, Steven Millhauser, and Jacob Epstein—more American Jews, in other words, came of age with parents who were publishers, scholars, editors, and writers—the inheritance of this kind of symbolic capital became more and more typical in American Jewish life (just as the rise in Jews' socioeconomic status made the inheritance of vast fortunes and stewardship of family foundations an increasingly normal facet of Jews' experiences in the late twentieth- and early twenty-first-century U.S.).[59] This corresponded to a period of generally decreasing support for estate taxes, the primary measure that had been used to constrain inheritances in the U.S. since the early twentieth century.[60] A complete list of contemporary Jewish writers and critics whose parents had been successful in related fields (as editors, literary scholars, or critics) before them would be nearly impossible to compile, and if it covered even a fraction of cases, it would stretch to hundreds of pages long. Still, a brief but representative list, focusing on children who published fiction, poetry, and criticism, in particular, could include the following people: the *Los Angeles Times* book reviewer Robert Kirsch's son Jonathan (1949–), who published his first novel in 1977; Bernard Malamud's daughter Janna Malamud Smith (1952–), who published her first book in 1997; Arthur Miller's daughter Rebecca (1962–), who published her first novel in 2001; the novelist Norma Rosen's son Jonathan (1963–), an editor and critic whose first novel was published in 1997; the novelist Rosellen Brown's daughter Adina Hoffman (1967–), who published her first book, a collection of literary essays, in 2000; Robert Kirsch's grandson and Jonathan Kirsch's son Adam (1976–), a poet and literary critic who published his first book of poems in 2002 and his first book of criticism in 2005; the novelist and critic Rebecca Goldstein's daughter Yael Goldstein Love (1978–), who published her first novel in 2007 and now runs a publishing company; the novelist and scholar Erich Segal's daughter Francesca (1980–), whose novel *The Innocents* was published in 2012 and won the Sami Rohr Prize for Jewish Literature; Norman Podhoretz and Midge Decter's grandson Sam Munson (1981–), who published his first novel in 2010; and the novelist and

—

153

scholar Jonathan Wilson's son Adam (1983–), who published his first novel in 2012.[61]

To be clear, that list does not include the children of writers who mostly or only have written memoirs about their famous parents (like Margaret Salinger and Gregory Bellow), nor does it even begin to cover the Jewish literary scholars and critics whose parents had made careers in similar fields to their own in the previous generation.[62] It also does not include people like Michael Kazin, David Bell, Dan Hofstadter, James Trilling, Nicholas Howe, John Podhoretz, and Adam Bellow, who found success as editors, academics, and intellectuals like their celebrated parents.[63]

In a sense, of course, such lists are unexceptional. As mentioned earlier, one could easily make even longer lists of non-Jewish Americans and non-Americans with major literary careers in the twentieth and twenty-first centuries whose parents had been well positioned in the literary field, and one could find innumerable examples of similar inheritances among Jews and other groups in many other cultural and professional fields.[64] Social scientists have noted the typicality of "microclass reproduction" (children taking up occupations identical or related to the occupations of their parents).[65] Perhaps even more than other fields, publishing and literature for centuries had been aristocratic or at least upper-class pursuits that were open more to the children of the gentry and those in the upper-middle class, including writers and scholars, than to workers.[66] What makes the preceding list of American Jewish second-generation literary professionals meaningful is, simply, the specific timing of the literary enfranchisement of American Jews in the middle of the twentieth century. Before that, because Jews were emphatically and deliberately excluded from that aristocratic literary system in the U.S., no such list could have been compiled. The generational transfer of literary prestige in the form of education, taste, and connections simply was not a phenomenon to which American Jews, as a group, were privy before the middle of the twentieth century. While Pat Knopf, Steven Millhauser, and Jacob Epstein represent somewhat pioneering examples, the proliferation of such inheritances in the decades that follow reflects the scale of American Jews' literary enfranchisement in the mid-twentieth century.

What did it mean to this later generation of American Jews to receive a specifically literary inheritance? How did it change what and how they wrote

—

that the anxiety of influence they experienced was not metaphorically Oedipal, as in Harold Bloom's famous formulation, but, as in Freud's Oedipal complex, a struggle between actual children and parents?[67] To some degree, of course, the answers to these questions continue to vary from one writer to another, but as diverse as the individual experiences of these writers might be, what they increasingly share after the 1980s is a less ambivalent acceptance of their inheritances. These writers may at times chafe lightly against parental influence or wonder about what they have gained and lost in receiving it, but whereas Knopf, Millhauser, and Epstein found striking ways to challenge, complicate, or even repudiate their parents' influence, increasingly American Jewish writers have found ways to overcome any guilt they might experience. They manifest a tendency toward reverence for their forbears rather than an agonistic struggle against their influence.

Take Francesca Segal, for example. She has been more than happy to answer interviewers' questions about her father, Erich Segal, the son of a rabbi, raised in Brooklyn, who went to Harvard in the 1950s, became a classics scholar, and then wrote the major bestseller *Love Story* (1970), among other popular novels. "My father was an enormous source of inspiration," she told one interviewer, "both for the example that he set and for the passionate love of reading that he instilled in our whole family."[68] When another interviewer gently raised the issue of nepotism ("often the kids of successful people end up doing well in the same profession"), Segal did not react defensively but effusively: "I adored my father and when I was a child, I wanted to do anything he did, but mostly I think his passion for language permeated and informed my childhood."[69] In an essay she published in *Granta* in 2008, Segal explained that her "earliest memories of [her] father are inextricably linked with his identity as a writer," and she unselfconsciously linked her vocation to this inheritance she received from him and her mother: "Writing was the centre of our family, the language we spoke. . . . My father the writer, my mother the editor — theirs are the only skills to which I've ever aspired."[70]

Segal's embrace of her inheritance resonates with the plot of her first, prize-winning novel, *The Innocents* (2012). Modeled on Edith Wharton's *The Age of Innocence* but set among well-off Jews in suburban London, the novel focuses on a young man named Adam Newman who is engaged to marry his high school

—

sweetheart, Rachel. The novel's conflict concerns Adam's attraction to Rachel's New York cousin, Ellie, and the novel's jacket copy is not at all subtle in explaining that what Ellie "offers" Adam is "a liberation that he hadn't known existed: a freedom from the loving interference and frustrating parochialism of [Jewish] North West London."[71] This is, of course, the familiar triangular plot structure of ethnic American literature that Werner Sollors identified in his classic readings of Abraham Cahn's *Yekl* and Charles Chesnutt's "The Wife of His Youth," in which two potential romantic partners offer the protagonist a choice between "consent" and "descent," the opposite poles of a "central conflict" in which the protagonists will either "love and cherish their ethnic past or . . . abandon it."[72] Fittingly, Segal's novel describes its symbol of descent, Rachel, as having a host of babyish "tics and mannerisms," derived from "a lifetime of her parents' infantilizing worship," like holding her arms "out to [Adam], like a toddler asking to be carried" (243), while when Adam meets up with Ellie, she congratulates him for having "escaped NW11" (London's Jewish neighborhood) and suggesting they "toast [his] night of freedom" (146). Rachel represents infants, toddlers, and the perpetuation of a family line, while Ellie represents escape and freedom.

Similar conflicts animate hundreds of novels, but Segal resolves hers in an unexpected way. After Adam goes through with his wedding to Rachel, he plans to leave her and pursue a life with Ellie instead; but then it turns out that Rachel is pregnant, and her family, having discovered Adam's attraction to Ellie, conspires to let Ellie find out about the pregnancy, which convinces her that it is too late to be with Adam, and sends her back to New York. As an obstacle to Adam and Ellie's relationship, this seems formidable enough, but Segal goes further: Rachel miscarries only six days after telling Adam that she is pregnant, meaning that to whatever degree the pregnancy had tipped the balance of whether he should stay with Rachel or leave with Ellie, that motivation has disappeared. But Adam still stays with Rachel, and the novel suggests how hard he has to work to assure Rachel that he is committed to her (and finished with Ellie): "It had taken strength he hadn't known he had, love he hadn't known he'd felt, to make her turn back to him. It was only the force of Adam's will, his sudden clear and urgent longing that had convinced her" (281). This odd passage suggests that at a moment in time when Rachel is no longer pregnant and when Adam is fully aware that she has conspired with her family to separate him from the woman he loves—from Adam's perspective, the novel describes Rachel and her family as moving "together like fronds of coral, to expel the predator," with the purpose of "shielding Rachel" but also "shielding Adam from himself" (270) – he feels a new intensity of emotional desire ("sudden clear and urgent longing," a "love he hadn't known he'd felt") for Rachel. The source of that new longing, the novel implies, is precisely that Rachel, who has always seemed childish to Adam, has now impressed him with the facility with which she and her family have manipulated him; "with the sacrifice of her innocence . . . she had bought her strength" (281), he notes. Adam is able to marshal new "strength," then, because he newly perceives Rachel's. Strikingly, the novel ends with Adam locking eyes with his smiling father-in-law, as if to underline the point that in the choice between an insular, protective family and Jewish community, on the one hand, and "freedom" from "frustrating parochialism," on the other, Adam has definitively chosen the former, and even more remarkably, the novel records no ambivalence on Adam's part about that choice. Perhaps such an acceptance of the prerogative of a family to protect its members makes particular sense in the work of a writer who understands literature as her own family's business, an inheritance she embraces without cavil.

Another striking case of contemporary literary nepotism is Sam Munson, the grandson of the legendary *Commentary* editor Norman Podhoretz.[73] Podhoretz's "editorship by bloodline"—that is, his enthusiasm for hiring and publishing his relatives—has been widely noted, and Munson certainly appears to have benefited from his literary inheritance.[74] Born in 1981, Munson began to publish criticism while still an undergraduate at the University of Chicago; in 2002, he contributed the first of several book reviews to a relatively unlikely venue for a young aspiring writer, the Hoover Institution's *Policy Review*, a publication that was aligned with his family's neoconservative politics and that regularly hosted and praised his grandfather and uncle.[75] Munson graduated from the University of Chicago on June 15, 2003, and that same month, the issue of *Commentary* on newsstands contained Munson's first contribution to the magazine, a book review.[76] Over the next half decade, Munson would contribute another review or two each year.[77] Starting in 2006, he blogged regularly for *Commentary,* and at some point—around the time his uncle, John Podhoretz,

—

was named the magazine's editor – Munson was hired as online editor.[78] During this period, Munson worked on a novel. The first time the project was mentioned in the press was when, in January 2009, the *New York Observer* ran a piece titled "Sam Munson, Grandson of Norman Podhoretz, Taking Debut Novel to Market."[79] The book, titled *The November Criminals,* was eventually published in 2010. Munson had apparently stopped working for *Commentary* by then. The magazine's review of Munson's novel, by a frequent contributor, D. G. Myers, noted that Munson "worked at *Commentary* as its online editor from 2007 to 2009" (but not that he was related to many of the magazine's contributors and editors) before calling the book a "deeply satisfying first novel" and Munson "a remarkable new voice in American fiction."[80] It would be difficult to imagine a novelist's debut more intensely marked by his family members' achievements.

While Munson has generally avoided discussing his famous grandfather and other family members when giving interviews or writing essays, his novel is written from the perspective of a young man who spends quite a bit of his time thinking about his parents and doing so within a context that emphasizes the transfer of symbolic capital from one generation to another: the novel is written in the form of an unusually long college application essay, meaning that its protagonist is submitting this piece of writing to a system, U.S. college admissions, in which "legacy status" plays a significant role.[81] The novel's protagonist and narrator, Addison Schacht, is the son of artist-intellectuals, a book-editor mother who died young and a potter whom Addison judges "a failed artist."[82] The choice of these professions seems not entirely unrelated to those of Munson's parents; Munson's mother, Naomi, is a writer and "public relations executive" whose published work has appeared in *Commentary,* as well as in some other neoconservative venues, while Munson's father, Steven, was an editor and writer who published art criticism in *Commentary.*[83] Additionally, Addison is, the reader quickly learns, named after his grandfather.[84] While in many ways this character seems to have been designed to resist being seen as too dutifully the product of a well-known Jewish, neoconservative family – Addison is an antisocial drug dealer – one of the book's main interests is in the relations between a white, Jewish young man and his African American peers at school and in his neighborhood (one reviewer noted, "Race and the exposure of racism are the novel's central concerns").[85] This strikingly and inevitably recalls Norman Pod-

—

horetz's most notorious and widely discussed essay, "My Negro Problem — and Ours" (1963).[86]

In fact, Addison's experiences with race and his perspectives on the subject often echo Munson's grandfather's very particularly. In "My Negro Problem," Podhoretz remembers going to elementary and middle schools where "each grade had been divided into three classes, according to 'intelligence,'" with the result of "a preponderance of Jews in '1' classes and a corresponding preponderance of Negroes in the '3's," though "at least a few Negroes had always made the '1's" (95); in *The November Criminals,* Addison notes that his high school is "segregated," with a "90 percent white" school-inside-the-school, "the Gifted and Talented Program," which nonetheless "let in six black kids or so every year" (5). Addison blames his school's segregation on "the kind of [white] parents who *just love* black people — in the abstract" (4), while Podhoretz, in 1963, described with disdain those "white middle-class liberals" whose "abstract commitment to the cause of Negro rights will not stand the test of a direct confrontation" (98) and whose residential and policy choices lead to de facto school segregation.

The plot of *The November Criminals* concerns Addison's attempts to investigate the murder of one of his few African American classmates in the Gifted and Talented Program, and this often entails Addison's reflections on what he and the murdered boy have in common and what they do not, along the lines of Podhoretz's musings comparing himself and his African American neighbors and colleagues and Podhoretz's and other neoconservatives' ideas about race in the U.S. more generally.[87] In the novel, this all goes on for a couple of hundred pages, while "My Negro Problem" is, if nothing else, brief; and while one could find more correspondences between the two texts — not to mention between the novel and other bits and pieces across the rest of Podhoretz's extensive oeuvre — the point is not to reduce *The November Criminals* to a commentary on a family obsession. It is an admirably proficient novel that received at least a few admiring notices by people who are not members of Munson's extended family or their employees, and it was adapted to film by producers, writers, and a director who, presumably, felt that it provided worthwhile source material.[88] But the overlapping concerns visible from the book's beginning do suggest that, however Munson might feel on any given day about his famous family and whatever his intent may have been in writing the novel, it is not unfair to say that it reads, at least in part, as an attempt to update and translate into the form of fiction one of the issues that have been that family's core intellectual concerns for more than half a century.

That said, Munson still feels it necessary to avoid talking about his famous relatives (both in published interviews or essays and in not answering requests for an interview for this book).[89] Other writers of this generation have, like Segal, been less reticent, occasionally offering deeply adulatory portraits of their famous parents, like Rebecca Miller's film *Arthur Miller: Writer* (2017).[90] Others have cheerfully described how their parents' success helped them: Jonathan Rosen, who as a teenager already coauthored, with his novelist mother, a book for children called *A Family Passover,* has reflected on the ways that growing up with parents who were a writer and professor of comparative literature and whose "writer friends" included "Cynthia Ozick and Lore Segal and Johanna Kaplan" helped him to believe in the power and value of literature and gave him an understanding that "books are attached to people and to actual lives and words that flow around books and keep them afloat."[91] Katie Roiphe, a critic and novelist and the daughter of the novelist and memoirist Anne Roiphe, has been discussed in the press as "very much her mother's daughter" since the publication of her first book, when she was twenty-five, and she has often published praise of her mother's work, calling her, for one example, "a transcendently good storyteller."[92] Sam Apple, an essayist and nonfiction author whose father, Max, is a noted fiction writer, explained in an email that his father's reputation "probably helped open some doors" for him: "I recall once meeting Cynthia Ozick after a talk she gave. I had just graduated from college and was nervous about approaching a literary icon. But when I said I was Max Apple's son, she seemed more excited than I was."[93] Often the capital passed on from one generation to another takes a form as minor and unremarkable as this—it simply makes it easier for a young writer to talk to someone important in the field or to pitch their work, to take a risk or to give themselves permission to experiment in a way that less-well-connected people might not feel they have the right to do.

An impressively frank literary child of a literary parent, Yael Goldstein Love is the author of a novel, *Overture* (2007), and more recently the cofounder and editorial director of a digital publishing venture called Plympton. Her mother is the prominent novelist and philosopher Rebecca Goldstein, author of more

—

than ten books of fiction and nonfiction and the winner of many prestigious awards, including a MacArthur Fellowship and the National Humanities Medal. As Goldstein Love reflects on her experiences as the child of a successful writer, she notes that her mother's experiences in the field made her own literary career "seem possible, even inevitable" and "definitely helped [her] some with early connections." Goldstein Love insists that this was not by any means an unalloyed good: "people tended to think I was a lot better connected than I was and to attribute my early success to that."[94] All of this manifests itself in Goldstein Love's novel *Overture,* which, as an early profile noted, concerns "a famous artist and her talented daughter's struggle to assert her own autonomy as an artist outside of her mother's rather all-encompassing shadow."[95] Many other writers of this generation would seem to share Goldstein Love's mix of gratitude and uneasiness. A number of them whom I asked to comment on the subject responded uncomfortably to my questions and decided, in the end, not to answer on the record. But few of them, to date, have repudiated their families' influences with the vigor of a Pat Knopf or a Jacob Epstein—they have, instead, pursued literary careers in which they have been able to benefit from their parents' influence and connections, usually acknowledging the advantages they have derived from their parents, when asked, either enthusiastically or more quietly but without drawing undue attention.

Is Literary Nepotism Inevitable?

It is easy and tempting to be critical of writers (or professionals in any industry) who appear to have derived an enormous amount of benefit from their parents' successes in that same field. But like more general objections to a literary mafia, such criticism often leaves unexamined the assumptions of what a truly meritocratic or fair system would look like. Is it reasonable to expect that parents will not use their accrued symbolic and cultural capital on their children's behalf or that children will reject that support from their parents? Adam Bellow, in his book *In Praise of Nepotism,* distinguishes between what he calls "New Nepotism" and "Old Nepotism" (which, at one point he also characterizes as "*good* nepotism and *bad*") and describes himself as a beneficiary of the former: "I am the son of a famous writer (novelist Saul Bellow) who has made his career in the publishing business. Though my father had nothing to do with my getting a job, my employers were well aware of the connection, and they undoubtedly assumed not only that I had 'the right stuff' to be an editor by virtue of my parentage, but that my name and social background would be useful in my publishing career."[96] In Bellow's schema, he "can't be called a beneficiary of nepotism in the conventional sense" because his father "had nothing to do" with his "getting a job" – except that, as he goes on to describe, his father did have *plenty* to do with his getting a job. He conferred a valuable name, offered "social background" and a "connection" of which employers were aware. So in what sense did Saul Bellow have "nothing to do" with his son's literary employment? Only in the narrow sense that "the Old Nepotism involved parents hiring their children outright or pulling strings on their behalf" and that the New Nepotism "combin[es] the privileges of birth with the iron rule of merit."[97]

From Bellow's perspective, one might want to argue that of all the parents discussed in this chapter, only Jason and Barbara Epstein, with their willingness to pull strings on their son's behalf, and the Podhoretz family (which often hired relatives "outright"), and probably some of the publishing families in which children succeeded parents, would be guilty of "Old Nepotism," and the rest would be judged blameless practitioners of the New Nepotism. But that would mean accepting Bellow's fantasies about an "iron rule of merit" and about the contemporary U.S. as a place where "the playing field is much more level than it was one hundred, fifty, or even twenty years ago," where "it is no longer possible for nepotism to be practiced indiscriminately, or in a way that masks incompetence," and where "a famous name may get you in the door," but "you have to prove your worth or face the consequences."[98]

Those fantasies – that an "iron rule of merit" could possibly apply in a business like publishing, where Adam Bellow made his career, or that it is clear and widely agreed on what constitutes "incompetence" (or its opposite) in that field – are the threads one expects a beneficiary of nepotism to cling to. If repeated often enough, they might help to allay that person's guilt and self-doubt. But since, as this book has argued, there is nothing that can be called merit, per se, in literary culture or any general agreement about what constitutes competence in literature or publishing, Bellow's distinction between New Nepotism and

Old Nepotism begins to blur. Indeed, despite the emphasis he places on his father having "had nothing to do" with his "getting a job," Bellow elsewhere explains that in the contemporary U.S., "intervention" — an active pulling of strings — "isn't necessary": "Growing up around a business or vocation — learning how it works, getting to know the people in it — creates a powerful advantage," and this "works for the most part subtly and invisibly, creating opportunities for those who have connections in a given field, and increasingly excluding those who don't."[99] In acknowledging this, Bellow agrees with a leading scholar of inheritance, Jens Beckert, who observed despondently in 2013 that "societies seem once again willing to allow the disconnection of life chances from individual performance."[100]

One can hope that at least some of the beneficiaries of this system recognize its injustice. Social scientists reviewing Bellow's book noticed a tinge of desperation underneath the book's carefully balanced tone, and the tension is not especially subtle.[101] When he articulates a set of rules for how to practice nepotism so as to make it "constructive and positive," Bellow employs phrases — "Don't embarrass me" and "Don't embarrass yourself. . . . You have to work harder than anyone else" — that speak directly to the predicament that the children of celebrated and famous parents find themselves in.[102] Bellow is probably right that nepotism is so deeply ingrained in human psychology that it will never cease to be a factor in decision-making and most especially in a field, like literature, shot through with "radical quality uncertainty."[103] But what he unintentionally helps to expose, consonant with the careers of the editors and writers discussed in this chapter, is the degree to which, along with powerful benefits, nepotism carries a cost.

Unless the beneficiaries of nepotism can find a way to establish their independence from their parents — and convince not only their audiences and critics of this but also, which is more difficult (for most reasonable people), themselves — they will never be free from the doubt that they do not deserve the opportunities and acclaim that they receive. That is perhaps small comfort to people competing for the same opportunities who are not themselves beneficiaries of inheritances and who see these capital transfers as helping to perpetuate the prodigious and growing inequalities in the literary field. But it is something.

—

CONCLUSION

We Need More Literary Mafias

From the perspective of the present — as I finish my work on the manuscript of this book, amid an ongoing pandemic, in the summer of 2021 — the enfranchisement of Jews in U.S. literary culture, which began in the early decades of the twentieth century and made every opportunity and position in U.S. literary culture available to Jews by the end of the 1960s, seems to have been a lasting, perhaps even permanent transformation of U.S. culture. A casual survey of contemporary U.S. publishing and literary culture demonstrates that American Jews now enjoy the same full, unrestricted, even privileged access to the field that they have benefited from for half a century.

Many of the most consequential gatekeeping roles in U.S. literary culture are currently, or were until very recently, held by people who are Jewish or partly Jewish or have Jewish ancestry. The *New Yorker* continues to publish short fiction in almost every issue after most other U.S. magazines with large circulations have stopped doing so, and it has become even more influential than ever before in launching careers of fiction writers in the U.S. over the past two or three decades. Its editor since 1998, David Remnick, is Jewish, and its fiction editor since 2002, Deborah Treisman, called a "gatekeeper for literature" in the *New York Times*, considers herself "of mixed heritage — mother with Protestant roots, Jewish father, neither of them religious."[1] *Poetry*, the most well-resourced and influential periodical focusing on the publishing of poetry in the U.S., was from 2013 to the fall of 2020 edited by Don Share, who is Jewish and has published poems of his own about his Jewish ancestors.[2] The current or recent editors of many influential, independent journals that publish new fiction and poetry are Jewish or have Jewish ancestry, including, for example, the *Paris Review* (Emily Nemens), *n+1* (Mark Krotov), *Fence* (Rebecca Wolff), *Boston Review* (Deborah Chasman and Joshua Cohen), and *electric literature* (Jess Zimmerman).[3] Both at big-five publishers and at successful independent publishing houses, many of the most prominent current editors are Jewish, too. These include the current president and chief executive officer of Simon & Schuster, Jonathan Karp; Robin Desser, the editor in chief of Random House; Ann Godoff, the president and editor in chief of Penguin Press; John Glusman, the editor in chief of Norton; Johnny Temple, the publisher and editor in chief of Akashic Books; Judith Gurewich, the publisher of Other Press; and Ethan Nosowsky, the editorial director of Graywolf Press.[4] Many of the journalists who cover the publishing industry for influential publications or edit book-review sections are likewise Jewish or have Jewish ancestry, including Pamela Paul, the editor of the *New York Times Book Review;* Katy Waldman, a staff writer at the *New Yorker* who covers publishing and literature; Marc Winkelman, the president and publisher of the book-industry service and review magazine *Kirkus;* Boris Kachka, books editor first at *New York* magazine and then at the *Los Angeles Times;* and Emily Greenhouse, coeditor of the *New York Review of Books.*[5] In compiling these lists, I have made no effort at comprehensiveness, and dozens of other prominent Jews in contemporary publishing could easily be added. An exhaustive list including senior and junior editors and other literary professionals throughout the publishing industry who are Jewish in one way or another would be *very* long.

In other words, even though we do not have concrete data to cite, it seems fair to say that the general sense is that so many Jews work throughout U.S. publishing that it is literally unremarkable to find a Jewish person occupying any position in the field.[6] People change positions frequently in publishing and literary journalism, and by the time this book is published, some of the people just named will probably have moved on to other jobs or left the industry. Also, many of them would probably object to being included in a list of Jewish editors

—

and literary professionals; they would protest—and might be protesting this minute, if they happen to be reading this—that their individual relationships to Judaism and Jewish culture are tenuous or eccentric and that Jewishness certainly does not play a decisive role in what they decide to publish or promote or in the formation of their tastes and did not help them in attaining their current positions. It would sound wrong, to most of them, if they were to be referred to as "Jewish editors."

But, as I have suggested throughout this book, they may not be able to perceive all of the patterns in their own tastes and editorial judgments or the features of the system that have privileged them, giving them professional advantages denied to others. It is clear that thanks to homophilous logics in hiring and career advancement and all the many ways that U.S. culture promotes the perpetuation of privilege and conservation of all forms of capital, the pioneering Jews who were the first to occupy a variety of positions in U.S. literary culture paved the way for successive generations of Jews to succeed in these fields. That said, my claim that Jewishness might be a factor in the professional achievements of many contemporary editors and other literary professionals is not intended to impose any reductive reading on their careers; the ways Jewishness has played out in their careers and editorial achievements cannot be understood or surmised without close and careful study of their individual professional records. It is furthermore quite clear, even without having undertaken such a study, that unlike the mostly imaginary literary mafia of the 1960s and 1970s, these contemporary Jews in publishing do not all know one another and socialize together. In many cases, the people listed previously are members of different generations and even different socioeconomic strata, and some have very little in common. Though pernicious, nonsensical anti-Semitic claims about Jewish media control continue to be promulgated by white nationalists and conspiracy theorists who have been gaining prominence in recent years in the U.S., no reasonable scholar or critic whom I know of has suggested that there is a Jewish literary mafia operating nowadays.[7]

What *has* been discussed and decried by reasonable observers since at least the early 1990s is the whiteness of contemporary publishing. In 1991, the Association of American Publishers surveyed its members and found that "out of a total of 69,550 employees, 9.3% were African Americans, and 20.8% could be considered minorities," mostly "in clerical categories." An extensive 1994 report in *Publishers' Weekly* remarked, "No one . . . dispute[s] the fact that the book publishing industry lacks representative numbers of African American, Asian and Hispanic employees," citing racism, low salaries, and homophily as explanations for why the business was so white. Two years later, a *New York Times* article reported that even while African Americans bought hundreds of millions of books each year, the publishing industry was 87.2 percent white, citing figures from Equal Employment Opportunity Commission, and noted that "there are so few Hispanic employees . . . that it's not unusual that a major publishing house like HarperCollins . . . runs its new Libros line of Hispanic literature without a Hispanic editor involved in the project."[8] (In such statistics, as in many U.S. demographic studies, Jews were counted as white, unless they identified also as black, Hispanic, Asian, or Indigenous.)[9]

Increasing diversity in publishing was, according to those journalists, a widely shared goal: "everyone agrees that there *should* be more minorities in the business," the *Publishers' Weekly* article phrased it, and both articles cited promising examples of imprints and companies that had been actively pursuing diversity.[10] In the intervening quarter century, though, it seems that almost nothing has changed. On an anecdotal level, people of color remain rare in the industry. In 2015, Anna Devries, a senior editor at St. Martin's Press, noted that in her "15 years working in publishing, [she had] only worked with two people of color in editorial positions."[11] When editors of color do succeed, like Sonny Mehta, the celebrated editor in chief of Knopf, they are seen as an "exception" to the rule.[12] Statistics gathered recently by Lee & Low Books, in what it calls the Diversity Baseline Survey, suggest how very little has changed since the 1990s: in 2015, 79 percent of the survey's total respondents identified as white, 82 percent in editorial; in 2019, 76 percent of total respondents, and 85 percent in editorial, identified as white.[13] In practice, these numbers have meant that even successful editors of color have often endured very unpleasant experiences: in 2020, Christine Pride, an African American editor who worked for fifteen years in publishing, including as a senior editor at Simon & Schuster, described book publishing this way: "an egregiously and aggressively — I would argue, obscenely — white space."[14] This all raises a crucial question: If virtually everyone in publishing agreed thirty years ago that the industry needed to at-

—

tract more minority employees, and if efforts were made to do so at a variety of imprints and larger and smaller publishers in the intervening decades, why have we not already seen more change?

A few typical answers to this question—for example, that starting salaries in publishing are too low to attract a broad range of candidates—have been repeated decade after decade and have their value.[15] But the history of the so-called Jewish literary mafia and the relevant work of sociologists and economists who study minority experiences in employment suggest another way of understanding what has gone wrong in publishing and how to fix it. It seems at least possible that the gradualist approach that the industry has undertaken, and its far-off, unattained goal of a broadly diverse workforce, has been doomed to fail for structural reasons. The classic articulation of the problem of "tokenism," Rosabeth Moss Kanter's *Men and Women of the Corporation* (1977), explains that in her study of employees of one particular large U.S. company, "women who were few in number among male peers [in their sections or departments] . . . sometimes . . . had the advantages of those who are 'different' and thus were highly visible in a system where success is tied to becoming known, . . . [but more often] they faced the loneliness of the outsider, of the stranger who intrudes upon an alien culture and may become self-estranged in the process of assimilation, [and so] their turnover and 'failure rate' were known to be much higher than those of men in entry and early grade positions."[16] Somewhat controversially, Kanter suggests that this experience was not primarily the effect of gender, per se, but of minority status, explaining that these women's experiences "echoed the experiences of people of any kind who are rare and scarce: the lone black among whites, the lone man among women, the few foreigners among natives. Any situation where proportions of significant types of people are highly skewed can produce similar themes and processes."[17] Kanter's descriptions of loneliness and self-estrangement resonate with the experiences described by many people of color who have worked in contemporary publishing, and they go a long way to explaining why efforts to diversify the industry, since at least the 1990s, have not produced greater change.

But there are other ways a minority group can enter an industry or field. As discussed in the introduction, economists have shown that if a number of people enter a field as a group and establish themselves as at least a significant minority within that field, they can derive substantial benefits: "lower transaction and communication costs," "less noise in productivity signals," "better match quality," "better resource access," better information about who is and is not trustworthy, strengthened mechanisms of enforcement of contracts and censure of malfeasance, and so on.[18] More than theories about the dispositions or hereditary qualities of groups that have sometimes been proposed, these analyses of structural minority-group advantages help to explain the many concentrations of ethnic and immigrant groups in contemporary U.S. industries and fields — the fact that, for example, "one-third of all US motels are owned by Gujarati Indians" and that "the concentration of Korean self-employment in dry cleaners is 34 times greater than other immigrant groups."[19] While discrimination also in some cases clearly contributes to minority-group employment patterns and concentration in one or another area, this vein of economic argument suggests that such concentrations can also help the members of an "ethnic niche" to succeed and prosper within a field.[20]

It is clear that Jews who entered publishing did so, emphatically, not as tokens but as an ethnic niche. Alfred Knopf worked briefly at Doubleday, where he was certainly a token, but he quickly left that position to found Alfred A. Knopf, Inc., with his wife, father, and other Jewish employees, where he was part of a group. Within a decade, the handful of other publishing firms founded by Jews, which like Knopf hired both Jews and non-Jews (but showed no particular discrimination against Jews) built up a network of Jews in publishing — and many of the personnel across these different firms were related either by family or by social ties (Thomas Seltzer, who published on his own and advised others, was the uncle of Albert and Charles Boni; the founders of Random House and Simon & Schuster had previously worked at Boni & Liveright; and so on). Such interconnections would increase and ramify in the ensuing decades, as discussed in this book's chapters, through professor-student relationships, marriages and affairs, and parents' support of their children. These networks were exactly what inspired the critiques of a Jewish literary mafia, and though they were generally not conspiracies, they did very often provide the benefits of an ethnic niche, which were especially meaningful advantages in a field like literary publishing, where, as we have seen, one of the primary challenges at least since midcentury has been finding a signal within the ever-increasing noise (whether one is a

—

slush-pile reader, an agent or editor filtering through submissions, a book-review editor choosing which titles to assign for review, or a prize judge staring down a massive stack of submissions).[21]

Understanding Jews as having constituted a successful ethnic niche within U.S. publishing suggests one way, a new way, for the publishing industry to achieve the diversity that it apparently seeks but has not been able to realize. Rather than hiring and promoting relatively small numbers of people who iden-tify as BIPOC (Black, Indigenous, and People of Color), hoping to increase the percentage of such publishing employees over years and decades, the publishing industry could commit to seeding ethnic niches. This would mean hiring many more such people, hiring them in positions of greater authority, and investing in BIPOC-led new ventures. But probably it would also mean targeting one or two specific disenfranchised groups across the industry, rather than all such people. This seems like it would be more likely to succeed because, while there is some precedent for broad political and social coalitions drawing equally on all BIPOC, there is considerably more precedent for professional ethnic niches that are much, much more specific than that. It is not Asian Americans, in gen-eral, whom economists have identified as specializing in various U.S. fields and industries but immigrants specifically from states or countries like Gujarat, Vietnam, Korea, Laos, Tonga, Sri Lanka, and so on.[22]

If such a strategy were undertaken, and if it were to succeed and produce a vast transformation of U.S. literary culture, the end result would not be exactly the picture of diversity that one might expect or hope for. Using the current success of Jews in the field as a model, we might imagine a U.S. literary culture, say, optimistically, in the year 2030, in which African Americans were the editors of the *New Yorker* and the *Atlantic Monthly, Poetry,* the *Paris Review,* and *n+1,* the editors in chief of Random House and Simon & Schuster and Norton and Graywolf, the editors of the *New York Times Book Review* and the *New York Review of Books,* and the founders and editors in chief of a handful of new, thriving, and critically acclaimed publications and publishing houses, and in which these leaders supervised hundreds of African American employees throughout the ranks of all of their institutions. Plus, in this scenario, African Americans would be a third or more of the faculty at all the best English de-partments and most prestigious and well-funded creative-writing programs. In

—

such a situation, a typical item in the industry newsletter *Publishers Lunch* might note, without comment, that an African American literary agent had just sold a first novel, written by the protégé of a beloved African American MFA-program director, to an African American editor at one of the most prominent U.S. publishing houses, which is of course also led by an African American publisher and editor in chief. The novelist in question might be from any background, and the novel might be about absolutely anything or, in the way that some of the best novels often are, about nothing in particular.

The same scenario could be imagined with the privileged group being Latinx (or maybe even, more specifically, Chicanx) or Chinese American or Bengali or Indigenous or trans or many other possibilities or many combinations of different groups. What we can learn from the history of the so-called Jewish literary mafia in the twentieth and early twenty-first centuries is that whatever its composition, this new literary mafia would not end up being a literary mafia, really. That is, it would not be coherent, collusive, or ideologically or aesthetically uniform – but some critics would certainly come along to polemicize against it for being that way. We can easily imagine the kinds of critiques that would be leveled against such an emergent ethnic niche because, in the fantasies of American racists, any slight progress toward more opportunity for BIPOC in U.S. publishing has been met with the specter of a BIPOC takeover, of "brown nepotism" or a "black literary mafia" or, more generally, a fear of BIPOC becoming *over*represented in publishing.[23] One of the signals that white supremacy in publishing has been overcome might turn out to be that someone a little like Kostelanetz in temperament, identifying as a member of the newly enfranchised group but alienated from the successful people in the publishing world from that background, would sit down to write a long, exhausting survey of all the distressing connections and collusions driving this new literary mafia.

Though such an attack might be overheated and polemical, it, like Kostelanetz's, would have its merits. Because even if an embrace of ethnic niches were to succeed in dramatically increasing the influence of one or two groups of BIPOC in U.S. publishing and even if, as a result, the industry as a whole became much more equitable than the industry currently is, this transformation would not mitigate all claims of privilege and inequality in U.S. literary culture. In addition to individual cases of injustice, which would surely persist, there would

—

also still be other groups, not included in the successful ethnic niches, who would continue to suffer broad literary disenfranchisement. So, after some reasonable period of time — twenty years? fifty? — it would be time again for the dominant ethnic niches in publishing to change.

Such demographic transformations do happen, seemingly naturally, in many fields and industries — think of the different ethnic and immigrant groups that have predominated in taxi driving over the history of that field in the U.S., in different cities — but not in all of them. It seems especially important for such a change to take place in publishing, if we continue to believe — as sociologists, historians, and literary scholars have claimed for centuries — that books are not just another consumer good (and not, as some claim, an anachronistic relic of previous centuries bound for extinction) but still in the third decade of the new millennium a privileged site of intellectual exchange, development, and debate.[24]

In this imagined future, Jews would, by necessity, become substantially less prominent in positions of literary influence through U.S. literary culture. Jewish college graduates might find it even more difficult to land entry-level jobs in publishing than it is for them now, even if their parents or cousins already work in the business, and harder to fund new ventures or get attention for the projects they promote. Importantly, though, this would not mean that Jews would be literarily disenfranchised, just as American whites are in no danger of being literarily disenfranchised even if they do finally lose their majority status and much of their influence. White Jews and non-Jews would continue to have the opportunity to participate in literary culture, and since few of them, as far as I can tell, genuinely aspire to conspiratorial, racist control of U.S. publishing and literary culture, they would be no less happy to do so — and indeed, most would be much happier to do so — in an industry that was no longer more than 80 percent white, as the current one is and has been for a century, but rather one led by people of color.

However we imagine this future of U.S. literary culture and whatever groups we imagine being newly enfranchised and empowered within it, it seems clear that such a massive change of the demographics of the publishing industry would have profound and meaningful effects on which manuscripts would and would not be published and how literature would be talked about and also —

again, as long as we agree that books still play a pivotal role in changing the way Americans think—on the direction of U.S. culture as a whole. If so, the changes would take complex shapes that we cannot predict, sometimes benefiting the members of the group that had established an ethnic niche in literary culture, in a general sense, and sometimes not. If it came to pass, though—if, in 2030, we had a publishing industry that was 40 percent Chicanx or 30 percent Bangladeshi American—it would, I hope, be an aspect of U.S. literary culture that would not be taken for granted by literary journalists, scholars, and critics but one that would be discussed and carefully considered in every work of scholarship and criticism addressing the literature produced in that period, by writers from any background.

That hope—that scholars of American literature might pay more attention to who is influential and empowered within publishing and how that affects what is and is not published—is the one that has motivated this book. It may be frustrating, to some readers, that *The Literary Mafia* has not gestured more broadly at many of the consequential interventions Jews have made in the history of U.S. publishing. The reason why is simple: the scale of such interventions was so very large that it is not feasible to do so. A full history of Jews and Jewishness in twentieth-century U.S. publishing would be substantially similar in its scope to a history of twentieth-century U.S. publishing, overall—and that is not something that can be covered effectively in a short book. One can read through histories of the periods and facets of modern and postmodern American literature and find many places where Jewishness seems to have been relevant: for example, in the developments of modernism and postmodernism, the formation of modern literary canons, the postwar paperback boom, the flourishing of popular nonfiction after World War II, and the memoir boom of the 1990s. Some scholars of American literature have attended with care to the roles played by Jews in these developments, but in many cases, they have not done so yet.[25] There are many other aspects of U.S. literary history in which further research will be necessary to determine what, if any, influence Jews in publishing exerted. By way of example, one might ask how the knowledge, preferences, and prejudices of American Jews in publishing affected the history of literary translation in the U.S.: from a cursory survey of relevant bibliographies, it appears that for whatever complex and varied reasons, Jewish translators and publishers in the

—

173

United States may have been more interested throughout the twentieth century in translations from Japanese and Brazilian literatures than in translations from Arabic or Korean ones. Why that would have been the case, and what it has meant for the development of world literature, would seem valuable questions to answer.[26] Another area ripe for further study is the specific roles of Jews in the development and publishing of African American literature. Despite the proliferation of sophisticated comparative and intersectional studies of Jews and African Americans in U.S. culture (and some important emerging scholarly work that has begun to redress the erasure of African American Jews), too often Jews who played pioneering roles in publishing African American literature, from the Harlem Renaissance to the rise of Black pulp fiction and beyond, have been discussed simply as white publishers and editors—which in most cases they certainly were, but that may not always have been quite the whole story.[27]

Though I have not been able to address such questions in *The Literary Mafia*, I have attempted to model a study of American literature that attends to the influential roles Jews played in publishing and in literary culture more generally. One further hope is that such a perspective can inform, much more than it has in the past, the study of twentieth- and twenty-first-century American Jewish writers. It seems absolutely crucial, in order for scholars and critics to understand a Jewish novelist's or poet's project, to know who they were writing for and whether their editors valued them for writing about a recognizable social reality to which the editors had access or appreciated them for providing glimpses into an exotic and unknown world or valued them as a means to prove to themselves and others that they were not anti-Semites. When Jewish editors published American Jewish texts, did they expect their writers to shore up their own Jewish bona fides or assist them in grinding their axes about their childhood experiences or seek to reach a perceived book-buying demographic by catering to its alleged interests? Knowing what was at stake emotionally, psychologically, politically, and commercially for all the people involved in what we have come to call, however uncertainly, American Jewish literature will help to elucidate why it developed in the ways that it did.

A wider scholarly awareness of Jews' roles in publishing also might help to clarify why non-Jewish American authors have tended to devote so much time and energy to writing about Jews. From Theodore Dreiser and Willa Cather

—

to Richard Wright and Sylvia Plath — and many, many other canonical American writers one could name — very often non-Jewish writers' representations of Jews have been interpreted and analyzed in terms of anti-Semitism or its absence and according to various understandings about the ethics of representation.[28] But given how often American writers from all backgrounds have had Jewish agents, editors, and publishers, surely part of all of these representations — as we have seen in the case of Raymond Chandler's basing a character on Alfred Knopf — can be understood in relation to the personalities, ideas, and influence of Jewish literary professionals with whom the authors had come into contact. Contemporary white authors, from Thomas Pynchon to Joshua Ferris and Nell Zink, as well as writers of color like Gish Jen, Sherman Alexie, and Zadie Smith, have continued to turn to such representations, and at least part of the reason these non-Jews write about Jews again and again, despite the tiny number of Jews in the U.S., is for the same reason that so many stand-up comics, who travel the country for their shows, joke about airplanes: it is virtually unavoidable that in pursuing a literary education and a literary vocation that a writer in the United States has encountered many Jews, whether as teachers, agents, editors, or other participants in literary culture.[29]

As a literary scholar and cultural historian, I am in no position to predict the future, and I have no idea whether the publishing industry will manage to achieve the greater equity and inclusion to which it has long aspired, as it previously changed to accommodate and accept Jews, who flourished and succeeded, transforming U.S. culture as they did. (A few hopeful signs appeared, during the time I was finishing this book, including the hiring of Dana Canedy as senior vice president and publisher of Simon & Schuster's namesake imprint and of Lisa Lucas as senior vice president of Knopf and head of the Schocken and Pantheon imprints, as well as Don Share, the editor of *Poetry*, announcing that he was stepping down from his position as part of the Poetry Foundation's attempts to address critiques of institutionalized racism, noting, "I hope that my departure makes space for others.")[30] What I can predict with some certainty is that literature will never be objective or meritocratic. Which literary texts succeed, find their readerships, win acclaim, and command attention will always have something to do with who the publishers, editors, agents, teachers, and readers are. In other words, whatever does change, large or small, in U.S. pub-

—

lishing and literary culture in the years to come, it will continue to be the case that knowing who can and cannot, and does and does not, occupy positions of influence and power within that system should always be an absolutely foundational facet of what it means to study that literature.

—

ACKNOWLEDGMENTS

Extensive and detailed acknowledgments sections have become increasingly conventional over the past several decades, not only in academic books like this one but in novels and poetry collections, too. Whatever else one might want to say about this phenomenon, these acknowledgment sections have been a remarkable boon to those of us who are interested in how literature and literary culture get made, and I am grateful to every author who has publicly thanked their agent, editors, writing teachers, and partner in painstaking detail. With that in mind, it seems only fair, especially given the subject of *The Literary Mafia*, that I use this section to explain how this book came to be published, through a process that was neither fair nor in any real sense meritocratic, though also, I hope, not corrupt.

At the Yiddish Book Center, where I worked as academic director from 2011 until the summer of 2020, I was given the opportunity to create and lead a residency we called Tent: Creative Writing. In 2016, the novelist and writing teacher Sam Lipsyte was kind enough to accept my invitation to teach in the program (I had asked him out of the blue, not knowing him, because I admired his work and had heard he was a talented and generous teacher). During his time at the center that summer, he suggested that I might be interested in reading Gordon Lish's novel *Extravaganza*. I knew of Lish, at that point, as the in-

—

177

famous editor of Raymond Carver and a few other writers, but I was surprised to discover Lish's intense interest in Jewishness in *Extravaganza* and then, as I read more, throughout Lish's published fiction. I applied for and received a fellowship from the Lilly Library at Indiana University, and I spent a few days there in January 2018, photographing thousands of pages of Lish's papers. Sam generously put me in touch with Lish himself, who granted me a phone interview. I wrote up a journalistic essay about Lish's Jewishness and his support of Cynthia Ozick, and when I had a solid working draft, I tried to figure out where to publish it. I thought this was a piece that might resonate with contemporary writers and MFA students, and I wanted to place it in a general-interest publication that such people would read (rather than one of the more specifically Jewish publications I often prefer to write for). I asked for suggestions from one of the participants in the 2017 Tent: Creative Writing program, Nathan Goldman, who had impressed me with some essays he had placed as a freelancer in magazines and journals. Using Nathan's name and email addresses he supplied, I pitched the essay to a few editors, and Jess Bergman, at *Literary Hub*, eventually agreed to publish it. When it was published, in the fall of 2018, I was teaching as a visiting professor in American Studies at Princeton, a position I had been offered largely thanks to the support of Esther Schor. (Schor is a Princeton English professor and poet whom I first met when she gave a talk at the University of Michigan, back when I was in graduate school there; she came at the invitation of her friend, my advisor, Jonathan Freedman, and I got to know her better when we served together on the judging panel for the Sami Rohr Prize for Jewish Literature in the 2010s.) The same day the *Literary Hub* piece was published, with an author's bio noting that I was teaching at Princeton and working on a book called *The Literary Mafia*, I received an email from an editor at Yale University Press, who asked if I would be attending the Modern Languages Association conference in Chicago that coming January and whether I would like to meet her there. I was going to Chicago — to serve on a roundtable, to see friends, and to watch our kids while my wife, who is also a literary scholar, moderated a panel and went to some meetings — and so I was able to meet with that editor in the book exhibit at MLA. I told her about my plans for the book, she mentioned some of the nepotistic conflicts she had observed during her own editorial career, and she said she would be interested in seeing a proposal. Now,

—

after a couple rounds of peer review and thanks to a different editor and her editorial assistant and many others at the press (as well as anonymous reviewers), here the book is, finally.

That is not a scintillating story, I realize. But I hope it might be helpful in illustrating how such things work, these days, especially for graduate students or junior academics reading this who have not had similar experiences yet or for some future scholar looking back at our time. There is also a more specific reason I wanted to tell the story. If the Yiddish Book Center had not had the funding to pay Sam Lipsyte to teach, I would not have met him and maybe would not have gotten his nudge to read Lish's fiction. If I had not known a young writer, like Nathan Goldman, who had a connection at *Literary Hub* and was willing to vouch for me, I may never have placed my piece there. If I had not been visiting at Princeton, thanks to Esther Schor's support, at that moment, my *LitHub* piece probably would not have commanded the same attention from an editor at Yale University Press. None of these people helped me because we were related, but all of them helped me. In fact, again and again, over the course of my career as an academic and writer, people have been kind and generous to me — see the copious acknowledgments that follow — and they have helped me to get to where I wanted to go. Part of that has been my dumb luck, surely, but some of it has been quid pro quo (people doing me a favor because I had done them one); and most of it can be said to owe to privilege of one sort or another. A lot of it, inseparable from the privilege, can be understood as owing to homophily, a sense of shared interests and values. Part of the reason I wanted to write this book about how relationships influence the development of U.S. literary culture is my sense of being deeply enmeshed in a network of such relationships myself, a network that is fueled by goodwill and generosity but that, all the same, often perpetuates inequity.

All that said, I had better get on with the more conventional thanking of the people who and institutions that enabled the research and writing that went into making this book.

At Yale University Press, I am grateful to Sarah Miller, who first reached out to me and expressed an interest in the project; to Ash Lago, who assisted her; to Heather Gold, who took over the book with aplomb during a challenging time; to Eva Skewes, who managed the review and publishing process gracefully; and to Andrew Katz, for thoughtful and painstaking copyediting. Thanks also to the anonymous reviewers of the initial proposal and of the full manuscript for their careful reading and thoughtful suggestions.

For most of the decade that I worked on *The Literary Mafia*, I was employed by the Yiddish Book Center, in Amherst, Massachusetts. It is a remarkable institution, too complex to capture here, and I owe my gratitude to its founder, Aaron Lansky, and executive director, Susan Bronson, who invited me to take the position of academic director in 2011 and made it possible for me to pursue my scholarly research agenda while I served in that role, with support both material and otherwise. I am also thankful for the colleagues I worked with there and especially those who discussed literature and culture with me, including Mindl Cohen, Gretchen Fiordalice, David Mazower, Jessica Parker, Sylvia Peterson, Eitan Kensky, Asya Vaisman Schulman, Sebastian Schulman, Lesley Yalen, and so many other colleagues, visiting faculty members, and fellows who spent a year or two at the center, as well as hundreds of program participants and students who listened to me talk about material related to this book and helped to shape my research agenda with their suggestions and responses. Many of these fellows and program participants have gone on to extraordinary literary and cultural careers of one sort or another and have done me favors and enriched my life with their work and conversation. When I think about how lucky I am to be a teacher, it is all of these people I think of.

During that same period, I taught one course each fall at UMass Amherst in the English department, and if ever a professional association could be frictionless, that one was. I enjoyed the teaching; the department gave me latitude to choose my topics; the students filled the courses unfailingly and helped me to see texts in new ways, in some cases texts that I discuss in this book, especially the students in my fall 2017 course, Jews and American Literature. I never attended a single department meeting, and I did not get to know my colleagues too well; but being a visiting assistant professor for all those years allowed me to feel that I was being taken seriously as an academic, and that was invaluable in keeping my research on track. My thanks go to Joseph Bartolomeo, Deborah Carlin, Suzanne Daly, and Randall Knoper, as well as Meg Caulmare, Mary Coty, and Celeste Stuart. I am deeply in the debt of the staff at the W. E. B. DuBois Library at UMass Amherst, especially Jim Kelly and the Interlibrary Loan staff,

—

who scanned and delivered hundreds of documents related to this project over the years.

Beginning in July 2020, I have found a new professional home at Wellesley College. Though 2020–21 has been one of the most challenging academic years on record to get to know a new institution, I am very excited to be joining a new scholarly community at Wellesley and in greater Boston, and I am specifically grateful to Andrew Shennan, Larry Rosenwald, Barbara Geller, Pat Giersch, and Kristin Butcher, to Susan Meyer and Jonathan Imber, and to other members of the English Department who in the spring of 2019 workshopped what became chapter 2 of this book.

The archival research for *The Literary Mafia* took place at the Harry Ransom Center at the University of Texas at Austin (thanks especially to Rick Watson); the Columbia Rare Book and Manuscript Library at Columbia University (thanks to David Olson, Tara Craig, and Karen Green, among others); the Lilly Library at Indiana University (thanks to Penny Ramon, Erika Dowell, and those who administrate the Everett Helm Visiting Fellowship); the Manuscripts, Archives, and Rare Books Division and Berg Collection of the New York Public Library (thanks to Tal Nadan, Brandon Westerheim, Meredith Mann, among others); and Special Collections and Archives at Queens College (thanks to Annie Tummino and her staff). I remain in awe of the archivists and leaders who keep these institutions running, organize inconceivable mountains of paper, and make this kind of humanities scholarship possible. I also want to thank the Internet Archive for its National Emergency Library initiative, which, notwithstanding the degree to which it may have infringed on the rights of authors and publishers, allowed for my research to continue during the early months of the pandemic.

Earlier drafts, excerpts, and elements of this book appeared in the following publications: "Publishing Jews at Knopf," *Book History* 21 (2018): 343–69 (with thanks to Greg Barnhisel); "Fictions of Anti-Semitism and the Beginnings of Holocaust Literature," in Christopher Vials, ed., *American Literature in Transition, 1940–1950* (Cambridge University Press, 2017); "Identity Recruitment and the 'American Writer': Steven Millhauser, Edwin Mullhouse, and Biographical Criticism," *Contemporary Literature* 54:1 (Spring 2013): 23–48 (with thanks to Steven Belletto, Thomas Schaub, and Mary Mekemson); "The Gordon Lish Lineage of Jewish American Writing," *Literary Hub* (September 25,

—

2018) (with thanks to Jess Bergman); "The History of Prestige: Blanche Knopf and Literary Culture," *Los Angeles Review of Books* (May 30, 2016) (with thanks to Tom Lutz); "The Problem of Too Many Books, or, Publishing History," *Michigan Quarterly Review* 53:3 (Summer 2014): 447–54 (with thanks to Jonathan Freedman); "Big Bang," Nextbook (February 12, 2009) (with thanks to whoever it was — I am deeply embarrassed that I cannot remember and cannot find the relevant email, but either Joanna Smith Rakoff or Sara Ivry, I think — who sent me a copy of Sam Astrachan's *An End to Dying* and asked me to see what I could do with it, which was what got me started down the rabbit hole of Lionel Trilling's papers and thereby got this project started). In each case, I am grateful for the permission to reprint material and especially for the opportunity to try my ideas out in print as I worked toward this book.

I am likewise grateful to the colleagues who invited me to give talks on topics related to this book at their institutions and gave me feedback. These events included the Yiddish Book Center's 2020 Melinda Rosenblatt Lecture, generously sponsored by Lief and Melinda Rosenblatt; a talk at Laura Hobson-Faure's invitation at Paris III — La Sorbonne Nouvelle; a workshop at Indiana University, at the invitation of Judah Cohen and his colleagues; a presentation at the Modern Jewish Literatures Symposium held in honor of Anita Norich at the University of Michigan; and a (highly memorable but not in a good way) job talk for Harvard's English department where some people, especially Elisa New, Leah Price, Stephen Greenblatt, and Louis Menand, went out of their way to be supportive.

I am deeply fortunate to have had a large academic and intellectual community to engage with while I worked on this book. Rachel Gordan, Lori Harrison-Kahan, Ronnie Grinberg, Adam Kirsch, and Morris Dickstein generously read chapter drafts and offered feedback (as did Irving Feldman, at the very last moment). People who organized and served with me on panels and seminars at SHARP, ACLA, and AJS conferences, where I tried out some of this material, and offered their support and suggestions include Omri Asscher, Lila Corwin-Berman, Jodi Eichler-Levine, Allison Fagan, Kirsten Fermaglich, Dean Franco, Rachel Gordan, Markus Krah, Rachel Kranson, Julian Levinson, Samantha Pickette, Kinohi Nishikawa, Maeera Schreiber, Benjamin Schreier, and J. Logan Wall. Many people in publishing and related fields who answered my questions, on the phone or over email, are cited in the book's notes, but I also want to express my gratitude to them here and also to a handful of people I cannot name because they answered questions off the record.

Many fellow academics, archivists, writers, editors, and readers offered suggestions and assistance, often in casual conversations in person or by email. Thanks to Victoria Aarons, Nathan Abrams, Arielle Angel, Sam Ashworth, Sam Axelrod, Gal Beckerman, Tova Benjamin, Marc Berley, Jeffrey Berlin, David Brendel, Eli Bromberg, Erika Jo Brown, Japonica Brown-Saracino, Lee Conell, Jeremy Dauber, Valerie Feldman, Dory Fox, Jay Gertzman, Mollie Glick, Jessica Gross, David Hadar, Carolyn Hessel, Michele Lent Hirsch, June Howard, August Imholtz, Gordon Hutner, Binnie Kirshenbaum, Patrick Lawrence, Andrew Leland, B. J. Love, Michael Maguire, W. David Marx, Tony Michels, B. J. Novak, Shelley Salamensky, Jan Schwarz, Sasha Senderovich, Justin Taylor, Marian Thurm, Jim Wald, Ruth Wisse, and Stephen Whitfield — and so many more people I am surely forgetting to mention. Chloe Hawkey, Taelour Cornett, Dylan Kaufman-Obstler, and Annabel Brazaitis pitched in with excellent research assistance. People who went above and beyond to help me get my hands on rare materials include Samantha Baskind, Kimberly King Parsons, and Michael Casper. Friends whose support has meant a lot over the decade I worked on this book include Vanessa Bartram, Lia Brozgal, Laure Cohen, Greg Cohen, Kevan Choset, Nicole Dudukovic, Steve Jeppson-Gamez, Philip Johnson, Brice Kuhl, Aaron Izenberg, Lida Maxwell, Avi and Ivy Patt, Audrey Plonk, Andy Romig, David Silver, and Bill Woodcock. I am so lucky to continue to be able to call on Deborah Dash Moore and Anita Norich as my teachers and mentors and to learn from them whenever I have a chance to talk to them (and, of course, when I read and reread their work), and I am grateful for the encouragement, support, and inspiration of Eileen Pollack, Riv-Ellen Prell, Esther Schor, and Jeffrey Shandler, all of whom have given me models for the kind of scholar and writer I would like to be. Jonathan Freedman's influence on my thinking and research in general and on this book in particular really could not be overstated, and I hope he knows that.

In addition to offering all kinds of motivation and encouragement over the years, my siblings, niece and nephews, and in-laws have all sharpened my thinking about questions of inheritance, nepotism, and cultural capital. Thanks to all

—

ACKNOWLEDGMENTS

the Lamberts and Kippurs. I cannot possibly express here how the changes that have been happening in the lives of my parents, Robert and Elaine Lambert, influenced and inspired my thinking about this project. I remain appreciative for the educational path they set me on and for all the freedom they gave me to discover who I wanted to be, and I am also grateful for the model they have provided, lately, of courage and strength.

Sara Kippur read every word when I asked her to, talked through every question, covered for me every time I traveled to an archive or to give a talk, called bullshit when necessary, and generally made my life worth living—so, you know, pretty helpful.

Asher and Noemi, I am so glad we have a "relationship." I love you, and so I am doing my best not to do to you what some of the parents in this book did to *their* kids.

—

NOTES

Epigraph: Robert DeMaria to Ann Birstein, November 30, 1976, folder 6, box 2, Ann Birstein Papers, Department of Special Collections and Archives, Queens College, City University of New York (hereafter ABP). Quoted with the permission of Robert DeMaria.

INTRODUCTION

1. Jack McClintock, "This Is How the Ride Ends," *Esquire* (March 1970), 188.

2. Mario Puzo, "A Modest Proposal to Enrich These Gentlemen," *Chicago Tribune* (April 7, 1968), L4.

3. Hank Lopez, "A Country and Some People I Love," in Joan Givner, ed., *Katherine Anne Porter: Conversations* (Jackson: University Press of Mississippi, 1987), 134. Originally in *Harper's* (September 1965).

4. Marvin Mudrick, "The Holy Family," *Hudson Review* 17:2 (1964): 299.

5. "The *Playboy* Interview: Truman Capote," *Playboy* 15 (March 1968): 169.

6. See, among other pieces by the same researchers, Charles Kadushin, Julie Hover, and Monique Tichy, "How to Find the Intellectual Elite in the United States," *Public Opinion Quarterly* 35:1 (1971): 6–7.

7. Robert Gutwillig, "What Ails the Book Trade," *New Leader* (May 15, 1961): 14–16. In 1965, Richard Kostelanetz quoted the publisher Arthur Wang, founder of Hill & Wang, as having said something similar: "there is good reason to believe, as Arthur Wang suggests, that a majority of the book buying public today, particularly of hardbacks, is Jewish; and this, rather than the gentiles' philo-Semitism, may better explain the preponderance of Jewish authors and subjects on the best-seller lists." Kostelanetz, "Militant Minorities," *Hudson Review* 18:3 (1965): 478.

—

8. Ernest van den Haag, *The Jewish Mystique* (1969; repr., New York: Dell, 1971), 119.

9. For an alternative perspective on Jewish readers, see a 1951 article by Harold Ribalow, in which he surveyed publishers and came to the conclusion that even "the finest Jewish fiction . . . sell[s] poorly," that "books on Israel and Zionism sell very badly," and "the sales of general Jewish non-fiction reflect no better upon the acumen of Jewish readers." Ribalow, "Do Jews Read?," *Congress Weekly* (October 8, 1951), 8–12. The classic statement on U.S. book publishers' lack of knowledge about their markets is O. H. Cheney's *Economic Survey of the Book Industry 1930–1931* (New York: R. R. Bowker, 1949). Nonetheless, wild claims about Jewish readers and book buyers, based on no evidence and straining plausibility, have been regularly made. In 1979, for example, a *Publishers' Weekly* article reported that among editors and others at major publishing houses, "estimates range anywhere from 33⅓% to 70% of all buyers of hardcover books and quality paperbacks" are Jews. Lily Edelman, "The Changing World of Jewish Publishing," *Publishers' Weekly* (February 12, 1979), 64.

10. In *The Publishing Game* (1971), Anthony Blond notes that "mostly, New York publishing is lateral, air-conditioned and, with the strong exception of Scribner's, Jewish." Quoted in William Targ, *Indecent Pleasures: The Life and Colorful Times of William Targ* (New York: Macmillan, 1975), 208. In 1975, when James T. Farrell was asked by an interviewer if he felt he had been a victim of a literary mafia, he answered, "Absolutely." See Ira Berkow, "James T. Farrell Is Alive and Well," *Longview News-Journal* (September 3, 1975), 40. For an editor who invoked the "Jewish mafia" in the early 1980s, see Lewis A. Coser, Charles Kadushin, and Walter W. Powell, *Books: The Culture and Commerce of Publishing* (New York: Basic Books, 1982), 88. Ted Solotaroff noted, in an essay published in 1982, "In literary matters, New York is perceived to be the corrupt and corrupting center of things which operates through a kind of conspiracy made up mostly of Jews." Solotaroff, "The New York Publishing World," in Bernard Rosenberg and Ernest Goldstein, eds., *Creators and Disturbers: Reminiscences by Jewish Intellectuals of New York* (New York: Columbia University Press, 1982), 416.

11. Eduoard Drumont's *La France Juive* (1886) and Telemachus Thomas Timayenis's translation and adaptation of it, *The Original Mr. Jacobs* (1888), railed against "Jew editors" who "willfully degrade the profession of journalism." Timayenis, *The Original Mr. Jacobs: A Startling Exposé* (New York: Minerva, 1888), 280. The twelfth protocol of the fraudulent, widely disseminated anti-Semitic text *The Protocols of the Elders of Zion* describes how the Jews will exert control over "literature and journalism," with the specific aim of editorial control of the horizon of the publishable: "if there should be any found who are desirous of writing against us, they will not find any person eager to print their productions." Henry Ford's *The International Jew* claimed that while "thirty years ago the New York press was free, . . . today it is practically all Jewish controlled," and suggested that the result of that control was that articles critical of Jews could not get published. Ford, *The International Jew,* vol. 2, *Jewish Activities in the United States* (Dearborn, MI: Dearborn, 1921), 212. On claims about Jews and media control in contemporary white-supremacist discourse, see Jessie Daniels, *White Lies: Race, Class, Gender, and Sexuality in White Supremacist Discourse* (New York: Routledge, 1997). One example of a contemporary Islamic extremist claim about Jewish

—

media control can be observed in a broadcast on El Sharq TV, an Istanbul-based channel known for its support of the Muslim Brotherhood, on April 28, 2020, in which the host claimed that, per the *Protocols,* Jews created and control cinema and other media forms as part of their efforts to "take over the world." MEMRI, "Muslim Brotherhood TV Host Maged Abdallah: Jews Founded Egyptian Cinema in Order to Control the World through the Media in Accordance with the Protocols of the Elders of Zion" (May 13, 2020), https://www.memri.org/reports/muslim-brotherhood-tv-host-maged-abdallah-jews-founded-egyptian-cinema-order-control-world.

12. J. Michael Lennon, *Norman Mailer: A Double Life* (New York: Simon & Schuster, 2013), 275; "Norman Mailer versus Nine Writers," *Esquire* (July 1963), 63.

13. Charles J. Sopkin, "Strange Bookfellows," *Boston Globe* (April 12, 1970), 20.

14. Harry Smith, "Publishing and the Destruction of Values," *Smith* 22–23 (1973): 26. On Gross's career, see Al Silverman, *The Time of Their Lives: The Golden Age of Great American Publishers, Their Editors and Authors* (New York: St. Martin's, 2008), 438.

15. "Can a Literary Mafia Affect Your Choice of Books?" (advertisement), *New York Times* (October 12, 1972), 43. For the context of this statement and Levin's struggles vis-à-vis Anne Frank's diary, see Lawrence Graver, *An Obsession with Anne Frank: Meyer Levin and the Diary* (Berkeley: University of California Press, 1995).

16. Richard Kostelanetz, *The End of Intelligent Writing* (New York: Sheed & Ward, 1974). Subsequent citations of this book appear parenthetically in the text.

17. An example of a serious scholar who relied on Kostelanetz's work can be found in Richard Ohmann, "The Shaping of a Canon, 1960–1975," *Critical Inquiry* 10:1 (1983): 199–222.

18. Aristides (Joseph Epstein), "A Literary Mafia?," *American Scholar* 44:2 (1975): 183, 184, 192.

19. "The Reader Replies," *American Scholar* 45:1 (1976): 853–54.

20. In the *New York Times Book Review,* a frequent contributor to the *New York Review of Books* explained, "in all my dealings with established New York reviews I have never once encountered the kind of malicious calculation about who is to review what that Kostelanetz alleges to be the constant practice of these periodicals." Roger Sale, "The End of Intelligent Writing," *New York Times* (December 29, 1974), 198. Dennis H. Wrong, meanwhile, described Kostelanetz's book as "reeking with *ressentiment.*" Wrong, review of Charles Kadushin, *The American Intellectual Elite, American Journal of Sociology* 81:4 (1976): 933.

21. Curt Johnson to Gordon Lish, January 10, 1968, Lish mss., Lilly Library, Indiana University, Bloomington, IN.

22. Curt Johnson to Gordon Lish, July 6, 1969, Lish mss.

23. Curt Johnson to Gordon Lish, December 1, 1968, Lish mss.

24. Curt Johnson, "Letting George Do It, or Fun and Shell Games with the Beautiful People," *Chicagoland* (August 1969), 33.

25. On Johnson generally, see Geoffrey Johnson, "On Curt Johnson, 'December' Magazine, and Raymond Carver," *Chicago* (July 6, 2010), https://www.chicagomag.com/Chicago-Magazine/June-2010/On-Curt-Johnson-December-magazine-and-Raymond-Carver/.

—

26. Richard H. Brodhead, *Cultures of Letters: Scenes of Reading and Writing in Nineteenth-Century America* (Chicago: University of Chicago Press, 1993), 115.

27. Rachel Malik, "Horizons of the Publishable: Publishing in/as Literary Studies," *ELH* 75:3 (Fall 2008): 709, 721, 720.

28. Among the challenges to women and minority writers Olsen lists, she includes "*Climate in literary circles for those who move in them,*" noting that "writers know the importance of being taken seriously, with respect for one's vision and integrity," as well as "how chancy is recognition and getting published." Tillie Olsen, *Silences* (New York: Delta/Seymour Lawrence, 1978), 41.

29. While Amy Kaplan uses the term "literary enfranchisement" in a slightly different sense, to describe the way that William Dean Howells felt that "realism extends literary representation to ordinary people" (see Kaplan, *The Social Construction of American Realism* [Chicago: University of Chicago Press, 1992], 16), at least a couple of scholars—Tilar J. Mazzeo and Gregory Maertz—have used it the same way I do here. See Mazzeo, *Plagiarism and Literary Property in the Romantic Period* (Philadelphia: University of Pennsylvania Press, 2013), 180; and Maertz, *Literature and the Cult of Personality: Essays on Goethe and His Influence* (Stuttgart: Ibidem, 2017).

30. Discrimination against people of color and other marginalized groups in both U.S. higher education and publishing was pervasive and taken for granted until at least the 1960s and 1970s, with few exceptions. With regard to prestigious institutions of higher education, which were often the training grounds for literary critics and editors from the start of the twentieth century, one historian estimates that only about 160 African Americans attended Harvard between 1890 and 1940 and notes that, as such, "blacks were a small enough group to be segregated or ignored," and another notes that African Americans "were completely excluded from Princeton": "not until 1947 would a black . . . receive an undergraduate degree" there. Roger L. Geiger, *The History of American Higher Education: Learning and Culture from the Founding to World War II* (Princeton, NJ: Princeton University Press, 2015), 451; Marcia Graham Synott, *The Half-Opened Door: Discrimination and Admissions at Harvard, Yale, and Princeton, 1900-1970* (Westport, CT: Greenwood, 1979), 47, 81, 174. See also Lavelle Porter, *The Blackademic Life: Academic Fiction, Higher Education, and the Black Intellectual* (Evanston, IL: Northwestern University Press, 2019). In publishing, the exclusion of people of color was almost complete and taken for granted and persisted even after prestigious and previously exclusionary colleges and universities began accepting more students of color. Al Silverman notes that in 1949, Doubleday was "the biggest publishing house in the country," with "about 5,000 employees," and had "but one African-American employee" (*Time of Their Lives,* 193-94), and in a long, capacious book that mentions more than a hundred editors and other influential employees of major U.S. trade publishers in the postwar decades, Silverman names only two African Americans: Charles Harris, "the first African-American editor at a major book publishing house" (195), and Toni Morrison. The sociologists Coser, Kadushin, and Powell note, without further comment, that the sample they used to assess the publishing industry "was overwhelmingly white; only one editor interviewed was black" (*Books,* 113). Looking back, the editor Michael Korda reflected, "Book

—

publishing, as an industry, was pretty much a white man's business. . . . It was hard to find a single black person outside the mailroom in most publishing houses." Korda, *Another Life: A Memoir of Other People* (New York: Random House, 1999), 203. Faith Berry has recounted a dispiriting meeting as late as 1971 with Thomas Guinzburg, president and editor in chief of Viking Press; in the previous decade, under his direction, she noted, the firm "had published [only] one book by a black author." Berry, "A Question of Publishers and a Question of Audience," *Black Scholar* 17:2 (1986): 45. See the conclusion of this book for more recent statistics and observations about the persisting whiteness of contemporary U.S. publishing.

31. While Robert Darnton's model of "the communications circuit" is the most influential in book history scholarship, Clayton Childress's more recent model, which breaks down the life cycle of literary texts into three overlapping fields (creation, production, and reception) is perhaps even more flexible and precise for thinking about the dynamics of twentieth- and twenty-first-century publishing in the U.S. See Darnton, "What Is the History of Books?," *Daedalus* 111:3 (1982): 65–83; and Childress, *Under the Cover: The Creation, Production, and Reception of a Novel* (Princeton, NJ: Princeton University Press, 2017). Laura J. Miller, in an admirable study of bookselling in the U.S., *Reluctant Capitalists: Bookselling and the Culture of Consumption* (Chicago: University of Chicago Press, 2006), notes that despite her deep historical research and many interviews, she can "make no claim to representativeness" (19), and she also explains that she cannot give "definitive answers" about the book selections at independent and chain bookstores because it would be "extremely unlikely" to receive "the cooperation of" chain and independent bookstores (84). For a scholar's excellent recent attempt to explore an even less accessible site in the field of production, which concludes by acknowledging "the inscrutable nature of the supply chain," see Matthew Kirschenbaum, "Bibliologistics: The Nature of Books Now, or a Memorable Fancy," *post45* (April 8, 2020), https://post45.org/2020/04/bibliologistics-the-nature-of-books-now-or-a-memorable-fancy/.

32. On American Jews in law and medicine, see Leon Hühner, "Jews in the Legal and Medical Professions in America Prior to 1800," *Publications of the American Jewish Historical Society* 22 (1914): 147–65; Jerold S. Auerbach, "From Rags to Robes: The Legal Profession, Social Mobility, and the American Jewish Experience," *American Jewish Historical Quarterly* 66:2 (1976): 249–84; Eli Wald, "The Jewish Law Firm: Past and Present," in Ari Mermelstein, Victoria Saker Woeste, Ethan Zadoff, and Marc Galanter, eds., *Jews and the Law* (New Orleans: Quid Pro Books, 2014), 65–124; and Theodore M. Brown, "Jewish Physicians in the United States," in Natalia Berger, ed., *Jews and Medicine: Religion, Culture, Science* (Philadelphia: Jewish Publication Society, 1997), 221–33. Publications like Kurt F. Stone's *The Jews of Capitol Hill: A Compendium of Jewish Congressional Members* (Lanham, MD: Scarecrow, 2011) and L. Sandy Maisel and Ira N. Forman's edited volume *Jews in American Politics* (Lanham, MD: Rowman and Littlefield, 2001) chronicle the election and appointment of Jews to political positions.

33. See Amnon Raz-Krakotzkin, *The Censor, the Editor, and the Text: The Catholic Church and the Shaping of the Jewish Canon in the Sixteenth Century* (Philadelphia: University of Pennsylvania Press, 2007); and Dmitry A. Elyashevich, "Censorship in the Russian Empire," in

Gershon Hundert, ed., *The YIVO Encyclopedia of Jews in Eastern Europe* (2010), https://yivoencyclopedia.org/article.aspx/Censorship/Censorship_in_the_Russian_Empire. On the suppression of Native American languages, see Jon Reyhner, "American Indian Language Policy and School Success," *Journal of Educational Issues of Language Minority Students* 12 (Summer 1993): 35-59. On antiliteracy laws, see, e.g., Birgit Brander Rasmussen, "'Attended with Great Inconveniences': Slave Literacy and the 1740 South Carolina Negro Act," *PMLA* 125:1 (2010): 201-3.

34. On a Jewish scholar's conversion to Christianity to take a position at Harvard in the eighteenth century, see Michael P. Kramer, "Beginnings and Ends: The Origins of Jewish American Literary History," in Hana Wirth-Nesher and Michael P. Kramer, eds., *The Cambridge Companion to Jewish American Literature* (Cambridge: Cambridge University Press, 2003), 12-30. Gerald Graff's *Professing Literature: An Institutional History* (Chicago: University of Chicago Press, 1987) offers an account of the rise of academic literary studies in the late nineteenth century.

35. On Noah, see Jonathan Sarna, *Jacksonian Jew: The Two Worlds of Mordecai Manuel Noah* (New York: Holmes and Meier, 1981). For a survey of Jewish publishers before the late nineteenth century, including a short biography of Abraham Hart (1810-85), "one of America's most prominent publishers" before the Civil War, see Charles Madison, *Jewish Publishing in America: The Impact of Writing on American Culture* (New York: Sanhedrin, 1976), 246-85; and Jacob Rader Marcus, "Jews as Publishers," in *United States Jewry, 1776-1985,* vol. 1 (Detroit: Wayne State University Press, 1989), 192-97.

36. On the Ochs and Sulzberger families and the *New York Times,* see Susan E. Tifft and Alex S. Jones, *The Trust: The Private and Powerful Family behind the "New York Times"* (Boston: Little, Brown, 1999); and on Joseph Pulitzer and the *New York World,* see James McGrath Morris, *Pulitzer: A Life in Politics, Print, and Power* (New York: Harper, 2010).

37. Brief introductions to all these publishing houses can be found in John Tebbel's standard, four-volume *A History of Book Publishing in the United States* (New York: R. R. Bowker, 1972-81).

38. Madison, *Jewish Publishing in America,* 246-85, remains a useful introductory survey. For more on the publishers mentioned, see also Ann Catherine McCullough, "A History of B. W. Huebsch, Publisher" (PhD diss., University of Wisconsin-Madison, 1979); Amy Root Clements, *The Art of Prestige: The Formative Years at Knopf, 1915-1930* (Amherst: University of Massachusetts Press, 2014); Tom Dardis, *Firebrand: The Life of Horace Liveright* (New York: Random House, 1995); Boris Kachka, *Hothouse: The Art of Survival and the Survival of Art at America's Most Celebrated Publishing House, Farrar, Straus, and Giroux* (New York: Simon & Schuster, 2014); on Simon & Schuster and on Basic Books, Charles A. Madison, *Book Publishing in America* (New York: McGraw-Hill, 1966), 346-54, 376-77; on Pantheon, André Shiffrin, *The Business of Books: How the International Conglomerates Took Over Publishing and Changed the Way We Read* (London: Verso, 2000); Loren Glass, *Counterculture Colophon: Grove Press, "The Evergreen Review," and the Incorporation of the Avant-Garde* (Stanford, CA: Stanford University Press, 2013); Blake Butler, "FC2's 40 Years of Brain-

bending," *Vice* (July 27, 2012), https://www.vice.com/en_us/article/4wq4kw/fc2s-40
-years-of-brainbending. On Shatzkin's hiring and tenure at Doubleday, see Silverman, *Time of Their Lives,* 192–94.

39. On the *American Mercury* and the *New Republic,* see Frank Luther Mott, *A History of American Magazines,* vol. 5 (Cambridge, MA: Harvard University Press, 1968), 3–26, 191–224. On the *Menorah Journal,* see Daniel Greene, *The Jewish Origins of Cultural Pluralism: The Menorah Association and American Diversity* (Bloomington: Indiana University Press, 2011). On *Seven Arts,* see Victoria Kingham, "Commerce, Little Magazines and Modernity: New York, 1915–1922" (PhD diss., University of De Montfort, Leicester, 2009), 43–81. On the *New Masses* and *Partisan Review,* see Joseph Robert Conlin, ed., *The American Radical Press, 1880–1960,* vol. 2 (Westport, CT: Greenwood, 1974), 539–46, 548–54.

40. On the development of literary studies in this period, see Gerald Graff, *Professing Literature: An Institutional History* (Chicago: University of Chicago Press, 1987), 55–120.

41. Ludwig Lewisohn believed that he was repeatedly denied academic positions because he was Jewish, with some reason; writing to the chairman of the German department at the University of Wisconsin, to recommend Lewisohn for a job there, in 1910, Calvin Thomas, a professor and advisor to Lewisohn at Columbia, lied, saying that Lewisohn "is a Jew by his father's beard only, a Christian by his mother's. His sympathies and tempers are Christian." Lewisohn got that job. See Ralph Melnick, *The Life and Work of Ludwig Lewisohn,* vol. 1, *"A Touch of Wildness"* (Detroit: Wayne State University Press, 1998), 137–39, 145. Isaac Goldberg received his PhD in Romance languages and literature from Harvard in 1912 and outlined an autobiographical novel in which a character sharing those experiences believes that "no position [was] forthcoming" because of "his Jewish origin and radicalism." See Josh Lambert, "Isaac Goldberg and the Idea of Obscene Yiddish," in Lara Rabinovitch, Hannah Pressman, and Shiri Goren, eds., *Choosing Yiddish: Studies in Yiddish Literature, Culture, and History* (Detroit: Wayne State University Press, 2012), 147. Stanley Kunitz was reportedly told, at Harvard in 1926, that "Anglo-Saxons would resent being taught English by a Jew." See Kostelanetz, *End of Intelligent Writing,* 18.

42. On Jews in academic literary studies, see Stephen Steinberg, *The Academic Melting Pot: Catholics and Jews in American Higher Education* (New York: Transaction, 1977), 122; and Jonathan Freedman, *The Temple of Culture: Assimilation and Anti-Semitism in Literary Anglo-America* (New York: Oxford University Press, 2000), 175–86.

43. See Theodore Peterson, *Magazines in the 20th Century* (Urbana: University of Illinois Press, 1964); Frank Luther Mott, *A History of American Magazines,* vol. 4 (Cambridge, MA: Harvard University Press, 1957); and Richard Ohmann, *Selling Culture: Magazines, Markets, and Class at the Turn of the Century* (London: Verso, 1998).

44. While an accounting of the ethnic, geographic, and religious backgrounds of the editors in chief of all the widely circulating U.S. magazines has not yet, to my knowledge, been published, a few examples can be offered that suggest the general trend. The *Saturday Evening Post*'s first editor in chief, George Horace Lorimer, was the Kentucky-born son of a Baptist minister, and his two immediate successors, Wesley Winans Stout and Ben Hibbs

—

(whose editorships lasted until 1962) were both born and raised in Kansas. The guiding spirit of *Esquire* from the magazine's founding in 1933 until 1976, Arnold Gingrich, was the Michigan-born son of Mennonites, and Harold Hayes, who was editor in chief from 1961 to 1973, was, in Gay Talese's words, "an Anglo-Saxon Protestant . . . from the South." Carol Posgrove, *It Wasn't Pretty, Folks, but Didn't We Have Fun? "Esquire" in the Sixties* (New York: Norton, 1995), 144. Linda Bell Wallace, who with her husband, DeWitt Wallace, founded *Reader's Digest* and edited it until 1964, was the daughter of a Presbyterian minister.

45. On the "intimate tone" of magazines' "conversation[s] with the reader" and the "persona" used in many early magazines to foster such a tone, see Susan L. Greenberg, *A Poetics of Editing* (London: Palgrave Macmillan, 2018), 92.

46. Robert Vanderlan, *Intellectuals Incorporated: Politics, Art, and Ideas inside Henry Luce's Media Empire* (Philadelphia: University of Pennsylvania Press, 2010), 222.

47. One exception was Theodore White, a Jewish Harvard graduate who started as a stringer for *Time* in China in 1939 and then joined the magazine's New York editorial staff in 1941. See White's memoir, *In Search of History: A Personal Adventure* (New York: Harper-Collins, 1978). On Howe's and Bell's hiring, see Vanderlan, *Intellectuals Incorporated*, 277; and Edward Alexander, *Irving Howe: Socialist, Critic, Jew* (Bloomington: Indiana University Press, 1998), 67.

48. On the founding of the *New Yorker* and Raoul Fleischmann's role in it, see Ben Yagoda, *About Town: The "New Yorker" and the World It Made* (New York: Scribner, 2000).

49. Advertisements mention "restricted clientele" in the December 1940 issue of *Esquire*, in an advertisement for the Versailles in Miami Beach; in the April 1942 issue of *Harper's*, for Clafonte-Haddon Hall in Atlantic City and the Cavalier in Virginia Beach; and in the January 1943 issue of the *Atlantic Monthly*, for the Cloister in Sea Island, Georgia.

50. Only one employee of the (fictional) magazine, the protagonist's secretary, is Jewish, and she has changed her name and passed for gentile so as to get the job despite an anti-Semitic hiring policy. In one passage in the novel, a book publisher suggests that if a major exposé of anti-Semitism were to be published by "one of the Jewish [book publishing] houses, . . . people might think it was just special pleading," which suggests that the magazine, by contrast, labors under no such perception of Jewish influence. Laura Z. Hobson, *Gentleman's Agreement* (New York: Simon & Schuster, 1947), 100–101, 254.

51. The *Time* stories are unsigned, so it is difficult to know who wrote or edited them, but given the composition of the magazine's staff, it seems relatively unlikely that these were the work of Jewish reporters or editors. See "A Trumpet for All Israel," *Time* (October 15, 1951), 52–59; and "The Wouk Mutiny," *Time* (September 5, 1955), 48–52. The article in *Look* was written by William Attwood, a graduate of Choate and Princeton who had been a foreign correspondent for the *New York Herald Tribune* during the war and later went on to a career as a diplomat. See Attwood, "The Position of the Jews in America Today," *Look* 19:24 (November 29, 1955): 27–35.

52. Albert Q. Maisel, "The Jews among Us," *Reader's Digest* 66 (April 1955): 31.

53. Circulation data from Peterson, *Magazines in the Twentieth Century*, 81.

—

54. See Josh Lambert, "My Son, the Pornographer," *Tablet* (February 24, 2010), https://www.tabletmag.com/sections/arts-letters/articles/my-son-the-pornographer.

55. See Kadushin, Hover, and Tichy, "How to Find the Intellectual Elite"; as well as Julie Hover and Charles Kadushin, "The Influential Intellectual Journals: A Very Private Club," *Change* 4:2 (March 1972): 47; and Charles Kadushin, *The American Intellectual Elite* (Boston: Little, Brown, 1974), 23.

56. For an excellent survey of the different kinds of anti-Semitism at work in the postwar U.S., see Kirsten Fermaglich, *A Rosenberg by Any Other Name: A History of Jewish Name Changing in America* (New York: New York University Press, 2018).

57. For a useful overview of U.S. publishing in this period, see Beth Luey, "The Organization of the Book Publishing Industry," in *A History of the Book in America,* vol. 5, *The Enduring Book: Print Culture in Postwar America* (Chapel Hill: University of North Carolina Press, 2009), 29–54. On the international expansion of U.S. publishing, see also Alistair McCleery, "The Book in the Long Twentieth Century," in Leslie Howsam, ed., *The Cambridge Companion to the History of the Book* (Cambridge: Cambridge University Press, 2015), 169–70.

58. Paula Rabinowitz, *American Pulp: How Paperbacks Brought Modernism to Main Street* (Princeton, NJ: Princeton University Press, 2015); Glass, *Counterculture Colophon*. Scholars with a variety of interests have been exploring the vast (and often nefarious) influence of the U.S. on literary culture around the world in the twentieth century; for examples, see Amy Kaplan and Donald E. Pease, eds., *Cultures of United States Imperialism* (Durham, NC: Duke University Press, 1993); Frances Stonor Saunders, *The Cultural Cold War* (New York: New Press, 2000); and Sarah Brouillette, *UNESCO and the Fate of the Literary* (Stanford, CA: Stanford University Press, 2019).

59. Jews living in the Middle East, Europe, Asia, and Africa had throughout history published books and periodicals in Jewish and non-Jewish languages for Jewish audiences and had attained positions of influence in some other non-Jewish publishing contexts. For overviews of publishing by Jews, see Emile G. L. Schrijver, "Jewish Book Culture since the Invention of Printing (1469–c. 1815)," in Jonathan Karp and Adam Sutcliffe, eds., *The Cambridge History of Judaism*, vol. 7, *The Early Modern World, 1500–1815* (Cambridge: Cambridge University Press, 2017), 291–315; and Kenneth Moss, "Print and Publishing after 1800," in Hundert, *YIVO Encyclopedia of Jews in Eastern Europe*. On publishing companies aimed specifically at Jewish audiences in the U.S., see Jonathan Sarna, *JPS: The Americanization of Jewish Culture, 1888–1988* (Philadelphia: Jewish Publication Society, 1989); and Sarna, "Two Ambitious Goals: American Jewish Publishing in the United States," in *A History of the Book in America*, vol. 4, *Print in Motion: The Expansion of Publishing and Reading in the United States, 1880–1940* (Chapel Hill: University of North Carolina Press, 2014), 376–91.

60. See David Hollinger, *Science, Jews, and Secular Culture: Studies in Mid-Twentieth-Century American Intellectual History* (Princeton, NJ: Princeton University Press, 1996), 11.

61. "The Publishers Who Lunch: The Social Networking of American Book Publishers," *Book History* 18 (2015): 273–301, quotation on 292.

—

62. John Tebbel's standard, four-volume *A History of Book Publishing in the United States* and the five-volume *A History of the Book in America* edited by David D. Hall (Chapel Hill: University of North Carolina Press, 2007-9) both mention Jews and Jewishness many times in passing, but aside from Jonathan Sarna's essay, cited earlier, they do not offer any sustained exploration of the role of Jews in the U.S. publishing industry. Charles Madison's overview of Jews' involvements in U.S. publishing tends toward the boosterish ("the increase in the number of readers and their cultural enhancement, was initiated and furthered in large measure by Jews active in American book publishing" [*Jewish Publishing in America*, 285]), and even Jonathan Freedman's more sophisticated treatment of Jews in publishing offers a somewhat inaccurate, essentializing perspective on Jews as sharing "a strong antipathy to censorship and a questioning of authority over the dispersion of words, which has been a strong impulse in Jewish culture from the Haskalah forward" (*Temple of Culture*, 175) — which certainly does not account for Alfred Knopf's capitulation to censorship — though more generally Freedman's sensitivity to the complexity and contingency of Jews' involvement in the U.S. publishing industry inspired this project and much of my scholarly work. See Freedman, *Temple of Culture*, 168-75. One very recent work that exemplifies the way that inattention to Jewishness can undermine otherwise sophisticated and incisive scholarship on the history of U.S. publishing is Richard Jean So's *Redlining Culture: A Data History of Racial Inequality and Postwar Fiction* (New York: Columbia University Press, 2020). So notes, as a parenthetical "sidebar," that despite "the high number of Jewish writers on" the list of most-reviewed authors he has generated, he has "bracket[ed] out the question of how Jewishness articulates a specific type of 'whiteness,'" with a passing acknowledgment of "the complicated history by which Jews became 'white' in this period" (81). The missed opportunity here is not just to think through the complexity of Jews' whiteness in the U.S. (as important as that project is) but to understand the effects of Jewishness as a key variable in the very fields — publishing, literary gatekeeping, and literary texts — that interest So. Indeed, elsewhere in his study, So discovers but does not interpret the seemingly striking fact that "Jew" appears among the "most similar terms to the 'black character' vector," according to his analysis, from the 1960s to the 1990s (see table 1.3, 54).

63. See Brodhead, *Cultures of Letters*, 107-14.

64. Relevant institutional histories of American literature include Evan Brier, *A Novel Marketplace: Mass Culture, the Book Trade, and Postwar American Fiction* (Philadelphia: University of Pennsylvania Press, 2010); Glass, *Counterculture Colophon;* Mark McGurl, "Everything and Less: Fiction in the Age of Amazon," *Modern Language Quarterly* 77:3 (2016): 447-71; and Dan N. Sinykin, "The Conglomerate Era: Publishing, Authorship, and Literary Form, 1965-2007," *Contemporary Literature* 58:4 (2017): 462-91. On Hollywood, see Neil Gabler, *An Empire of Their Own: How the Jews Invented Hollywood* (New York: Crown, 1988); on newspapers, see Laurel Leff, *Buried by the Times: The Holocaust and America's Most Important Newspaper* (New York: Cambridge University Press, 2006); on popular music, see Jeffrey Melnick, *A Right to Sing the Blues: African-Americans, Jews, and American Popular Song* (Cambridge, MA: Harvard University Press, 1999); on Broadway, see Andrea Most, *Making Amer-*

icans: Jews and the Broadway Musical (Cambridge, MA: Harvard University Press, 2004). In general, see Paul Buhle, ed., *Jews and American Popular Culture* (Westport, CT: Praeger, 2006).

65. On "ethnic capital," see George J. Borgas, "Ethnic Capital and Intergenerational Mobility," *Quarterly Journal of Economics* 107:1 (1992): 123–50; and for recent work on ethnic niches, see Michael Cohen, *Cotton Capitalists: American Jewish Entrepreneurship in the Reconstruction Era* (New York: New York University Press, 2017); and William R. Kerr and Martin Mandorff, "Social Networks, Ethnicity, and Entrepreneurship" (Working Paper no. 16-042, Harvard Business School, Cambridge, MA, June 14, 2016).

66. On Bellow's derision of the novel, see James Atlas, *Bellow: A Biography* (New York: Random House, 2000), 98–99. For a reading of the novel as a reaction to the Holocaust, see Josh Lambert, "Fictions of Anti-Semitism and the Beginnings of Holocaust Literature," in Christopher Vials, ed., *American Literature in Transition, 1940–1950* (Cambridge: Cambridge University Press, 2017), 44–58.

67. Saul Bellow, *The Victim* (1947; repr., New York: Penguin Books, 1996), 1. Subsequent citations of the novel appear parenthetically in the text.

68. This detail suggests that *Dill's* is a very important national magazine, as not many magazine publishers would have been successful enough to own a large building. The Curtis Company, the enormously successful publishers of the *Ladies Home Journal* and the *Saturday Evening Post,* built the Curtis Center in Philadelphia, while *Reader's Digest's* staff was housed, for most of its existence, in a four-story building in New Castle, New York. The Time & Life Building at 1271 Avenue of the Americas in Manhattan, which was built in the late 1950s, is only forty-eight stories high.

69. On Bellow's interview, see Atlas, *Bellow,* 90–91.

70. "Influence" is mentioned (sometimes more than once) on pages 74, 81, 107, 169, 200, and 236; and "connections," on 14, 41, 127, 174, and 220.

71. See Walter Benn Michaels's reading of Cather in *Our America: Nativism, Modernism, and Pluralism* (Durham, NC: Duke University Press, 1995) and his contention that "the emergence of nativist modernism involved . . . the transformation of the opposition between black and white into an opposition between Indian and Jew" (107). On more recent instances, see Karen Goodluck, "Far-Right Extremists Appropriate Indigenous Struggles for Violent Ends," *High Country News* (August 27, 2019), https://www.hcn.org/issues/51.16/tribal-affairs-far-right-extremists-appropriate-indigenous-struggles-for-violent-ends.

72. Harold Ribalow's anthology *The Land, These People* (New York: Beechhurst, 1950) offers one view of the prominent Jewish writers of the 1930s and 1940s, including work by Howard Fast, Waldo Frank, Ludwig Lewisohn, Jerome Weidman, and Irwin Shaw. Leah Garrett's *Young Lions: How Jewish Authors Reinvented the American War Novel* (Evanston, IL: Northwestern University Press, 2015) examines a handful of novels by Jewish writers that were bestsellers in 1948.

73. Bellow's former teachers Melville Herskovits and Alexander Goldenweiser not only were likely to have raised his sensitivity to issues of kinship in general but had both also specifically applied their theories about society to questions about Jews. Herskovits and

Goldenweiser were students of Franz Boas, and in the 1920s and 1930s, before Bellow encountered them, they had each published their ideas on the question of the interrelation of Jewish identity, anti-Semitism, and Jewish power, which would become Bellow's subject in *The Victim*. Herskovits, who focused on the impossibility of defining what a Jew is, for example, noted "the great imponderable fact that . . . [Jews] feel perhaps more at home among persons called Jews than with others who are not called this," while Goldenweiser, lamenting the persistence of racial prejudice in general and anti-Semitism in particular, mentions the case of Palestine, where Jews hold prejudicial views of Arabs "as a primitive race," suggesting how the victim can become victimizer. See Melville J. Herskovits, "When Is a Jew a Jew?," *Modern Quarterly* 4 (1927): 109–17, quotation on 117; and Alexander Goldenweiser, *History, Psychology, and Culture* (London: Kegan Paul, Trench, Trubner, 1933), 397–404, quotation on 400. On Bellow's studies with Herskovits and Goldenweiser, see Atlas, *Bellow*, 49–50, 57.

74. J.C., "His World Was Rich with Life," *New York Times Book Review* (April 4, 1943), BR12.

75. Saul Bellow, *Saul Bellow: Letters*, ed. Benjamin Taylor (New York: Viking, 2010), e.g., 27–28, 37–38.

76. See Atlas, *Bellow*, 82.

77. "Introspective Stinker," *Time* 43:19 (May 8, 1944): 106; *Merriam-Webster.com*, s.v. "pharisaical," https://www.merriam-webster.com/dictionary/pharisaical.

78. On such concerns in philosophy in general, see Diane Jeske, "Special Obligations," in Edward N. Zalta, ed., *The Stanford Encyclopedia of Philosophy* (Fall 2019), https://plato.stanford.edu/archives/fall2019/entries/special-obligations/; and Samuel Scheffler, "Families, Nations and Strangers," in *Boundaries and Allegiances: Problems of Justice and Responsibility in Liberal Thought* (Oxford: Oxford University Press, 2001), 48–65. Marc Dollinger's *Quest for Inclusion: Jews and Liberalism in Modern America* (Princeton, NJ: Princeton University Press, 2000) usefully surveys American Jews' debates about U.S. intervention in World War II and about Zionism in the 1930s and 1940s. Many Jewish writers and intellectuals, including Bellow, would later reflect on this period—and especially their first glimpses of newsreel footage of the extermination camps—as formative. See Bellow's recollection of his encounter with newsreel footage of the liberated camps and how he reacted, quoting a similar reminiscence from Lionel Abel's memoir, in Bellow, "A Jewish Writer in America—II," *New York Review of Books* (November 10, 2011), https://www.nybooks.com/articles/2011/11/10/jewish-writer-america-ii/. Another set of examples can be found in Kazin's repeated references to the moments in the spring of 1945 when he first heard and saw recordings and reports from Bergen-Belsen: Kazin recalls hearing a radio report from Belsen while in London, in *A Walker in the City* (New York: Harcourt Brace, 1951), 51–52, and remembers seeing newsreel footage from the liberated camp in *Starting Out in the Thirties* (Boston: Little, Brown, 1965), 166, and then refers to the audio again in *New York Jew* (New York: Knopf, 1978), 140, and then mentions a 1945 *London Times* report on Belsen in *Writing Was Everything* (1995; repr., Cambridge, MA: Harvard University Press, 1999), 80.

79. Norman Podhoretz, *Making It* (New York: Random House, 1967). On organized crime organizations as "patterns of relationship among individuals which have the force of kinship," "not based on blood, of course, but on the social and individual recognition that reciprocal rights and obligations exist between kin," see Francis A. J. Ianni with Elizabeth Reuss-Ianni, *A Family Business: Kinship and Social Control in Organized Crime* (New York: Russell Sage Foundation, 1972), 153, 165–66.

80. Walter Goodman, "The Lobbying for Literary Prizes," *New York Times* (January 28, 1988), C26.

81. Deborah Treisman, email to the author, August 8, 2013. On the *New Yorker*'s extraordinary support for Jewish, post-Soviet writers under Remnick and Treisman, see Josh Lambert, "Since 2000," in Hana Wirth-Nesher, ed., *The Cambridge History of Jewish American Literature* (New York: Cambridge University Press, 2015), 622–41.

82. For another example, the team behind Submittable, a leading online system for managing literary journals' submissions processes, suggested in a 2010 blog post that one solution to the problems of "nepotism in publishing" and "insiderism" would be wider use of "a system of blind reading" (in other words, obscuring the names and other identifying details of those who submit their work for consideration), as this "would allow [journals] to build a reputation for quality and discernment rivaling that of *The Paris Review*" and help to bring the "industry . . . closer to the meritocratic ideal." "Reading Blind," *Submittable* (blog) (December 23, 2010), https://blog.submittable.com/reading-blind/ (no longer available). As one might expect, many journals do follow this practice, and a more recent blog post by the Monadnock Writers' Group lists journals that "read submissions 'blind,'" explaining that such journals "hopefully" judge "your creative work . . . on its own merits." "17 Literary Journals That Read Submissions 'Blind,'" Monadnock Writers' Group (May 14, 2019), https://monadnockwriters.org/2019/05/14/17-literary-journals-that-read-submissions-blind/ (no longer available). The flaws in this reasoning have been pointed out by other contemporary editors. For example, the editors of *Apogee,* in a post titled "The Politics of 'Blind Submissions' Policies" (July 28, 2015), https://apogeejournal.org/2015/07/28/from-the-editors-the-politics-of-blind-submissions-policies/, critique the "myth, prominent in the literary world, of an objective standard for literary excellence; one whose criteria has nothing to do with a writer's or reader's identity or background," and they quote the poet Kazim Ali's remark that "claiming to judge work solely based on literary merit is inherently and inescapably racist."

83. As early as 1974, Gerald Graff noted, "No idea of the New Critics seemed to inspire more protest than their assumption of the 'objective' nature of literary text, their view that a poem was an object whose meaning could be analyzed by the detached, disinterested critic." Graff, "What Was New Criticism? Literary Interpretation and Scientific Objectivity," *Salmagundi* 27 (1974): 72.

84. Walter Benn Michaels, *The Trouble with Diversity: How We Learned to Love Identity and Ignore Inequality* (New York: Metropolitan Books, 2006), 197–98.

85. Walter Benn Michaels, "Last Words," *New York Times* (October 1, 2006), https://www.nytimes.com/2006/10/01/magazine/01wwln_essay.html. One might expect the author of *The Gold Standard and the Logic of Naturalism* to be less sanguine about his ignorance of a major text of late-nineteenth-century European literature satirizing the failures of the Enlightenment. On Abramovitch's novel, see, for example, David Aberbach, "Enlightenment and Cultural Confusion: Mendele's 'The Mare' and Dangarembga's 'Nervous Conditions,'" *Comparative Literature Studies* 41:2 (2004): 214–30.

86. Another example is Philip Fisher, a leading scholar of American literature, who sees "childhood, adolescence, Yuppiedom or senior-citizenship" as "full cultural programs, not inferior in complexity to being gay or being Jewish," and insists that "it is only in relation to catastrophic politics and apocalyptic conditions that a collapse occurs in which poly-identities disappear into what we might call a single hunted identity, as happened to European Jews 1930 to 1945" (which could be read, for example, as Fisher suggesting that to insist that Toni Morrison's race or Philip Roth's ethnicity, rather than their age, might be the most important thing about them would, in effect, make you a Nazi). Fisher, *Still the New World: American Literature in a Culture of Creative Destruction* (Cambridge, MA: Harvard University Press, 1999), 162, 163. Even a writer as committed to Jewish texts and issues as Cynthia Ozick, writing from the perspective of a leading critic as well as a major novelist, can insist in her own way that one's background is irrelevant. She writes, "No writer should be expected to be . . . a representative of 'identity.' . . . I have never set out to be anything other than a writer of stories." Ozick, "Tradition and (or versus) the Jewish Writer," in Derek Rubin, ed., *Who We Are: On Being (and Not Being) a Jewish American Writer* (New York: Schocken Books, 2005), 22.

87. In a still-resonant study, *Scaling the Ivory Tower: Merit and Its Limits in Academic Careers* (Baltimore: Johns Hopkins University Press, 1975), Lionel S. Lewis concludes, on the basis of reviewing "well over three thousand letters of recommendation . . . from a number of disciplines written on behalf of both faculty and students" (65) for academic positions, that "extra-academic considerations play an extensive part in the recruitment of faculty" (63), including "references to a man's personality" (64) and "remarks bearing on the candidates' families and appearances" (69).

88. Gregory Jay, *American Literature and the Culture Wars* (Ithaca, NY: Cornell University Press, 1997), 209.

89. Coser, Kadushin, and Powell, *Books,* 166; Will Atkinson, "The Structure of Literary Taste: Class, Gender, and Reading in the UK," *Cultural Sociology* 10:2 (2016): 248.

90. Childress, *Under the Cover,* 75. Philippa Chong, *Inside the Critics' Circle: Book Reviewing in Uncertain Times* (Princeton, NJ: Princeton University Press, 2020), 28.

91. Childress, *Under the Cover,* 169, 171.

92. Coser, Kadushin, and Powell, *Books,* 73.

93. Frank Parkin, *Marxism and Class Theory: A Bourgeois Critique* (London: Tavistock, 1979), 44.

94. See Chong, *Inside the Critics' Circle,* 8.

95. Pat K. Chew and Robert E. Kelley observe that "judges of different races have different decision-making patterns," in "The Realism of Race in Judicial Decision Making: An Empirical Analysis of Plaintiffs' Race and Judges' Race," *Harvard Journal on Racial & Ethnic Justice* 28 (2012): 115. On racial inequality in the U.S. health-care system, see Dayna Bowen

—

Matthew, *Just Medicine: A Cure for Racial Inequality in American Health Care* (New York: New York University Press, 2015).

96. Cohen, *Cotton Capitalists,* 201.

97. An example of a Jew helping a Jew for no other reason than their shared Jewishness can be found in a story told by the game show host Monty Hall, in an oral history, about his immigrant grandfather's experience. At least according to the story, Hall's grandfather stepped off a train in late-nineteenth-century Winnipeg, knowing no one, and heard someone call, "S'iz do yidn?" (Are there Jews here?). The man took Hall's grandfather back to his home, gave him a meal and a bath, took him to the free loan society and got him a loan for five dollars, and then got him a room and a pushcart. Christa Whitney, "A Job, a Place to Live, and a Pray within 24 Hours: Mutual Aid for Jewish Refugees in Winnipeg," Wexler Oral History Project, Yiddish Book Center (March 11, 2014), https://www.yiddishbookcenter .org/collections/oral-histories/excerpts/woh-ex-0003225/job-place-live-and-pray-within -24-hours-mutual-aid-jewish-refugees-winnipeg. For the benefits of shared ethnicity, see Olof Åslund, Lena Hensvik, and Oskar Nordström Skans, "Seeking Similarity: How Immigrants and Natives Manage in the Labor Market," *Journal of Labor Economics* 32:3 (2014): 407; and Kerr and Mandorff, "Social Networks, Ethnicity, and Entrepreneurship," 2. See also Charles Kadushin, who in "Social Networks and Jews," *Contemporary Jewry* 31:1 (2011): 55–73, notes that "social circles not only create the conditions for trust, but make for enforceable trust" (61).

98. Though the loan societies were founded to help newly arrived immigrants and other financially disadvantaged Jews, they did not give loans to any Jew who walked in the door. Instead, they relied on a system of endorsers that emphasized the power of ethnic networks (because, to be approved for a loan, one needed to be endorsed by known members of the community, and if one defaulted on the loan, the endorsers were held responsible). Tanenbaum shows, moreover, that the endorsement system was decisive in the success of loan societies: "when philanthropic organizations, rather than individuals, cosigned loans, many borrowers failed to pay." So it is emphatically not the case that Jews seeking loans were inherently trustworthy borrowers – the endorsement system, which drew on the knowledge of their communities about individuals, allowed the loan societies to determine *which* Jews were good bets. See Tanenbaum, *A Credit to Their Communities: Jewish Loan Societies in the United States, 1880–1945* (Detroit: Wayne State University Press, 1993), especially 70–73, quotation on 72.

99. Again, Tanenbaum notes that free loan societies would "warn each other that a person with a delinquent loan history had moved to a new area" (71).

100. See Sigmund Freud, *Civilization and Its Discontents,* trans. and ed. James Strachey (New York: Norton, 1961), 72.

101. See Atkinson, "Structure of Literary Taste," 250, discussing the limitations of "the reliance on *genre* categories" in sociological studies of reading taste.

102. See Aristides, "Literary Mafia?," where Joseph Epstein unconvincingly suggests as evidence against the existence of a Jewish literary mafia the "extreme disputatiousness" and "intense rivalries" (184) among Jewish writers and intellectuals in New York.

—

CHAPTER 1. JEWS EDITING JEWS

1. Associated Press, "National Book Awards Presented in New York," *Hartford Courant* (March 24, 1960), 5.

2. See Rita N. Kosofsky, *Bernard Malamud: A Descriptive Bibliography* (New York: Greenwood, 1991); and Bernard F. Rodgers, *Philip Roth: A Bibliography* (Metuchen, NJ: Scarecrow, 1984). On *Commentary* as an organ of the Jewish literary mafia, see, e.g., Marvin Mudrick, "The Holy Family," *Hudson Review* 17:2 (1964): 299; and Richard Kostelanetz, *The End of Intelligent Writing: Literary Politics in America* (New York: Sheed & Ward, 1974), 45–47.

3. See Evan Brier, *A Novel Marketplace: Mass Culture, the Book Trade, and Postwar American Fiction* (Philadelphia: University of Pennsylvania Press, 2009), 45–53; James F. English, *The Economy of Prestige: Prizes, Awards, and the Circulation of Cultural Value* (Cambridge, MA: Harvard University Press, 2008); John B. Hench, *Books as Weapons: Propaganda, Publishing, and the Battle for Global Markets in the Era of World War II* (Ithaca, NY: Cornell University Press, 2010).

4. "Book Trade Plans to Honor Writers," *New York Times* (January 22, 1950), 68.

5. See W. J. Stuckey, *The Pulitzer Prize Novels: A Critical Backward Look* (Norman: University of Oklahoma Press, 1981), 181.

6. Robert R. Kirsch, "Books and People: NBA's Purpose a Moot Question," *Los Angeles Times* (March 22, 1959), 94.

7. Joyce Carol Oates, "A Conversation with Philip Roth," in George J. Searles, ed., *Conversations with Philip Roth* (Jackson: University Press of Mississippi, 1992), 89; quoted in English, *Economy of Prestige*, 134–35n55; Carol Iannone, "Literature by Quota," *Commentary* (March 1991), 52.

8. English, *Economy of Prestige*, 212.

9. "Clipping Featuring the 1959 National Book Award Nominations Including May Swenson for *A Cage of Spines*," Washington University Digital Gateway, Image Collections & Exhibitions, accessed December 1, 2020, http://omeka.wustl.edu/omeka/items/show /9056.

10. Joe Moran, *Star Authors: Literary Celebrity in America* (London: Pluto, 2000), 44.

11. Louis Harap notes in his study of the period, *In the Mainstream*, that at the beginning of the 1950s, "the growing importance of Jews in literature had not yet emerged into full awareness," although Norman Mailer, Alfred Kazin, Lionel Trilling, Saul Bellow, and others had already produced noteworthy work and though, as Harap knew very well, Jewish authors and characters had been a noticeable presence in American literature for about seven decades. Harap, *In the Mainstream: The Jewish Presence in Twentieth-Century American Literature, 1950s–1980s* (New York: Greenwood, 1987), 17. On early periods, see Harap's *The Image of the Jew in American Literature: From Early Republic to Mass Immigration* (Philadelphia: Jewish Publication Society, 1974), which remains the most useful overview of Jews and Jewishness in American literature in the nineteenth century and earlier. It was, Harap continues, "only as the 1950s wore on, with its parade of best-sellers by Jews" such as Herman

Wouk and Leon Uris "and the emergence of widely discussed new novelists like Bernard Malamud and Philip Roth, that a full realization of the new literary importance of Jewish writers moved into the center of public consciousness" (*In the Mainstream*, 17, 21). See also the aptly titled 1964 anthology *Breakthrough;* the editors write, "For the first time in history a large and impressively gifted group of serious American-Jewish writers has broken through the psychic barriers of the past to become an important, possibly a major reformative influence in American life and letters." Irving Malin, Irwin Stark, and Paul Goodman, introduction to Irving Malin, Irwin Stark, and Paul Goodman, eds., *Breakthrough: A Treasury of Contemporary American-Jewish Literature* (Philadelphia: Jewish Publication Society of America, 1964), 1. In a recent survey essay, Benjamin Schreier reproduces the language of these earlier critics — titled "Making It into the Mainstream" the piece argues that "this period screams out to be read through, read as, a narrative of emergence" — and, relevant to my argument here, emphasizes that it was the period "in which the Jewish American writers who would go on to win all the major U.S. literary awards entered the scene." He goes on to argue that what really emerged in this period was "Jewish American literary culture as a disciplined object of interpretation," though the coalescing of an academic field, which interests Schreier and serves as the basis for that claim, only began toward the end of the period he discusses, in the late 1960s. Schreier, "Making It into the Mainstream, 1945–1970" in Hana Wirth-Nesher, ed., *The Cambridge History of Jewish American Literature* (Cambridge: Cambridge University Press, 2016), 124–43, quotations on 124, 132. Schreier has more recently mounted a critique of the "breakthrough" narrative, though his attention is more on the critics who shaped that narrative in the postwar decades, rather than on earlier moments in American Jewish literary history; see Schreier, "The History of Jewish American Literary History: A Critical Genealogy of Emergence," *American Literature* 91:1 (2019): 121–50; and Schreier, *The Rise and Fall of Jewish American Literature: Ethnic Studies and the Challenge of Identity* (Philadelphia: University of Pennsylvania Press, 2020).

12. It is worth mentioning that Nelson Algren, who won the first National Book Award for Fiction, in 1950, was Jewish, but according to one contemporary observer, Algren was "scarcely known as a Jewish writer" when he won the award and has not often been mentioned as one since then. See Harold Uriel Ribalow, *A Treasury of American Jewish Stories* (New York: T. Yoseloff, 1958), 483.

13. "National Book Awards Presented in New York," 5.

14. Writing in 1969, Ernest van den Haag noted that "Mary McCarthy has long been a member of the Jewish cultural establishment." Van den Haag, *The Jewish Mystique* (1969; repr., New York: Dell, 1971), 113. On Edel, see his posthumously published memoir, *The Visitable Past: A Wartime Memoir* (Honolulu: University of Hawai'i Press, 2000). He remembers himself as having been a "Euro-centered youth" who felt himself to be "rather cosmopolitan" but with an "unorthodox . . . Jewish upbringing" that "made [him] feel that warring against the Nazis was self-defense" (5), which he pursued by enlisting in the U.S. Army.

15. See James Atlas, *Bellow: A Biography* (New York: Random House, 2000), 142, 210; and Frances Kiernan, *Seeing Mary Plain: A Life of Mary McCarthy* (New York: Norton, 2002), 357.

—

16. Chad Walsh, "A Turmoil of Desires," *New York Times Book Review* (September 28, 1952), 5.

17. Nathan Rothman, "Poets of Wander," *Saturday Review* (August 9, 1952), 19. This review also correctly notes the problem with the novel's title, and the oddness or wrongness of Martin's translating *landslayt* — which, as Rothman points out, means "kinsmen" (or, really, "kinfolk") — as "landsmen" (19).

18. Arnold Rampersad, *Ralph Ellison: A Biography* (New York: Knopf, 2007), 269.

19. Kostelanetz, *End of Intelligent Writing*, 84–86.

20. When Ellison is mentioned in Kostelanetz's *The End of Intelligent Writing*, it is always as a *victim* of the literary mafia; see especially 35 and 132–33.

21. Rampersad, *Ralph Ellison*, 273.

22. Lawrence Jackson has described the contradictory effects of the prize on the field: "After Ellison had received the National Book Award for Fiction, black writers were uneasy about his membership as an organic part of the black community, in part undoubtedly because they could not match the recognition accorded Ellison from elite publishers, top-tier white colleges and universities, foundations, media organs and award-granting bodies." At the same time, Jackson explains, "It was becoming obvious that after Ellison's National Book Award, everyone [i.e., African American critics] would retreat from the initial criticism of *Invisible Man* and use the work as a new kind of benchmark." Jackson, *The Indignant Generation: A Narrative History of African American Writers and Critics, 1934–1960* (Princeton, NJ: Princeton University Press, 2011), 381–82, 393.

23. See Amy Root Clements, *The Art of Prestige: The Formative Years at Knopf, 1915–1929* (Amherst: University of Massachusetts Press, 2014).

24. On Samuel's background and Alfred's early years, see Clements, 16–20.

25. Laura Claridge, *The Lady with the Borzoi: Blanche Knopf, Literary Tastemaker Extraordinaire* (New York: Farrar, Straus & Giroux, 2016), 17.

26. Clements, *Art of Prestige*, 76; Claridge, *Lady with the Borzoi*, 14. "Knopf, Samuel," of "61 E. Ninety-first [Street]," in New York, is listed as a member in the "Report of the Twelfth Year of the Jewish Publication Society of America, 1899–1900," *American Jewish Year Book* 2 (1900–1901): 701. He was listed regularly as a member, over the next decades, up to the "Report of the Thirty-Fourth Year of the Jewish Publication Society of America, 1922–1923," *American Jewish Year Book* 24 (1922–23): 489, where he was listed as residing at "220 W. 42d" in New York.

27. See, e.g., Jonathan Freedman, *The Temple of Culture: Assimilation and Anti-Semitism in Literary Anglo-America* (New York: Oxford University Press, 2000), 168.

28. See Robert Nathan, *Road of Ages* (New York: Knopf, 1935).

29. Bill Cole, note, manuscript record for *Commentary on the American Scene*, May 10, 1951, Alfred A. Knopf, Inc. Records, 958.3, Harry Ransom Center, University of Texas at Austin (hereafter cited as AAKR). Quoted with the permission of the Estate of William Rossa Cole.

30. Though Strauss occupied an important role at the firm, he was regularly disparaged and dismissed by the Knopfs; for more details, see Josh Lambert, "Publishing Jews at Knopf," *Book History* 21 (2018): 346.

—

31. Harold Strauss, note, manuscript record for *Commentary on the American Scene,* AAKR, 958.3. It is noteworthy that Strauss's sense of the Jewish market's interests aligns quite nicely with Laurence Roth's retrospective observation of "the three Jewish experiences . . . that proved compelling to a mass American readership and exploitable to general publishers: the traumas of the Holocaust, the struggle for Jewish national and cultural self-determination, and the social and psychological hardships of acculturation." Roth, "Literature, United States: Popular Fiction," in Judith R. Baskin, ed., *The Cambridge Dictionary of Judaism and Jewish Culture* (Cambridge: Cambridge University Press, 2011), 396. That said, the same year Strauss made these comments, Harold Ribalow surveyed publishers and came to the conclusion, contrary to Strauss's, that "books on Israel and Zionism sell very badly." Ribalow, "Do Jews Read?," *Congress Weekly* (October 8, 1951), 8–12.

32. Strauss, note, manuscript record for *Commentary on the American Scene.*

33. Such ideas about the market have almost always been projections (how could Strauss know which of the millions of Jews in the United States constituted and contributed to the "Jewish market" for books—which numbered in the tens of thousands, at most—and how could he know whether it was a member of that Jewish market who had bought a copy of a Knopf title in a bookstore in Texas or Oklahoma or New York?); in other words, publishing houses and their employees in Strauss's time simply did not know "where books are bought and who buys them." See O. H. Cheney, *Economic Survey of the Book Industry, 1930–1931* (New York: R. R. Bowker, 1949), 18.

34. On Hollywood, see Neil Gabler, *An Empire of Their Own: How the Jews Invented Hollywood* (New York: Crown, 1988), 300–301; and for an earlier example of this dynamic in U.S. book publishing, see Barbara Cantalupo and Lori Harrison-Kahan's introduction to Emma Wolf's 1900 novel *Heirs of Yesterday* (Detroit: Wayne State University Press, 2020), especially 25–50.

35. Harold Strauss to Leslie Fiedler, March 15, 1954, AAKR, 979.12.

36. Blanche Knopf to Joyce Weiner, June 15, 1955, and Walter Allen, "SON OF A SMALLER HERO by Mordecai Richler," n.d. (ca. spring 1955), AAKR, 993.3.

37. In an "informal sales conference" that took place on December 10 and 11, 1946, Alfred Knopf told his sales representatives that Philip Frank's forthcoming biography, *Einstein: His Life and Times,* would have appeal, even "apart from the great publicity that its subject is always enjoying . . . to the world of mathematics and the world of physics, and particularly . . . the Jewish groups." "Knopf Dept.—Sales—Informal Sales Conference—1946," December 10–11, 1946, AAKR, 1513.9, 63; Alfred Knopf, note, manuscript record for Samuel Chotzinoff, *A Paradise Lost,* June 11, 1953, AAKR, 958.2.

38. See Josh Lambert, "Fictions of Anti-Semitism and the Beginning of Holocaust Literature," in Christopher Vials, ed., *American Literature in Transition: 1940–1950* (New York: Cambridge University Press, 2017), 44–58.

39. See, e.g., Clements, *Art of Prestige,* 85–86; Claridge, *Lady with the Borzoi,* 62; and Geoffrey T. Hellman, "II: Flair Is the Word," *New Yorker* (November 27, 1948), 51.

40. Donald Pizer, *American Naturalism and the Jews: Garland, Norris, Dreiser, Wharton, and Cather* (Urbana: University of Illinois Press, 2008), 61.

—

41. Willa Cather, "Scandal," *Century* 98:4 (August 1919): 440.

42. Clements, *Art of Prestige,* 86.

43. Knopf, Inc., *The Borzoi 1920: Being a Sort of Record of Five Years' Publishing* (New York: Knopf, 1920), iv.

44. Knopf, Inc., 81–82.

45. See, for example, Anthony Julius, *T. S. Eliot, Anti-Semitism, and Literary Form* (Cambridge: Cambridge University Press, 1996), 75–110; and Ronald Suchard, "Burbank with a Baedeker, Eliot with a Cigar: American Intellectuals, Anti-Semitism, and the Idea of Culture," *modernism/modernity* 10:1 (2003): 1–26.

46. H. L. Mencken, *A Treatise on the Gods* (New York: Knopf, 1930), 345–46.

47. Quoted in Marion Elizabeth Rodgers, *Mencken: The American Iconoclast* (New York: Oxford University Press, 2005), 355.

48. Quoted in Rodgers, 354.

49. "Dr. Margoshes, Editor of 'The Day,' Finds Anti-Semitism in H. L. Mencken's Latest Work, 'Treatise on the Gods,'" *Jewish Daily Bulletin* (March 23, 1930), 4.

50. Clements, *Art of Prestige,* 82.

51. Raymond Chandler to Miss Aron, January 11, 1945, in Cathy Henderson and Richard W. Oram, eds., *The House of Knopf, 1915–1960: A Documentary Volume,* Dictionary of Literary Biography 355 (Detroit: Gale Cengage Learning, 2010), 189.

52. Raymond Chandler, *The High Window,* in Frank McShane, ed., *Stories and Early Novels* (New York: Library of America, 1995), 1060, 1134.

53. Chandler, 1093.

54. Chandler to Aron, 189.

55. Raymond Chandler to Alfred Knopf, March 22, 1945, in Henderson and Oram, *The House of Knopf,* 190–91.

56. For example, compare Raymond Chandler, *The High Window* (New York: Vintage, 1976), 114.

57. Strauss wrote, in a report on Robbins's *Never Love a Stranger,* that it was "in that special class of novel which *appears* to have enough serious ideas about society (in this case, unemployment, race relations, racketeering, and the problem of orphan children) to titillate the women's clubs, but actually is featherweight, superior slick-magazine writing with strong element of tear-jerking sentimentality." Quoted in Andrew Wilson, *Harold Robbins: The Man Who Invented Sex* (New York: Bloomsbury, 2007), 44.

58. Harold Ribalow, "American Jewish Writers and Their Judaism," in Jacob Freid, ed., *Jews in the Modern World,* vol. 2 (New York: Twayne, 1962), 424; Meyer Levin, "The East Side Gangsters of the Paper-Backs: The 'Jewish' Novels that Millions Buy," *Commentary* (October 1953), 339. A more recent appraisal remarks that Danny is "cynical, anti-clerical, anarchistic, suspicious, materialistic and dangerous." Marc Lee Raphael, "From Marjorie to Tevya: The Image of Jews in American Popular Literature, Theatre and Comedy, 1955–1965," *American Jewish History* 74:1 (1984): 67.

59. See Harold Robbins, *Never Love a Stranger* (New York: Pocket Books, 1962), 68, 232.

60. Arthur Miller, "Concerning Jews Who Write," *Jewish Life* (March 1948), 9.

—

61. Strauss's report and the flap copy are quoted in Wilson, *Harold Robbins,* 63, 64.

62. Harold Robbins, *The Dream Merchants* (New York: Pocket, 1961), 416, 451, 492.

63. Compare the discussions of Laura Hobson's *Gentleman's Agreement* at Simon & Schuster in the late 1940s. The company's founder, Richard Simon, who was Jewish, shared Hobson's concerns about genteel anti-Semitism, but he doubted that her novel would be able to change readers' minds. See Rachel Gordan, "Laura Z. Hobson and the Making of *Gentleman's Agreement,*" *Studies in American Jewish Literature* 34:2 (2015): 231–56.

64. Christian Lorentzen, "Gordon Lish: The Art of Editing, No. 2," *Paris Review* 215 (Winter 2015), https://www.theparisreview.org/interviews/6423/gordon-lish-the-art -of-editing-no-2-gordon-lish.

65. See, for example, Steven X. Rea, "He Holds the Hands of Writers," *Philadelphia Inquirer* (January 10, 1984), E1; Amy Hempel, "Captain Fiction," *Vanity Fair* (December 1984), 91–93, 126–29; Mimi Kramer, "What I Know about Gordon Lish . . . So Far," *Spy* (October 1986), 36–40; Carla Blumenkranz, "Captain Midnight," *n+1* 12 (Fall 2011), https://nplusonemag.com/issue-12/essays/captain-midnight/, and 14 (Summer 2012), https://nplusonemag.com/issue-14/essays/captain-midnight-part-two/; and Alexander Nazaryan, "An Angry Flash of Gordon," *Newsweek* (June 19, 2014), https://www.newsweek .com/2014/06/27/angry-flash-gordon-255491.html.

66. On Perkins as the paradigm of the literary editor's changing role in the prewar decades, see Clayton Childress, *Under the Cover: The Creation, Production, and Reception of a Novel* (Princeton, NJ: Princeton University Press, 2017), 89–90. For an example of critical discussion of Lish's Carver edits, see Matthew Blackwell, "What We Talk about When We Talk about Lish," in Loren Glass, ed., *After the Program Era: The Past, Present, and Future of Creative Writing in the University* (Iowa City: University of Iowa Press, 2017), 113–22. For an example of how Lish's edits are discussed far beyond strictly literary venues, see Ken Jennings and John Roderick's podcast *Omnibus,* episode 51 (May 22, 2018), https://www .omnibusproject.com/51.

67. Mark McGurl, *The Program Era: Postwar Fiction and the Rise of Creative Writing* (Cambridge, MA: Harvard University Press, 2009), 293.

68. David Winters, "Theory and the Creative Writing Classroom: Conceptual Revision in the School of Gordon Lish," *Contemporary Literature* 57:1 (2016): 112, 114.

69. For example, see Michael Hemmingson's extensive blog, *Gordon Lish Edited This,* https://gordonlisheditedthis.wordpress.com/ (published circa 2011–12); Megan Hamilton, "Glamour, Good Money, and Glossy Magazines: The *New Yorker, Esquire,* and 20th Century Magazine Fiction" (PhD diss., Brandeis University, 2014); and Carla Blumenkranz, "Seduce the Whole World: Gordon Lish's Workshop," *New Yorker* (February 20, 2014), https://www.newyorker.com/books/page-turner/seduce-the-whole-world-gordon-lishs -workshop.

70. See, e.g., Robert Gottlieb, *Avid Reader* (New York: Farrar, Straus & Giroux, 2016), 14–15, 24, 29.

71. Lorentzen, "Gordon Lish."

72. This is consistent with Lish's vision of himself as a paranoid Jew in an interview published thirteen years earlier, in which he remarks, "It must be, in every Jew's terror, that this will be his destiny, that this will be his fate. Somehow the most intimate part of himself will be measured against other men and found wanting. . . . I've been that way all my life." Rob Trucks, "A Conversation with Gordon Lish," in *The Pleasure of Influence: Conversations with American Male Fiction Writers* (West Lafayette, IN: Purdue University Press, 2002), 110.

73. David Winters, "An Interview with Gordon Lish," *Critical Quarterly* 57:4 (2015): 95.

74. Winters, 95.

75. Lorentzen, "Gordon Lish."

76. Winters, "Interview," 102. Another published example in which Lish invokes a Yiddish word this way was in 1988, when asked why he puts up with some of Harold Brodkey's bad behavior; he remarks, "it's all a question of *ku-vit* [*sic*] (Yiddish for 'honor' or 'tribute')." Dinita Smith, "The Genius: Harold Brodkey and His Great (Unpublished) Novel," *New York* (September 19, 1988), 66.

77. Martha Bayles, "What Gordon Knew," *New Republic* 194:3720 (May 5, 1986): 40–41.

78. Edward Hirsch, "The Oldest Stories Made New," *New York Times Book Review* (December 20, 1987), 1, 24; review of David Rosenberg, ed., *Testimony: Contemporary Writers Make the Holocaust Personal*, *Publisher's Weekly* (November 28, 1989), https://www.publishers weekly.com/978-0-8129-1817-5.

79. The piece's title evokes Salinger's story "For Esmé — with Love and Squalor," and its chatty first-person voice, with interjections like "Actually" and "I suppose," seem designed to make readers wonder if the story might have been written by Salinger, whose work they probably know from *The Catcher in the Rye*. Gordon Lish, "For Rupert — with No Promises," *Esquire* (May 1977), 83–87. Lish once told an interviewer that "art is a stunt, . . . a provocation, and quite properly." John Blades, "Admired and Vilified, Writer-Editor Gordon Lish Can Be Counted on for Wild Words," *Chicago Tribune* (January 7, 1997), https://www .chicagotribune.com/news/ct-xpm-1997-01-07-9701080289-story.html.

80. Gordon Lish, "Note to Story," *New England Review* 1:2 (1978): 144.

81. Lish published a short story in 1962; see Gordon Lish, "Flower," *Chrysalis Review* 1:2 (Spring 1962): 18–21.

82. See Lish, "Note to Story," 145.

83. Lish, "For Rupert," 87.

84. Compare Cynthia Ozick, "Usurpation," *Esquire* (May 1974), 173, to Lish, "For Rupert," 87. A few examples: Ozick: "So why come to me? You made your decision already." Lish: "Why come to me? You made your decision already." Ozick: "The father asks, 'What is the law on this?' 'The law is, Don't kill.'" Lish: "The father says, 'What is the law on this?' The rabbi answers, 'The law is, don't kill.'" Ozick noted the use of her work, with pleasure, in a letter to Lish praising "For Rupert" before it was published: "Thank you for including a part of my story in your story." Cynthia Ozick to Gordon Lish, December 21–22, 1976, Lish mss., Lilly Library, Indiana University, Bloomington.

85. "For Jerome" is singled out, for example, in Carl Senna, "Marvelously Funny Collection of Sketches," *Christian Science Monitor* (May 24, 1984), 20.

86. Whether accidentally or for some difficult-to-discern purpose, the story ignores well-known biographical facts about the authors it mentions, such as that Saul Bellow changed his first name, from Solomon, and that Irving Howe changed his last name, from Horenstein.

87. Gordon Lish, "Squeak in the Sycamore" and "Narratology to the People!," in *Collected Fictions* (New York: OR Books, 2010), 286–88, 418–20.

88. Gordon Lish, "In Defense of NYLE," in Bill Henderson, ed., *The Publish-It-Yourself Handbook: Literary Tradition and How-To* (Yonkers, NY: Pushcart Book Press, 1973), 335–40.

89. Cynthia Ozick remarked on Lish's willingness to publish his students in a 1983 letter, responding to a profile of Lish in *Publishers' Weekly,* "after this confession (but it's Well-Known, anyhow) of your genuine accessibility, and your getting contracts for your students, your life will be squeezed more than ever by importuning hordes of scribblers." Ozick to Lish, May 11, 1983, Lish mss.

90. Gordon Lish, telephone interview with the author, March 6, 2018.

91. Gordon Lish and Don Erikson, memo, March 18, 1970, Lish mss.

92. Lish interview.

93. On Lish's mixed feelings about Roth and Singer, see memos dated May 14, 1970, and December 11, 1973, Lish mss.

94. Contributor biographies, *Genesis West* 1:1 (Fall 1962): 98. The "panegyric" that Lish is referring to is, presumably, the one that appeared in Herbert Feinstein, "Contemporary American Fiction: Harvey Swados and Leslie Fiedler," *Wisconsin Studies in Contemporary Literature* 2:1 (1961): 79–98, especially 81–82, where Swados says that Paley "is at least as interesting as J. D. Salinger."

95. "Special Offer," *Genesis West* 1:3 (Spring 1963): 284.

96. Irving Malin, "The Verve of Grace Paley," *Genesis West* 2:1 (1964?): 73, as well as the issue's list of contributors.

97. Gordon Lish, "I Make This Choice Every Day of My Life: An Interview with Herbert Gold," *Genesis West* 2:2–3 (Winter–Spring 1964): 193.

98. Grace Paley, "Living" and "Gloomy Tune," *Genesis West* 3:1–2 (Winter 1965): 11–15.

99. Editorial note, *Genesis West* 3:1–2 (Winter 1965): i.

100. Gordon Lish, ed., *New Sounds in American Fiction* (Menlo Park, CA: Cummings, 1969).

101. Gordon Lish to Don Erikson, February 24, 1971, Lish mss.

102. Gordon Lish to Tom [Ferrell?], October 1, 1973, Lish mss.

103. Cynthia Ozick to Gordon Lish, March 28, 1970, Lish mss.

104. Ozick to Lish, October 9, 1973, Lish mss.

105. Ozick to Lish, January 1, 1974, Lish mss.

106. Ozick to Lish, June 3, 1975, Lish mss.

107. Gordon Lish to Don Erikson, June 14, 1974, Lish mss.

—

108. Ozick to Lish, June 3, 1975, Lish mss.

109. Ozick to Lish, May 11, 1983, Lish mss.

110. "Biographies," in Gordon Lish, ed., *All Our Secrets Are the Same: New Fiction from "Esquire"* (New York: Norton, 1976), 142.

111. Lish interview. See also John F. Baker, "*PW* Interviews Gordon Lish," *Publishers' Weekly* (May 13, 1983), 58–59; and Gordon Lish, "Levitation, or My Career as a Pensioner," in *White Plains: Pieces and Witherlings* (Stroud, UK: Little Island, 2017), 131–39.

112. Paley has explained how the voice of her fiction owed much of its uniqueness to the linguistic environment of her childhood home, where Russian and Yiddish jostled with English. See Grace Paley, "Clearing My Jewish Throat," in Derek Rubin, ed., *Who We Are: On Being (and Not Being) a Jewish American Writer* (New York: Schocken Books, 2005), 12–18; and Jonathan Dee, Barbara Jones, and Larissa MacFarquhar, "Grace Paley, The Art of Fiction No. 131," *Paris Review* 124 (Fall 1992), https://www.theparisreview.org/interviews/2028/the-art-of-fiction-no-131-grace-paley. Syntax, cadence, volume, and vocal markers (such as the sound "ach" in "The Loudest Voice," for example), serve in Paley's fiction, as Hana Wirth-Nesher has argued, as "the remainder of the Yiddish speech that the written page cannot convey." Wirth-Nesher, *Call It English: The Languages of Jewish American Literature* (Princeton, NJ: Princeton University Press, 2008), 23. As for Elkin, a *Kirkus* reviewer noted in 1987 that "all of Elkin's work is saturated with Jewish-American, Yiddish-tinged rhythms"; review of Stanley Elkin, *The Rabbi of Lud*, *Kirkus Review* (September 15, 1987), https://www.kirkusreviews.com/book-reviews/stanley-elkin/the-rabbi-of-lud/. Michaels, for his part, wrote, "Until I was five, I spoke only Yiddish. . . . To some extent, my intuitions and my expression of thoughts remain basically Yiddish." Michaels, "My Yiddish," *Threepenny Review* (Fall 2003), https://www.threepennyreview.com/samples/michaelslenny_f03.html.

113. The novelist and short story writer Sam Lipsyte, who has taught in and directed the MFA in creative writing at Columbia, has explained, "I'd read Ozick and Paley and Brodkey before, but it was the way [Lish] talked about certain stories of theirs [in his classes] that made me revisit them and read them in a more interesting way"; Lish also introduced him to stories by Michaels and Elkin that were "major" for him. Sam Lipsyte, email to the author, March 8, 2018. Adam Wilson confirmed, in an email, that though he had not himself met Lish, Lipsyte had "turn[ed him] onto those writers" (Michaels, Elkin, and Brodkey, especially). Adam Wilson, email to the author, March 14, 2018. Rebecca Schiff recalled that on the first day of the first course she took with Lipsyte, he handed out a list of writers, with some first lines of stories, including Elkin, Leonard Michaels, Grace Paley, and Harold Brodkey. Rebecca Schiff, telephone interview with the author, March 16, 2018. See also Justin Taylor, "Textual Dysfunction," *Bookforum* (June–July–August 2016), 43; and Josh Lambert, "The Gordon Lish Lineage of Jewish American Writing," *LitHub* (September 25, 2018), https://lithub.com/the-gordon-lish-lineage-of-jewish-american-writing/. On the "MFA canon," see Chad Harbach, "MFA vs NYC," in Chad Harbach, ed., *MFA vs NYC: The Two Cultures of American Fiction* (New York: n+1/Farrar, Straus & Giroux, 2014), 19–20.

114. Jess Row, *White Flights: Race, Fiction, and the American Imagination* (Minneapolis: Graywolf, 2019), 73. Row suggests, further, that "whether Lish deliberately avoided working with nonwhite writers is a significant question for his biographers" (73). As sensitive and thoughtful as Row's essay on Lish is, he ignores Lish's own fiction and his support for writers like Ozick, Paley, and Michaels, and as a result, Row erroneously describes Lish as "operat[ing] in a parallel aesthetic universe that deals neither in culture nor multiplicity" (73).

115. McGurl, *Program Era*, 273–81.

116. Mitchell S. Jackson, "Dear Gordon Lish," *Tin House* (February 26, 2015), http://tinhouse.com/dear-gordon-lish/. See LeRoi Jones [Amiri Baraka], "The Screamers," *Genesis West* 5 (Fall 1963): 81–86; and William Melvin Kelley, "Not Exactly Lena Horne," in Gordon Lish, ed., *New Sounds in American Fiction* (Menlo Park, CA: Cummings, 1969), 81–92.

117. See Lish, *New Sounds in American Fiction;* and Lish, *All Our Secrets Are the Same.* At the end of *New Sounds,* Lish provides a longer list of 156 writers who represented "the best of contemporary American short fiction" and includes five African American writers among them (Ann Petry, James Baldwin, Paule Marshall, Ellison, and Baraka) (237–39).

118. For this list of 797 writers, see Series II, Subseries: "By Other Authors," boxes 39–80, Lish mss. Anatole Broyard, whose racial self-identification has been the subject of some discussion, also appears in there. According to Ellison's biographer, "after years of begging Ralph to offer him some material," Lish "rejected two sections" of Ellison's novel-in-press in February 1977. Rampersad, *Ralph Ellison,* 513. Working with a research assistant, I was able to make a reasonable inference about an author's ethnic, racial, or national background for 542 out of the 797 writers. According to that research, of these 542 writers, about 7 were from Asian or Asian American backgrounds (including Susan Choi, Akhil Sharma, and Rick Noguchi), and about a dozen more had partly or wholly Latin American, Middle Eastern, or other non-European backgrounds. Thanks to Annabel Brazaitis for extraordinary and careful help with this accounting.

119. On Liu's relationship with Lish, see Anne van Buren, "Interview with Timothy Liu," *Katonah Poetry Series* (n.d., ca. 2020), http://katonahpoetry.com/interview-with-timothy-liu/.

120. See Yung Lung, "The National Disgrace," *Quarterly* 9 (1989): 173; and Yung Lung, "Bastards," *Quarterly* 10 (1989): 18–21; as well as illustrations credited to Yung Lung or Ying Ling in issues 14, 17, and 18. While this pseudonym probably derived from 永隆, a fairly common Mandarin phrase (used as a name for people as well as a town in Hubei province) meaning roughly "forever prosperous," it seems likely that it was chosen by the contributor to the *Quarterly,* playfully, because of its English cognates (young lung) and possibly because *yingling* means "young man" in Yiddish. Thanks to Yipeng Shen and Jui-Chien Wang for their assistance. For Atticus Lish's drawings and writing, see his *Life Is with People* (New York: Tyrant Books, 2011) and *Preparation for the Next Life* (New York: Tyrant Books, 2014).

121. "Asked if he had ever considered showing his fiction to his father," Atticus Lish replied, "Absolutely not, no. If it had ever come up, I would have said to him, 'With all respect, I'm not going to have an editor-writer relationship with you.'" John Williams, "A Son Writes His Own Ticket," *New York Times* (November 21, 2014), C1, https://www.nytimes.com /2014/11/22/books/atticus-lishs-long-route-to-preparation-for-the-next-life.html.

—

122. Ozick, who had adored Atticus since his childhood and praised him for his studies of Mandarin, regarded the appearance of the Chinese pseudonym in the *Quarterly* as a delightful joke: "Yung Lung!!!! Ominous wit, scary comic power. . . . Congratulations to Yung and his Lusty Lung." Ozick to Lish, March 9, 1990, Lish mss. On the perniciousness of yellowface hoaxes, see Hua Hsu, "When White Poets Pretend to Be Asian," *New Yorker* (September 9, 2015), https://www.newyorker.com/books/page-turner/when-white-poets -pretend-to-be-asian; and Jenny Zhang, "They Pretend to Be Us While Pretending We Don't Exist," *Buzzfeed* (September 11, 2015), https://www.buzzfeed.com/jennybagel/they -pretend-to-be-us-while-pretending-we-dont-exist.

123. See Michael North, *The Dialect of Modernism: Race, Language, and Twentieth-Century Literature* (New York: Oxford University Press, 1998); and Joshua L. Miller, *Accented America: The Cultural Politics of Multilingual Modernism* (New York: Oxford University Press, 2011).

124. Lish told one interviewer, "Any writing with any prospect of making its way with me would have to have been done in English. The kinds of things I'm looking for in a piece of writing can only have been put there by somebody writing in English, or writing in American English." Trucks, "Conversation with Gordon Lish," 90.

125. A 1997 story on Lish in the *Chicago Tribune* noted Lish's "inability to find another position" in publishing after his time at Knopf. See Blades, "Admired and Vilified." In 2014, Lish was "persona non grata at the Big Five Publishers," per Nazaryan, "Angry Flash of Gordon."

126. Michael Korda, *Another Life: A Memoir of Other People* (New York: Random House, 1999), 211. Gottlieb describes Potok's *The Chosen* as "a novel by a complete unknown, on so obscure and parochial a subject" that "revealed to readers an exotic world they didn't know" (*Avid Reader*, 88). Gottlieb describes himself as "a Jew who knows nothing about Jewishness" and notes that later in his relationship with Potok, he asked Potok to write *Wanderings: Chaim Potok's History of the Jews* (1978) in the hopes that it "might instruct someone like [him]." Larissa MacFarquhar, "Robert Gottlieb: The Art of Editing I," *Paris Review* 132 (1994): 197.

127. Boris Kachka, *Hothouse: The Art of Survival and the Survival of Art at America's Most Celebrated Publishing House, Farrar, Straus and Giroux* (New York: Simon & Schuster, 2013), 114–15. Dorothea Straus notes in her book *Under the Canopy* (New York: George Braziller, 1982) that for her, when she was growing up, "the idea of any kind of Jewish club [had] always been embarrassing, even repugnant" (123) and that she carried a sense of "Jewish inferiority" but that, in part through her friendship, as an adult, with Singer, she experienced a "change of attitude" and began to "desire to learn something about the Jewish religion" (143).

128. See Theodore Solotaroff, *First Loves: A Memoir* (New York: Seven Stories, 2003), 205, 213, 216, 260.

129. A classic articulation of an antiessentialist approach to cultural studies can be found in the essays of Stuart Hall from the 1990s; see Hall, *Essential Essays,* vol. 2, *Identity and Diaspora,* ed. David Morley (Durham, NC: Duke University Press, 2019).

—

CHAPTER 2. TEACHERS AND STUDENTS

1. For numbers of Jewish students in colleges and universities in the early decades of the twentieth century, see Suzanne Klingenstein, *Jews in the American Academy, 1900–1940: The Dynamics of Intellectual Assimilation* (New Haven, CT: Yale University Press, 1991), 6. On discrimination against Jews by elite universities, see Jerome Karabel, *The Chosen: The Hidden History of Admission and Exclusion at Harvard, Yale, and Princeton* (Boston: Houghton Mifflin, 2005). Kirstin Fermaglich emphasizes that the discrimination against Jews did not stop, as some people assume, immediately after World War II but persisted "well into the late 1950s." Fermaglich, *A Rosenberg by Any Other Name: A History of Jewish Name Changing in America* (New York: New York University Press, 2018), 74.

2. There had been some exceptions, like Joel Spingarn, who was Jewish and taught comparative literature at Columbia from 1899 to 1911, and Horace Kallen, who taught in the English department at Princeton from 1903 to 1905, but in 1922, Ludwig Lewisohn remarked that while in other disciplines Jews had been hired as professors, "that prejudice has not . . . relented in a single instance in regard to the teaching of English." The appointments of Harry Levin at Harvard and Lionel Trilling at Columbia in 1939, both in English, marked a major opening of the field – both stayed in those posts for decades – though Klingenstein notes that "it took another two to three decades for Jewish appointments in this field to become a matter of course" (*Jews in the American Academy,* xi). See Lewis S. Feuer, "The Stages in the Social History of Jewish Professors in American Colleges and Universities," *American Jewish History* 71:4 (1982): 432–65; and Klingenstein, *Jews in the American Academy.*

3. Columbia was the alma mater of such legendary publishers as Bennett Cerf and Donald Klopfer (founders of Random House), Alfred Knopf, Richard Simon and Max Schuster (founders of Simon & Schuster), and many, many others.

4. One of his teachers, Mark Van Doren, included a brief profile of Trilling in an article about teaching Jewish students at Columbia: Van Doren, "Jewish Students I Have Known," *Menorah Journal* 13:3 (June 1927): 264–68.

5. Lionel Trilling, "A Light to the Nations," *Menorah Journal* 16 (April 1928): 402–8. See also Daniel Greene, *The Jewish Origins of Cultural Pluralism: The Menorah Association and American Diversity* (Bloomington: Indiana University Press, 2011), 171.

6. He issues a familiar-sounding call for academic egalitarianism: "The academic community must always be on guard against using any other criterion than intellectual power as demonstrated in intellectual accomplishment. The honors should go to the students with the best marks, and we ought always to resist the effort to make 'character' or 'leadership' or 'activities' equal in value to scholarship." Thanks to the debates about affirmative action in recent decades, this academic egalitarianism sounds immediately double-edged; for Trilling, it would have been perhaps even more so. To say that "the honors should go to the students with the best marks" is not only, as one hears it today, a conservative refusal to redress social inequality through affirmative action, though Trilling did later oppose affirmative action in his 1972 Jefferson Lecture in the Humanities; see Lionel Trilling, *Mind in the Modern World* (New York: Viking, 1973). With his references to "character" and "leadership," Trilling is also rejecting the admissions tactics that were used, from the 1920s until the 1960s, to reduce the number of Jewish students who enrolled at prestigious U.S. colleges, Columbia as much as anywhere.

7. "Seven Professors Look at the Jewish Student: A Symposium," *Commentary* (December 1951), 529.

8. Allen Ginsberg went to Trilling for help himself in the summer of 1944, after he was indirectly involved in a murder, and in March 1945, after an infamous incident involving some slurs written on his dorm window, and again in late 1946, when he wanted to start psychotherapy. He requested letters of recommendation in 1947 in support of his fellowship at Columbia, in 1948 for a job at the Associated Press, and in 1949 for a job teaching at Cooper Union. Ginsberg's father, Louis, sought Trilling's aid in January of 1945, when a dean suggested that Allen was not fitting in at school, and again in April of 1949, after Allen was arrested in connection with a friend's crimes. In the latter situation, Trilling ended up testifying at the trial that resulted in Allen being "released into his father's custody on the condition that he be admitted to a mental hospital for psychiatric treatment." See Bill Morgan, *I Celebrate Myself: The Somewhat Private Life of Allen Ginsberg* (New York: Viking, 2006), 43, 51, 58, 63, 77, 98, 107, 109, 114–16.

9. John Rodden lists some of Trilling's more prominent students in "Reputation and the Sociological Imagination: The 'Case' of Lionel Trilling," in *Explorations: The Twentieth Century* (October 4, 2012), https://explorations20th.wordpress.com/2012/10/04/reputation-and -the-sociological-imagination-the-case-of-lionel-trilling/: "Some of [Trilling's] students became well-known poets (Allen Ginsberg, Jack Kerouac, John Hollander, Richard Howard, Gerald Stern, Louis Simpson), academic and/or intellectual authorities ([Norman] Podhoretz, Steven Marcus, Quentin Anderson, Morris Dickstein, Charles Peters, Jeffrey Hart, Marshall Berman, Fritz Stern, Charles Kadushin, Dan Wakefield, Joseph Kraft, Philip Lopate), and prominent men in the publishing world (Jason Epstein, Robert Gottlieb, Sol Stein, Gilman Kraft)." On Trilling's relationships with Cynthia Ozick, Norman Podhoretz, Steven Marcus, and Carolyn Heilbrun, see Susanne Klingenstein, *Enlarging America: The Cultural Work of Jewish Literary Scholars, 1930–1990* (Syracuse, NY: Syracuse University Press, 1999), 207–72. For extended treatments of Trilling's relationships with some of these students, see also Carolyn G. Heilbrun, *When Men Were the Only Models We Had: My Teachers Barzun, Fadiman, and Trilling* (Philadelphia: University of Pennsylvania Press, 2002); Norman Podhoretz, *Ex-Friends: Falling Out with Allen Ginsberg, Lionel and Diana Trilling, Lillian Hellman, Hannah Arendt, and Norman Mailer* (New York: Free Press, 1999); Leon Wieseltier, introduction to Lionel Trilling, *The Moral Obligation to Be Intelligent: Selected Essays* (New York: Farrar, Straus & Giroux, 2000); Adam Kirsch, "Lionel Trilling and Allen Ginsberg: Liberal Father, Radical Son," *Virginia Quarterly Review* (Summer 2009), https://www.vqr online.org/essay/lionel-trilling-and-allen-ginsberg-liberal-father-radical-son; Morris Dickstein, *Why Not Say What Happened: A Sentimental Education* (New York: Liveright, 2015).

10. Diana Trilling, "A Jew at Columbia," *Commentary* (March 1979), 46.

11. Mark McGurl, *The Program Era: Postwar Fiction and the Rise of Creative Writing* (Cambridge, MA: Harvard University Press, 2011).

—

12. Mike McGuire offers the best capsule history to date of the book blurb in the United States, in "The Literary Blurb Economy," *Post45* (November 30, 2018), https://post45 .org/2018/11/the-literary-blurb-economy/.

13. For example, he wrote letters on behalf of the graduate students Robert Wagner, William Wasserstrom, John D. Rosenberg, and Walter Sokel. See Lionel Trilling to Robert B. Heilman, May 22, 1953; L. Trilling to George R. Anderson, January 20, 1955; L. Trilling to James D. Hart, February 19, 1957; John Rosenberg to L. Trilling, March 14, 1953; L. Trilling to Rosenberg, April 6, 1953; L. Trilling, recommendation letter for Walter Sokel, October 17, 1955; all in Lionel Trilling Papers, Rare Book and Manuscript Library, Columbia University Library, New York (hereafter LTP). For undergraduates he supported, see Robert Gottlieb's memoir *Avid Reader,* in which Gottlieb recalls how after failing to be awarded a scholarship, he "confronted" Trilling to argue that he deserved a place at Cambridge. Trilling dispatched a letter to England, with the result that "ten days later [Gottlieb] received not an application form but an acceptance letter"; Gottlieb calls this "a stunning (to me) illustration of how the Old Boy network operated." Gottlieb, *Avid Reader: A Life* (New York: Farrar, Straus & Giroux, 2016), 27. For another example of Trilling's assistance to an undergraduate, see L. Trilling to R. M. D. Richardson, November 23, 1953, LTP.

14. Lionel Trilling to Alan [?], July 1, 1953, LTP.

15. Trilling explained to his colleague Marjorie Nicolson that while he had not accepted a draft of one student's dissertation, he had nonetheless written a letter to the student's supervisors at Smith College, where he was working, "to protect him," a "friendly fiction" expressing confidence that Trilling did not genuinely feel. Trilling to Marjorie Nicolson, July 10, 1952, LTP. In another case, when a former student sent Trilling an essay he hoped to get published in *Partisan Review,* Trilling wrote to the editors of the journal, in a tone that, for Trilling, was refreshingly direct: "Here's another one. It isn't good, I think, and isn't for you, but the writer submits it to *PR* and I can't, without losing my amateur standing, tell him directly it won't do. So will you write him a little note?" Lionel Trilling to William Phillips and Philip Rahv, November 13, 1956, LTP.

16. Lionel Trilling to Pat Covici, May 27, 1953, and September 23, 1953, LTP.

17. John Marshall, "Interview with Lionel Trilling Regarding Saul Bellow," January 10, 1951, folder 2773, box 296, Projects, series 200.R, RG 1.2, Rockefeller Foundation Records, Rockefeller Archive Center, https://rockfound.rockarch.org/digital-library-listing/-/ asset_publisher/yYxpQfeI4W8N/content/interview-with-lionel-trilling-regarding -saul-bellow.

18. Lionel Trilling to Fon Boardman Jr., December 8, 1958, LTP.

19. Lionel Trilling to Marshall Best, February 2, 1960, LTP.

20. An example of a former student who requested but did not receive a blurb from Trilling is Ralph de Toledano; see Michael Kimmage, *The Conservative Turn: Lionel Trilling, Whittaker Chambers, and the Lessons of Anti-Communism* (Cambridge, MA: Harvard University Press, 2009), 386n10.

21. Gérard Genette, *Paratexts: Thresholds of Interpretation,* trans. Jane E. Lewin (Cambridge: Cambridge University Press, 1997), 111.

—

22. McGuire, "Literary Blurb Economy." Trilling was deeply invested in his reputation and the influence he wielded. Among the most frequently repeated anecdotes about Trilling is the one told by Alfred Kazin, who recalled when they met in the offices of the *New Republic*, sometime in the early 1940s: "Trilling astonished me by saying, very firmly, that he would not write anything that did not 'promote my reputation.'" Kazin, *New York Jew* (New York: Knopf, 1978), 43. While Kazin's account cannot necessarily be trusted, another of Trilling's most often quoted remarks from the same period, about knowing "no writer in English who has added a micromillimetre to his stature by 'realizing his Jewishness'" (*Contemporary Jewish Record* [February 1944], 17), also reinforces the idea that he was concerned, above all, with his reputation and influence: in place of "stature," he might have written "achievement," but what Trilling seems to be noting here is that assertions of Jewishness have not aided writers' *standing* with critics, readers, and the general public. Trilling also wrote, in his journals in 1952, that "reputation" was the thing he had "most wanted from childhood on." Lionel Trilling, "From the Notebooks of Lionel Trilling, Part II," *Partisan Review* 54:1 (1987): 7.

23. Lionel Trilling to Catharine Carver, May 5, 1963, LTP.

24. Elinor Grumet, "The Apprenticeship of Lionel Trilling," *Prooftexts* 4 (May 1984): 153–73.

25. "Under Forty: A Symposium on American Literature and the Younger Generation of American Jews," *Contemporary Jewish Record* (February 1944), 17.

26. See Robert Warshow, "The Legacy of the '30's: Middle-Class Mass Culture and the Intellectuals' Problem" *Commentary* (December 1947), 538–45; Leslie Fiedler, "The Fate of the Novel," *Kenyon Review* 10:3 (Summer 1948): 519–27. Michael Kimmage also reports on a letter on this subject from one of Trilling's readers; see Kimmage, "Lionel Trilling's *The Middle of the Journey* and the Complicated Origins of the Neo-Conservative Movement," *Shofar* 21:3 (2003): 50.

27. Irving Howe, *A Margin of Hope: An Intellectual Autobiography* (New York: Harcourt Brace Jovanovich, 1982), 229. On Trilling's work with book clubs and on his textbook, *The Experience of Literature,* see Mark Krupnick, *Lionel Trilling and the Fate of Cultural Criticism* (Evanston, IL: Northwestern University Press, 1986), 105–7, 140–43. While a full study of Trilling's appearances on radio and television has not been undertaken, listings in the *New York Times* record Trilling's appearances on radio programs in the early 1940s and mid-1950s.

28. See, for examples, David Hollinger, *In the American Province: Studies in the History and Historiography of Ideas* (Bloomington: Indiana University Press, 1985), 67; Alan Wald, *The New York Intellectuals: The Rise and Decline of the Anti-Stalinist Left from the 1930s to the 1980s* (Chapel Hill: University of North Carolina Press, 1987), 11; Kimmage, "Lionel Trilling's *The Middle of the Journey*," 63.

29. In a detailed study of Trilling's works, Suzanne Klingenstein credits Trilling with a "mitnagdic sensibility," derived from his "descent culture" – without entirely explaining why different members of the same descent culture can have such different intellectual orientations – in *Jews in the American Academy,* 140. Joshua A. Miller argues that "Trilling's stylistic project" is to "refashion Jewish stylistics within a silky and elite U.S. English cosmopolitanism." Miller,

Accented America: The Cultural Politics of Multilingual Modernism (New York: Oxford University Press, 2011), 264. In Jonathan Freedman's account, Trilling "perform[ed] a number of remarkable reversals . . . turning himself into a James, James into a Jew, and culture itself into a solution to the problem of anti-Semitism, rather than a powerful instantiation of it." Freedman, *The Temple of Culture: Assimilation and Anti-Semitism in Literary Anglo-America* (New York: Oxford University Press, 2002), 199. Emily Miller Budick meanwhile argues that "Trilling's writings are subtly pervaded by a Jewish consciousness" and that his "commitment to a personal self . . . is the distinctive marker" of that consciousness, "especially after the Holocaust." Budick, "The Holocaust and the Construction of Modern American Literary Criticism: The Case of Lionel Trilling," in Sanford Budick and Wolfgang Iser, eds., *The Translatability of Cultures: Figurations of the Space Between* (Stanford, CA: Stanford University Press, 1996), 136, 138. See also, for another example, Ben Schreier, *The Impossible Jew: Identity and the Reconstruction of Jewish American Literary History* (New York: New York University Press, 2015), 96–102, where once again Trilling's story becomes exemplary of the "revisionary critique" (102) that is Schreier's project.

30. Adam Kirsch, *Why Trilling Matters* (New Haven, CT: Yale University Press, 2011), 78.

31. Kimmage, *Conservative Turn*, 394n73.

32. Mark Krupnick, "Lionel Trilling, 'Culture,' and Jewishness," *Denver Quarterly* 18 (August 1983): 106.

33. Lionel Trilling to Robert Giroux, October 6, 1955, LTP.

34. Lionel Trilling to Elizabeth Ames, June 24, 1955, LTP.

35. Lionel Trilling to Elizabeth Ames, April 1, 1955, LTP.

36. Lionel Trilling to Robert Giroux, August 23, 1955, Farrar, Straus, & Giroux, Inc. Records, Manuscripts and Archives Division, New York Public Library, Astor, Lenox, and Tilden Foundations (hereafter FSGR).

37. Robert Giroux to Lionel Trilling, September 8, 1955; Roger Straus Jr. to L. Trilling, September 16, 1955; Straus to L. Trilling, September 28, 1955, LTP. Victor Gollancz would later say that a blurb from Trilling would be crucial in marketing the novel: "The use of that quote will make all the difference in the world." Gollancz to Giroux, April 4, 1956, FSGR.

38. Robert Giroux, "AN END TO DYING by Sam Astrachan (Lionel Trilling)," August 30, 1955, FSGR.

39. Lionel Trilling to Robert Giroux, September 13, 1955, LTP.

40. Sam Astrachan, *An End to Dying* (New York: Farrar, Straus & Cudahy, 1956), book jacket. Subsequent citations of the novel appear parenthetically in the text.

41. See Suzanne Silberstein, "'Hansen's Law' in Fiction," *Commentary* (August 1956), 191–92; and review of Sam Astrachan, *An End to Dying, Library Journal* (March 15, 1956), 713.

42. Review of Sam Astrachan, *An End to Dying, Booklist* (July 1, 1956), 458.

43. Sam Astrachan to Roger Straus Jr., December 5, 1955, FSGR. Quoted by permission of Isaac-Daniel Astrachan.

44. Victor Gollancz to Robert Giroux, May 31, 1956, FSGR. Gollancz predicted that if

he did publish the novel, it would be one of his "biggest flops" (Gollancz to Giroux, April 25, 1956, FSGR) and noted, defensively, that he had just purchased Adele Wiseman's *The Sacrifice* (1957), which treats similar material, because he felt its "superb" quality helped it to transcend what he called the "immense handicap" of its Jewish subject matter (Gollancz to Giroux, June 7, 1956, FSGR).

45. Silberstein, "'Hansen's Law' in Fiction."

46. Lionel Trilling, "Isaac Babel: Torn between Violence and Peace: The Intellectual and the Revolution," *Commentary* (June 1955), 561, 555, 560.

47. Krupnick, *Lionel Trilling,* 126.

48. See Krupnick, 23.

49. "Under Forty," 17.

50. Sam Astrachan to Lionel Trilling, June 25, 1955, LTP.

51. Sam Astrachan, interview with the author, December 18, 2008. Quoted with permission of Isaac-Daniel Astrachan.

52. Astrachan's books have not attracted much criticism, but he has published actively: *An End to Dying* was followed by *The Game of Dostoyevsky* (1965), *Rejoice* (1970), and *Katz-Cohen* (1978), the latter being a massive autobiographical saga. Since the 1990s, when he retired from his position teaching at Wayne State University and moved to the South of France, Astrachan's books have appeared mainly in French and have included *Malaparte in Jassy* (1989), *Hôtel Seville: Rockaway Beach 1947* (1996), and *Treife* (2004).

53. Irving Feldman, *Works and Days* (Boston: Little, Brown, 1961), back cover. Subsequent citations of the collection appear parenthetically in the text.

54. Lionel Trilling to Robert Giroux, January 4, 1955; Pascal Covici to L. Trilling, August 22, 1956; Seymour Lawrence to L. Trilling, April 18, 1960, LTP.

55. Irving Feldman to Lionel Trilling, February 5, 1954; Feldman to L. Trilling, July 17, 1955, LTP.

56. Irving Feldman to Lionel Trilling, December 23, 1956, LTP.

57. In one exchange, Feldman thanks Trilling for his letter: "It arrived at just the right moment—for I was just entering a dangerous state of theorizing about your failure to write. Chronologically, these stages have been: 1. He is too busy. 2. He doesn't know how to address me, as I am neither student nor close friend, not inferior and not equal. 3. Maybe something I wrote offended him. 4. He doesn't think I'm important enough to answer. 5. He doesn't like my poetry." In another, he begins addressing Trilling by his first name, noting, "It always seems to me like *lesé-majeste* to address a senior by his first name. But if you are agreeable, I'll begin that now." Irving Feldman to Lionel Trilling, n.d. (ca. November 1954); Feldman to L. Trilling, September 20, 1956, LTP.

58. Irving Feldman to Lionel Trilling, June 17, 1954, LTP.

59. Irving Feldman to Lionel Trilling, n.d. (ca. November 1954), LTP.

60. Irving Feldman to Lionel Trilling, April 3, 1957, LTP.

61. Irving Feldman to Lionel Trilling, July 15, 1961, LTP.

62. Lionel Trilling to Catharine Carver, April 21, 1955, LTP.

63. Alan Dugan, "Three Books, a Pamphlet, and a Broadside," *Poetry* 100:5 (August 1962), 311.

64. "Problems for Poets," *Times Literary Supplement* (February 16, 1962), 106.

65. John Malcolm Brinnin, "Man: From Ararat to 8th St.," *Saturday Review* (January 6, 1962), 71.

66. Ralph Mills Jr., "A Natural Poet," review of Irving Feldman, *Works and Days, Commentary* (July 1962), 91, 92.

67. Anthony Thwaite, review of Irving Feldman, *Works and Days, Spectator* (November 3, 1961), 634.

68. Leslie Fiedler, "On the Road, or the Adventures of Karl Shapiro," *Poetry* 96:3 (June 1950): 171.

69. Irving Feldman, "Abstract Jewishness," *Commentary* (November 1958), 448.

70. See Irving Feldman, "Two Poems," *Commentary* (January 1960), 43–44.

71. "Jewish Book Council Picks Outstanding Works of 1961 Jewish Literature," *Jewish Telegraphic Agency Daily News Bulletin* (May 17, 1962), 4. Adam Kirsch notes in his review of Feldman's *Collected Poems* that "Feldman, despite a long career that has brought him some of the highest honors in American letters, is little known to the general public—or even . . . to most other poets." Kirsch, "Spoken Bread," *New Republic* (April 18, 2005), 42.

72. "Under Forty," 15.

73. Lionel Trilling, "Wordsworth and the Iron Time," *Kenyon Review* 12:3 (Summer 1950): 482.

74. L. Trilling, 483.

75. L. Trilling, 483.

76. D. Trilling, "Jew at Columbia," 42.

77. It has been suggested that he condescended to it, given a remark he made about Irving Howe's 1953 anthology of Yiddish short stories. Edward Alexander, *Lionel Trilling and Irving Howe: And Other Stories of Literary Friendship* (Piscataway, NJ: Transaction, 2009), 3.

78. Edward Alexander, *Lionel Trilling and Irving Howe*, 3. Interestingly, this error, which appeared in Trilling's essay when it served as the introduction to *The Collected Stories of Isaac Babel* (New York: New American Library, 1955), 19, was corrected to "shtetlach" when the essay was published, the same year, in *Commentary* (see L. Trilling, "Isaac Babel," 555)—but somehow, despite being the subject of criticism well before Alexander mentioned it (see Maurice Friedberg, "A Non-Jewish Isaac Babel?," *Midstream* 19:4 [April 1973]: 74–77, especially 76), it persisted into the republication of the essay, not just in Trilling's *Beyond Culture* but even in the more recent *The Moral Obligation to Be Intelligent: Selected Essays* (Evanston, IL: Northwestern University Press, 2009), 320. It is noteworthy that Trilling gets much closer to getting the plural form of "shtetl" correct ("stetloch") in a letter written a few years after the Babel essay—though, there, he seems to confuse "mitzvah" (commandment) for "mikvah" (ritual bath), another seemingly telling error, although perhaps one that can be ascribed to the assistant who typed the letter for Trilling. See Lionel Trilling to Herbert Feinstein, August 28, 1958, LTP.

—

79. Jonathan Brent, "How Our Pious Literary Guardians Erase Ugly Truths and Leave Us Confused," *Tablet* (November 5, 2015), https://www.tabletmag.com/sections/arts -letters/articles/trilling-babel-howe-brent.

80. Lionel Trilling to Sam Astrachan, May 17, 1960, LTP.

81. Dan Wakefield, *New York in the Fifties* (Boston: Houghton Mifflin, 1992), 31.

82. Ivan Gold, *Sams in a Dry Season* (Boston: Houghton Mifflin, 1990), 122.

83. Wakefield, *New York in the Fifties*, 31.

84. Ivan Gold, *Nickel Miseries* (New York: Viking, 1963), back cover. Subsequent citations of the stories in this collection appear parenthetically in the text.

85. Lionel Trilling to Catharine Carver, May 5, 1963, LTP.

86. Lionel Trilling to Elizabeth Ames, April 9, 1957; Gordon N. Ray to L. Trilling, January 8, 1963, LTP.

87. Lionel Trilling to Catharine Carver, February 17, 1963, LTP.

88. Though acknowledging that *Sick Friends* had been published as a novel, one reviewer called it "essentially . . . a poignant, deeply etched memoir." Review of Ivan Gold, *Sick Friends*, *Kirkus Reviews* (September 30, 1969), https://www.kirkusreviews.com/book-reviews/a /ivan-gold/sick-friends/.

89. See, for example, Eugene Goodheart, "Compulsion, Pain, and Fear," *Saturday Review* 46 (April 20, 1963): 47; and Dan Wakefield, "Intensely Defying All the Literary Labels," *New York Herald Tribune Books* (May 5, 1963), 5.

90. Though the area between Houston and Fourteenth Street and between Broadway and the East River has been called the "East Village" since the 1960s, it was considered part of the Lower East Side, or just the "East Side," in the 1940s and 1950s, and I refer to it that way here. On the Lower East Side as a site of Jewish memory, see Hasia Diner, *Lower East Side Memories: A Jewish Place in America* (Princeton, NJ: Princeton University Press, 2002).

91. Details of Gold's childhood and parents are recounted, under a very thin veil of fiction, in Gold's *Sams in a Dry Season* and especially the chapter "A Death in the Family," 100–181. On his mother, 131.

92. Gold attended Seward Park High School, on Grand and Essex Streets; see Gold, 106.

93. See the description of "Rosie Beanbags" and her friends in Irving Shulman, *The Amboy Dukes* (New York: Pocket Books, 1971), 160–62.

94. Wakefield, *New York in the Fifties*, 28.

95. On the postwar period during which "religion became the major vehicle for Jewish identity, while secular Judaism as an ideology largely collapsed," see Jonathan Sarna, *American Judaism: A History* (New Haven, CT: Yale University Press, 2004), 275.

96. Thanks to W. David Marx for help with translations and identifying the dialect.

97. Compare Philip Roth, *Portnoy's Complaint* (New York: Random House, 1969), 189.

98. Krupnick, *Lionel Trilling*, 54. See also Trilling's posthumously published statement that the Jew in modernity "found the myths awaiting him. Sometimes he fought them, sometimes he accepted them to his own advantage, often he went off and contemplated them in great confusion of mind. When he came to write of himself he was not able to free himself of them." Lionel Trilling, "The Changing Myth of the Jew," *Commentary* (August 1978), 34.

—

99. O'Connor mentioned in a letter, in the spring of 1963, that at some earlier point, Gold arrived at her house "one night for a literary conversation – unannounced . . . a Brooklyn boy." Flannery O'Connor to "A.," n.d., *The Habit of Being: The Letters of Flannery O'Connor,* ed. Sally Fitzgerald (New York: Farrar, Straus & Giroux, 1979), 512.

100. Lionel Trilling "From the Notebooks of Lionel Trilling," *Partisan Review* 51:4, 52:1 (1984–85): 513; L. Trilling, "From the Notebooks of Lionel Trilling, Part II," 13. Cf. Krupnick, "Lionel Trilling," 115.

101. Lionel Trilling to John Gillard Watson, December 16, 1953, in *Life in Culture: Selected Letters of Lionel Trilling,* ed. Adam Kirsch (New York: Farrar, Straus & Giroux, 2018), 233–35.

102. According to Robert A. McCaughey's *Stand, Columbia: A History of Columbia University in the City of New York, 1754–2004* (New York: Columbia University Press, 2003), "The freshman class recruited in the spring of 1969 included 260 black, Hispanic, and Asian acceptances, up from 145 the year before" (472) – suggesting the total number of Asian (or Asian American) students on campus up to that point was extremely small.

103. One critic objected to the central African American character of the "The Nickel Miseries of George Washington Carver Brown," who "simply is not to be believed, except in the fond fantasies of white people, . . . a black-faced Jewish *schlmiel.*" Hoyt W. Fuller, "How We Live?," *Negro Digest* (March 1969), 85.

104. On these developments in Howe's and Kazin's careers, see Julian Levinson, *Exiles on Main Street: Jewish American Writers and American Literary Culture* (Bloomington: Indiana University Press, 2008), 143–91.

105. Lionel Trilling to Rabbi Isidor Hoffman, July 3, 1959, LTP.

106. It would be difficult to overstate the intensity of Trilling's relationship with Columbia. For one thing, he wanted to write fiction more than anything else, and almost every single piece of fiction he ever published – from his first story, "Impediments," which appeared while he was an undergraduate, thanks to a classmate's help, to his most famous story, "Of This Time, Of That Place" – takes as its setting a university campus, often a thinly fictionalized Columbia. He was particularly sensitive to the specific experiences of Jewish students, too: Trilling was one of the Jewish students Mark Van Doren described in a 1927 *Menorah Journal* article – "Jewish Students I Have Known" – and later Trilling reflected on his own experiences with Jewish students at Columbia in a *Commentary* symposium; see "Seven Professors Look at the Jewish Student."

107. The intense but finally ambivalent relationship between Trilling and Bellow is discussed at some length in Zachary Leader, *The Life of Saul Bellow: To Fame and Fortune, 1915–1964* (New York: Knopf, 2015), among other places; it is worth noting that Bellow's short-lived journal, *Noble Savage,* published both Feldman and Gold in the early 1960s, suggesting that Bellow and Trilling may have been in agreement about the merit of their work. There is no mention of Trilling in Philip Davis's biography of Malamud, *Bernard Malamud: A Writer's Life* (New York: Oxford University Press, 2010), but the two seem to have admired each other; both Trillings wrote to Malamud in praise of his story "The Magic Barrel" in 1954, and Lionel Trilling recommended Malamud for a Guggenheim Fellowship

—

in 1957, following up the next year to express his dismay when Malamud's application was not successful. See Lionel Trilling to Bernard Malamud, November 16, 1954, in *Life in Culture*, 241–42; and Diana Trilling to Bernard Malamud, December 8, 1954, and Lionel Trilling to Bernard Malamud, May 13, 1958, and September 26, 1959, folder 10, box 18, Bernard Malamud Papers, Harry Ransom Center, University of Texas at Austin. There is no mention of Philip Roth or Grace Paley in Trilling's selected letters, *Life in Culture*, and it is not clear that he interacted with either. It seems safe to say that whatever Trilling felt about them, his support for them was not as consequential or concrete as his support for Astrachan, Feldman, and Gold.

108. Richard Kostelanetz, *The End of Intelligent Writing: Literary Politics in America* (New York: Sheed & Ward, 1974), 51.

109. Kostelanetz, 95–96. Perplexingly, nowhere in Kostelanetz's extended polemic does he mention Astrachan, Feldman, or Gold, despite Kostelanetz himself having reviewed Gold's *Nickel Miseries* when it was first published and his almost certainly having been aware of the other two writers. A possible explanation for the omission is that because these were relatively young writers, in Kostelanetz's terms, who received the support of a powerful member of the putative literary establishment but still struggled to establish themselves, they contradict a major strand of his argument.

110. On the history of women at Columbia and debates about coeducation there, see Rosalind Rosenberg, *Changing the Subject: How the Women of Columbia Shaped the Way We Think about Sex and Politics* (New York: Columbia University Press, 2004).

111. Quoted in Wakefield, *New York in the Fifties,* 31.

112. Quoted in Susan Kress, *Carolyn G. Heilbrun: Feminist in a Tenured Position* (Charlottesville: University of Virginia Press, 1997), 49, 52.

113. Lionel Trilling to the Committee on Fellowships and Scholarships, University of Rochester, February 26, 1954, LTP.

114. Cynthia Ozick, "The Buried Life," *New Yorker* (October 2, 2000), 116.

115. Quoted in Klingenstein, *Enlarging America,* 225.

116. On the "negligible numbers" of "blacks or Puerto Ricans" at Columbia as late as the 1960s, see McCaughey, *Stand, Columbia,* 387–88. Relevantly, Trilling was an early and enthusiastic supporter of James Baldwin, who despite showing early academic promise did not attend university. See Jay Garcia, "James Baldwin, Lionel Trilling, American Studies, and the Freudian Tragic," *James Baldwin Review* 3:1 (September 2017): 65–88; see also Lionel Trilling to Paul Engle, April 1, 1955, and Elizabeth Ames to Lionel Trilling, June 20, 1955, LTP.

117. See Thomas Bartlett, "Rhyme & Unreason," *Chronicle of Higher Education* (May 20, 2005), A12–14; Kevin Larimer, "The Contester: Who's Doing What to Keep Them Clean," *Poets & Writers* (July–August 2005), https://www.pw.org/content/contester_who039s _doing_what_keep_them_clean.

118. See Klingenstein, *Jews in the American Academy;* and Stephen Steinberg, *The Academic Melting Pot: Catholics and Jews in American Higher Education* (New York: Transaction, 1977), 122.

—

CHAPTER 3. WOMEN AND SHITTY MEDIA MEN

1. In addition to a vast literature on female authors in the nineteenth century, scholars have addressed other roles played by women in the literary field in that period. On women's clubs and organizations, for example, see Anne Ruggles Gere, *Intimate Practices: Literacy and Cultural Work in U.S. Women's Clubs, 1880–1920* (Urbana: University of Illinois Press, 1997); and Elizabeth McHenry, *Forgotten Readers: Recovering the Lost History of African-American Literary Societies* (Durham, NC: Duke University Press, 2002). On female periodical editors in the nineteenth century, see especially Patricia Okker, *Our Sister Editors: Sarah J. Hale and the Tradition of Nineteenth-Century American Women Editors* (Athens: University of Georgia Press, 1995).

2. John Tebbel, *Between Covers: The Rise and Transformation of Book Publishing in America* (New York: Oxford University Press, 1987), 184.

3. On Knopf, see Laura Claridge, *The Lady with the Borzoi: Blanche Knopf, Literary Taste-maker Extraordinaire* (New York: Farrar, Straus & Giroux, 2016). On Seltzer, see Alexandra Lee Levin and Lawrence L. Levin, "The Seltzers & D. H. Lawrence: A Biographical Narrative" in D. H. Lawrence, *Letters to Thomas and Adele Seltzer,* ed. Gerald M. Lacy (Los Angeles: Black Sparrow, 1976), 177–201. On Harcourt, see "Our Founder and Visionary, Ellen Knowles Harcourt, 1889–1984," Alfred Harcourt Foundation, accessed December 1, 2020, https://www.aharcourt.org/about-mrs-harcourt; it is striking that Alfred Harcourt's memoir of publishing, *Some Experiences* (Riverside, CT: Alfred and Ellen Harcourt, 1951), was copyrighted in Ellen Knowles Harcourt's name but does not otherwise mention her.

4. Michael Korda, *Another Life: A Memoir of Other People* (New York: Random House, 1999), 94–95.

5. Tebbel, *Between Covers,* 184–85. Al Silverman's sense was, similarly, that "women were mostly out of the loop" in publishing during its golden age. Silverman, *The Time of Their Lives: The Golden Age of Great American Book Publishers, Their Editors and Authors* (New York: St. Martin's, 2008), 217. See, among other histories of second-wave feminism, Ruth Rosen, *The World Split Open: How the Modern Women's Movement Changed America* (New York: Penguin, 2000). On women's systematic relegation to lower-status roles at major journalistic outlets as late as 1970 and class-action lawsuits that fought to change that dynamic, see Lynn Povich, *The Good Girls Revolt: How the Women of "Newsweek" Sued Their Bosses and Changed the Workplace* (New York: PublicAffairs, 2012).

6. Lewis A. Coser, Charles Kadushin, and Walter W. Powell, *Books: The Culture and Commerce of Publishing* (New York: Basic Books, 1982), 165.

7. In a 1941 guidebook for women interested in editorial careers, "stenographic or secretarial work" is described as "by far the easiest entering wedge" to get into the industry. Marjorie Shuler, Ruth Adams Knight, and Muriel Fuller, *Lady Editor: Careers for Women in Publishing* (New York: Dutton, 1941), 179.

8. Coser, Kadushin, and Powell, *Books,* 165.

9. All of these editors are at least mentioned in Silverman's *The Time of Their Lives,* and several receive short profiles.

10. On Prashker, see Silverman, 182–85. On Helen Honig Meyer, see Silverman, 217, 408–20. On Nevler, see Silverman, 459–67. On Mayerson, see Lesley Pearl, "Mother's Anger, Loss Explored in Poems about AIDS," *j., the Jewish News of Northern California* (March 1, 1996), https://www.jweekly.com/1996/03/01/mother-s-anger-loss-explored-in-poems -about-aids/. On Shrifte, see "Evelyn Shrifte, 98, Publishing House President," *New York Times* (August 31, 1999), A18; and "History of Vanguard Press," box 4, Evelyn Shrifte Collection Relating to Vanguard Press, Syracuse University Libraries Special Collections Research Center, NY.

11. While a full study of these women's career trajectories is beyond the bounds of this book, it seems at least anecdotally the case that many of these Jewish women were first hired as assistants to Jewish men in the industry and then given opportunities to rise. This suggests that homophilous logics were at work when the barriers to women's participation in the industry were removed.

12. Christopher Ricks, "Mistaken Identity," *New York Review of Books* (March 28, 1968), https://www.nybooks.com/articles/1968/03/28/mistaken-identity/.

13. Christopher Ricks, response to Midge Decter, *New York Review of Books* (May 9, 1968), https://www.nybooks.com/articles/1968/05/09/couples/.

14. Barbara Lauren, letter to the editor, *New York Times Book Review* (November 12, 1972), BR34.

15. Midge Decter, letter to the editor, *New York Times Book Review* (November 26, 1972), BR40.

16. Midge Decter, *The Liberated Woman* (New York: Coward, McCann, & Geoghegan, 1971), dust jacket.

17. Marion Magid, letter to the editor, *New York Times Book Review* (July 27, 1975), BR20.

18. An example is Gore Vidal's "Some Jews & the Gays," *Nation* (November 14, 1981), https://www.thenation.com/article/culture/some-jews-gays/, where Vidal introduces her as "Mrs. Norman Podhoretz, also known as Midge Decter."

19. Harry Smith noted that he "began an investigation" after "a leading critic's complaint that [the *New York Review of Books*] is 'in effect, a house organ of Random House.'" Pursuing the kind of literary-quantitative analysis that has become much more typical in recent decades (pursued by nonprofit organizations like VIDA and academic digital humanists alike), Smith examined the *Review*'s 1968 issues and found that Random House publications were much more likely to be discussed, and discussed favorably, in the *Review* than books published by any other house; moreover, Random House purchased twice as many advertising pages in the *Review* as any other publisher. In that sense, Smith could be understood as having identified a quid pro quo relationship revealing how the *Review*'s editorial priorities were influenced by the flow of advertising income. But Smith did not neglect to mention another possible vector of and motivation for collusion between these two institutions: "NYR co-editor Barbara Epstein is the wife of Random House vice president & editor Jason Epstein." Harry Smith, "New York Review Gives Strong Preference to Random House Group," *Newsletter on the State of the Culture* (March 5, 1969), 1. That "leading critic" was of course

Kostelanetz, and for his remarks about the Epsteins (including his calling the relationship "collusive" and revealing of "bias"), see Kostelanetz, *The End of Intelligent Writing: Literary Politics in America* (New York: Sheed & Ward, 1974), 61–71, 107–12. In *Intellectual Sky-writing: Literary Politics and the "New York Review of Books"* (New York: Charterhouse, 1974), Philip Nobile refers to Barbara Epstein as "a nepotist by happenstance" who "fought for the appearance of equality" (84) and details Jason Epstein's roles at the *Review*: he "signed incorporation papers in 1963, sits on the board of directors, holds one-sixth of the voting stock, hired Silvers and Ellsworth [the *Review*'s coeditor and publisher, respectively], was a vice president of Review Presentations, edits the books of many prolific *NYR* contributors, distributes *NYR* books at Vintage," in addition to the indirect ways that his role at Random House allowed him to influence the weekly (101–2).

20. Kostelanetz, *End of Intelligent Writing*, 84–86. In Charles Kadushin's *The American Intellectual Elite* (Boston: Little, Brown, 1974), a list of "the seventy most prestigious contemporary American intellectuals," largely though not entirely overlapping with Kostelanetz's list, includes eight women (11.4 percent) (30–31).

21. On Kadushin's list, at least four of the eight women were at one point or another married to others on that list (again, not including Sontag). Kadushin, *American Intellectual Elite*.

22. Midge Decter, letter to the editor, *New York Review of Books* (May 9, 1968), https://www.nybooks.com/articles/1968/05/09/couples/.

23. Decter said this to the intellectual historian Ronnie Grinberg, in an interview conducted on November 21, 2011, and Grinberg shared it with me.

24. Jason Epstein, letter to the editor, *New York Times* (April 16, 1972), SM38.

25. Himmelfarb began publishing in *Commentary* while Kristol was an assistant editor there, in 1948, and then she first contributed to *Encounter* in 1955, while Kristol remained active there as its founding editor. Decter regularly published in *Commentary* while Podhoretz was its editor, and Podhoretz hired her, while they were married and after their children were born, as acting managing editor, in 1963. Alan Wald has called Decter "the coarchitect of [Podhoretz's] politics"—see Wald, *The New York Intellectuals: The Rise and Fall of the Anti-Stalinist Left from the 1930s to the 1980s* (Chapel Hill: University of North Carolina Press, 1987), 257—and Ronnie Grinberg's work in progress treats their mutual influence in greater detail. See note 18, above, for sources that treat the Epsteins' mutual influence.

26. One apposite example is Elihu Katz and Paul F. Lazarsfeld's classic *Personal Influence: The Part Played by People in the Flow of Mass Communications* (Glencoe, IL: Free Press, 1955), where among other findings in which spouses in their study influenced each other's preferences and behavior, "In the realm of movie-going," the authors find significant "influencing . . . between husband and wife" (329). A second example is Herbert J. Gans, who, while articulating his concept of "taste cultures," remarks that people who consume media "are not isolated individuals . . . but families, couples, and peer groups who use the media when and if the content is relevant to group goals and needs." Gans thus suggests "couples" as one relevant unit in which tastes tend to be shared. Gans, *Popular Culture and High Culture: An Analysis and Evaluation of Taste* (New York: Basic Books, 1974), 32. A third example is Pierre

—

Bourdieu's *Distinction: A Social Critique of the Judgment of Taste* (Cambridge, MA: Harvard University Press, 1984), where the family is everywhere a key object of analysis and often seems to consist, primarily, of a married couple and their children. More specifically addressing the ways that spouses influence each other's tastes, Bourdieu remarks, for example, that "there is every reason to suppose that . . . the weight [*poids*] of the man's own taste in choosing his clothes . . . depends not only on his own inherited cultural capital and educational capital . . . but also on his wife's educational and cultural capital and on the gap between them" (and "the same is true of the wife's own preferences in politics") (109).

27. Sean Latham, *The Art of Scandal: Modernism, Libel Law, and the Roman à Clef* (Oxford: Oxford University Press, 2009). Subsequent citations of this book appear parenthetically in the text.

28. Quoted in Lauren McCoy, "Literary Gossip: Caroline Lamb's *Glenarvon* and the *Roman à Clef*," *Eighteenth-Century Fiction* 27:1 (2014): 135.

29. McCoy, 129.

30. See, for example, Ashley Chantler and Rob Hawkes, "Introduction: The Brilliant Ford Madox Ford," in Chantler and Hawkes, eds., *An Introduction to Ford Madox Ford* (London: Routledge, 2016), 1–6. Max Saunder's two-volume biography of Ford deals with the affair with Rhys in some detail in its second volume, *Ford Madox Ford: A Dual Life*, vol. 2, *The After-War World*, 2nd ed. (Oxford: Oxford University Press, 2012), calling *Quartet* a "wild book" that has provoked "wild charges" (297) and noting (as if to justify any cruel treatment), "Ford had not only fostered [Rhys's] talent; he had — albeit inadvertently — given her her best subject: the misunderstanding and cruelty of human relations; the despair of the abandoned lover" (299).

31. On these dynamics, see Leigh Gilmore, *Tainted Witness: Why We Doubt What Women Say about Their Lives* (New York: Columbia University Press, 2017).

32. Roberta Rubinstein makes a claim of "literary identity theft" in *Literary Half-Lives: Doris Lessing, Clancy Sigal, and* Roman à Clef (New York: Palgrave Macmillan, 2014), 197. See Gilmore, *Tainted Witness*, 145–55.

33. Moira Donegan, "I Started the Media Men List: My Name Is Moira Donegan," *The Cut* (January 10, 2018), https://www.thecut.com/2018/01/moira-donegan-i-started-the-media-men-list.html.

34. In *Beyond Feminist Aesthetics: Feminist Literature and Social Change* (Cambridge, MA: Harvard University Press, 1989), Felski argues against "the assertion that experimental writing constitutes the only truly 'subversive' or 'feminine' textual practice, and that more conventional forms such as realism are [necessarily] complicit with patriarchal systems of representation" (7), and she includes in her "definition of feminist literature . . . all those texts that reveal a critical awareness of women's subordinate position and of gender as a problematic category, however this is expressed" (14). Such feminist works of the postwar period could be said to continue a tradition of female writers in the interwar period who "eschewed dramatic formal experimentation [and] were interested in using their fiction to persuade their audience of left-leaning political positions," on which see Jaime Harker, *America the Middlebrow: Women's Novels, Progressivism, and Middlebrow Authorship between the Wars*

—

(Amherst: University of Massachusetts Press, 2007), 3. Jaffe, Birstein, and Gertler are not included in *The Norton Anthology of Literature by Women*, 3rd ed. (New York: Norton, 2007), nor are they mentioned in Lisa Maria Hogeland's *Feminism and Its Fictions: The Consciousness-Raising Novel and the Women's Liberation Movement* (Philadelphia: University of Pennsylvania Press, 1998) or Maria Lauret's *Liberating Literature: Feminist Fiction in America* (New York: Routledge, 1994).

35. As an example, see Lori Harrison-Kahan, "The Seeds of #MeToo Started Growing 100 Years Ago," *CNN.com* (November 2, 2019), https://www.cnn.com/2019/11/02 /opinions/me-too-movement-history-jordan-michelson-harrison-kahan/index.html. A number of calls for papers in 2019 and 2020 have asked scholars to consider how #MeToo might be relevant to various subfields of literary studies.

36. Rona Jaffe, *The Best of Everything* (New York: Penguin Books, 2005), 293. Subsequent citations of the novel appear parenthetically in the text.

37. Julie Berebitsky, *Sex and the Office: A History of Gender, Power, and Desire* (New Haven, CT: Yale University Press, 2012), 183.

38. On Goodman, see Silverman, *Time of Their Lives*, 245–55, and "Jack A. Goodman, a Book Executive," *New York Times* (July 23, 1957), 27. On Wald, including his relationship with Jaffe, see M. J. Arlen, "At Last! The Mighty Marvelous Waldmachine," *Esquire* (May 1, 1962), 128. See also Andrew Spicer, "Producing Noir: Wald, Scott, Hellinger," in Robert Miklitsch, ed., *Kiss the Blood Off My Hands: On Classic Film Noir* (Urbana: University of Illinois Press, 2014), 132–36.

39. The novel, and Jaffe, were mentioned in several syndicated Hollywood columns, with specifics about whom Wald wanted to cast in the film adaptation, as early as December 1957, almost a year before the novel was set to be published, and in the months leading up to publication at the end of August 1958, the novel and its author were discussed in many syndicated columns and national and regional newspapers. See, for examples of this coverage, Hedda Hopper, "Hollywood," *New York Daily News* (December 11, 1957), 391; Louella O. Parsons, "Kathy Crosby Will Make TV Debut with Bing," *San Francisco Examiner* (December 26, 1957), 33; Herb Stein, "The Best of Hollywood," *Philadelphia Inquirer* (June 19, 1958), 7; Lee Segal, "Under the Dust Cover," *Louisville (KY) Courier-Journal* (July 6, 1958), 66; Dick Sinnott, "New England Vignettes," *Brattleboro (VT) Reformer* (August 7, 1958), 10.

40. For a sophisticated analysis of how actors are both empowered and exploited within the Hollywood star system, see Danae Clark, *Negotiating Hollywood: The Cultural Politics of Actors' Labor* (Minneapolis: University of Minnesota Press, 1995).

41. Patsi Farmer, "Story of the Working Girl Is Chronicled," *Shreveport (LA) Times* (August 24, 1958), 62; H. I. Phillips, "The Once Over," *East Liverpool (OH) Evening Review* (September 6, 1958), 4.

42. My reading here offers an alternative to Julie Berebitsky's claim that "getting groped by Mr. Shalimar, the married, fifty-year-old editor at the publishing house, . . . was simply an inescapable (and ultimately harmless) part of their initiation into office life." Berebitsky, *Sex and the Office*, 183.

43. On Levy's later career, "You Are Here," *This American Life*, episode 136, WBEZ Chicago (August 6, 1999), https://www.thisamericanlife.org/136/transcript.

44. The Lee & Low Diversity Baseline Survey in 2019 found that employees in the publishing industry are 76 percent white, 74 percent cis female, and 81 percent straight. See "Where Is the Diversity in Publishing? The 2019 Diversity Baseline Survey Results," *Lee & Low Books* (blog) (January 28, 2020), https://blog.leeandlow.com/2020/01/28/2019 diversitybaselinesurvey/.

45. Henry Popkin, "The Vanishing Jew of Our Popular Culture," *Commentary* (January 1, 1952), 46–55.

46. When Caroline goes to a church for a friend's wedding, the novel notes that "it made her feel religious to be in this kind of atmosphere" and that "she hadn't even gone to Sunday school after the first protesting year" and that "none of her friends went to their families' various places of worship oftener than once a year either." Jaffe, *Best of Everything*, 228. While "Sunday school" is a place that either Christians or Jews might attend (and then not attend), if Caroline and her friends were all Christian—and even if some were Catholic—it would seem unnecessary to mention "various places of worship," nor would the vagueness of "this kind of atmosphere" seem necessary. Caroline coins a description for the less-than-exciting man she is dating, "Bermuda Schwartz," which seems clearly to be a riff on the "Shirley" of Herman Wouk's recent bestseller *Marjorie Morningstar*, and Jaffe's pun on "Schwartz" seems at least plausibly to suggest that part of the boringness of this type is that they are nice Jewish boys. On Jaffe's representations of Jewish characters in other novels, see Rachel Shukert, "Chick Lit's Jewish Mother," *Tablet* (June 15, 2012), https://www.tabletmag.com/sections /arts-letters/articles/chick-lits-jewish-mother; and June Sochen, *Consecrate Every Day: The Public Lives of Jewish American Women, 1880–1980* (Albany: State University of New York Press, 2012), 100.

47. "Wins $1200 Literary Award," *CEA Critic* 10:5 (1948): 4.

48. E.A., memo (February 17, 1959), Yaddo Records, Manuscripts and Archives Division, New York Public Library, Astor, Lenox, and Tilden Foundations. Birstein notes in her memoir that it was Decter who reviewed her first novel for *Commentary*, in 1950—Decter's first piece published in that magazine. See Midge Decter, "A Rabbi, New Style," *Commentary* (October 1950), 402–4. It was only after Birstein married Kazin that she actually met Decter, as well as Himmelfarb, Barbara Epstein, Sontag, and many other literary intellectuals. The Epsteins became close enough friends that they visited when Birstein and Kazin lived in Amherst, Massachusetts, in the mid-1950s; see Ann Birstein, *What I Saw at the Fair: An Autobiography* (New York: Open Road Distribution, 2003), 123. Birstein mentions the Epsteins in her letters to Kazin from the period, noting, for example, that she "promised to stop by at the Epsteins for a drink." Ann Birstein to Alfred Kazin, February 11, 1958, Alfred Kazin Papers, The Henry W. and Albert A. Berg Collection of English and American Literature, New York Public Library, Astor, Lenox and Tilden Foundations (hereafter AKP). A few years later, on the Upper West Side, Himmelfarb would share her collection of "dozens of drinking glasses" with Birstein when the latter was throwing a party (at which the Epsteins were often guests), and in exchange, Birstein would lend Himmelfarb her "big coffee urn" for parties at the Kristols' apartment. Birstein, *What I Saw,* 132. In a letter to Kazin, Birstein describes one party at the Kristols, at which she met Leslie Fiedler for the first time, and remarks, "it's really touching how sweet your friends are to me." Birstein to Kazin, August 3, 1959, AKP. Later that year, she writes, "Typical example of this town: called Bea Kristol who asked me over for a drink today and then invited me to a party on Saturday. Accepted happily on both counts, only it turns out that party she invited me to on Saturday happens to be given by Danny Bell. Doesn't matter, accepted anyway. And so it goes." Birstein to Kazin, December 1959, AKP.

49. Part of the reason for her discomfort with and alienation from this crowd seems to have been her physical appearance. She herself reports on being perceived as "a glamorous young blond." Birstein, *What I Saw,* 88. Her friend Jules Feiffer remembered Birstein, in this period, as Kazin's "sexy blond wife, . . . also a writer, who found herself adrift in this sea of intellectuals when the person she really wanted to be was Ginger Rogers." Feiffer, *Backing into Forward: A Memoir* (New York: Nan A. Talese/Doubleday, 2010), 278.

50. Birstein, *What I Saw,* 85.

51. For example, see Birstein's retrospective reflection on "a symposium on the novel" organized while she and Kazin were living in Northampton, Massachusetts, at which Kazin, Ralph Ellison, and Saul Bellow presented: "Nobody . . . thought of my work in connection with the important public discourses being given on the novel. We all knew I had written two of them, but it was a matter politely swept under the rug." And when one invited speaker praised one of her novels and she mentioned this to Kazin, his response was "an almost painfully embarrassed shrug." Birstein, *What I Saw,* 117–18; and Richard M. Cook, *Alfred Kazin: A Biography* (New Haven, CT: Yale University Press, 2007), 191–92.

52. "Forum: Women on Women," *American Scholar* 41:4 (1972): 615. In a retrospective blog post, Birstein "confess[es]" her "spotty history as a feminist": Ann Birstein's blog (January 5, 2011), https://web.archive.org/web/20110912044349/http:/annbirstein.com/blog.htm.

53. Ann Birstein to Bede Hofstadter, November 27, 1970, folder 9, box 2, Ann Birstein Papers, Department of Special Collections and Archives, Queens College, City University of New York (hereafter ABP). Kostelanetz had written, "Since his first drafts are, by his own judgment, 'sloppy and idiosyncratic,' he joins his indispensable wife, Beatrice, in rewriting and editing the, literally, worked-up manuscript." Richard Kostelanetz, *Master Minds: Portraits of Contemporary American Artists and Intellectuals* (New York: Macmillan, 1969), 161. For a more recent discussion of the Hofstadters' collaboration, see Tim Lacy, "'Mrs. Hofstadter' and the Myth of the Heroic Lone Scholar," *U.S. Intellectual History Blog* (January 18, 2018), https://s-usih.org/2018/01/mrs-hofstadter-heroic-lone-scholar-myth/.

54. Ann Birstein, *Dickie's List* (New York: Coward, McCann & Geoghegan, 1973), 9. Subsequent citations of the novel appear parenthetically in the text.

55. Lois Gold, "A Literary Who's Who," *New York Times Book Review* (September 2, 1973), 4; Gynter Quill, "Literary 'Mafia' Gets Knife," *Waco (TX) News-Tribune* (August 22, 1973), 2C.

56. Roger W. Straus Jr. to Ann Birstein, September 14, 1973, folder 8, box 3, ABP.

57. Ann Birstein, "*Dickie's List:* General Notes" and "*Dickie's List:* Book Proposal," folders 9 and 10, box 16, ABP.

58. Birstein, "*Dickie's List:* Book Proposal."

59. Ann Birstein to Jack [?], February 1, 1973, box 22, ABP; Bel Kaufman, "Comment on *Dickie's List*/Ann Birstein," June 12, 1973, "Dickie's List" folder, box 22, ABP.

60. Ann Birstein, "*Dickie's List:* General Notes."

61. On libel and the modernist roman à clef, see Latham, *Art of Scandal,* 69–123. Of course, this is partly funny because Bellow was, by the time *Dickie's List* appeared, turning more and more to the roman à clef, with characters in *Herzog* easily recognizable to his friends as based on people in his life; this tendency would intensify in Bellow's later works like *Humboldt's Gift* (based on the life of Delmore Schwartz) and *Ravelstein* (based on the life of Allan Bloom). Scholars have often demonstrated how closely Bellow drew on the lives of his wives and friends in earlier novels. See, e.g., David Mikics, *Bellow's People: How Saul Bellow Made Life into Art* (New York: Norton, 2016).

62. Moshe Decter published in the magazine for the first time in September 1950; see Moshe Decter, "Two Centuries of Hebrew," *Commentary* (September 1950), 296–97. Midge Decter's first piece in the magazine, her review of Birstein's first novel, appeared in the following month's issue. See Midge Decter, "A Rabbi, New Style," *Commentary* (October 1950), 402–4.

63. See Birstein, *What I Saw,* 109.

64. John Leonard, "Gimme Shelter," *New York Magazine* (March 12, 2003), https://nymag.com/nymetro/arts/tv/reviews/n_8474/; Donna Seaman, "Women's Memoirs of Adversity, Work, and Revelation," *Booklist* (March 1, 2003), 1142. See also Sam Roberts, "Ann Birstein, Memoirist and Novelist, Dies at 89," *New York Times* (May 29, 2017), https://www.nytimes.com/2017/05/29/books/ann-birstein-dead-novelist-and-wife-of-alfred-kazin.html.

65. Birstein, *What I Saw,* 115, 154–57.

66. Joseph Epstein, *Gossip: The Untrivial Pursuit* (Boston: Houghton Mifflin Harcourt, 2011), 69.

67. Alfred Kazin to Esther Yntema, September 29, 1971; Yntema to Kazin, October 6, 1971, AKP. Kazin, *Bright Book of Life: American Novelists and Storytellers from Hemingway to Mailer* (Boston: Little, Brown, 1973), iii; in the book, Kazin credits Flannery O'Connor and other women writers for work "that erases our too-easy view of the world" (173), not acknowledging Birstein for doing the same.

68. Alfred Kazin, *New York Jew* (New York: Knopf, 1978), 257.

69. Alfred Kazin, *Alfred Kazin's Journals,* ed. Richard M. Cook (New Haven, CT: Yale University Press, 2011), 422.

70. Alfred Kazin, June 23, 1971, Journals, vol. 23, AKP.

71. Alfred Kazin, "Ann 1950–1978," 23–24, AKP.

72. Birstein, *What I Saw,* 109, 164.

73. Kazin does not mention anything about this incident in his journal entry recording Rahv's death, on December 24, 1973. Kazin, *Alfred Kazin's Journals,* 424.

74. Another roman à clef in which a character was modeled on Rahv is one of the most famous twentieth-century U.S. examples of the genre, Mary McCarthy's novella *The Oasis,* first published in *Horizon* 110 (1949): 75–152. There, the central character, William Taub, who was recognized from the first to be based on Rahv, reportedly much to his consternation, does not come off well: he is represented as having an inflated ego ("A transparent air of proprietorship emanated from his whole person" [87]) and an embarrassing relationship to his own Jewishness ("A kind of helplessness came over him when he came conscious of his Jewishness. . . . At such moments, he felt himself to be a mere mass of protoplasmic jelly . . . which could only quiver feebly in response to a stimulus that society sent through like an electric current" [89–90]); he is possibly a "coward" (98) and "moody" (115), and "concealment was second nature to him" (88). He is uncomfortable with "practical jokes" as well as "children, birds, cows, water, snakes, lightning, Gentiles, and automobiles" (99), with a "natural vindictiveness" (114) and a discomfort with money, if not stinginess (114, 138). All that said, only in two moments does the novella present Taub behaving in a way that would make a younger woman feel uncomfortable: early on, he ogles a "girl-student," with a woman observing as "his eye . . . ingested [the girl's] long legs . . . [which then] move[d] bulgingly down the tract of his appreciation, like a snake's dinner, to join the Jackson[s'] English bicycles and the breasts of the minister's wife" (89). Toward the novella's end, "a little drunk" and "swaying slightly on his feet," Taub "lean[s] caressingly down toward" a woman, "his eyes damp and glittering, like a magnetic confessor of women," and the woman feels "slightly repelled," at which point he "lean[s] still closer to her" (148). In neither case does Taub cross a line from creepy ogling to inappropriate touching, but these do suggest that among his other flaws are some kinds of sexual inappropriateness.

There is an enormous body of literature on the New York Intellectuals published after Birstein's *Dickie's List,* in which Rahv is often discussed in detail, but nowhere in any of these works have I found an explicit mention of Birstein's description of him or any discussion of Rahv having used his position to enable his sexual harassment of younger female writers. One would not expect to find such unpleasant aspects of his personality mentioned in his *New York Times* obituary or in the long essay Mary McCarthy published about him in the *New York Times Book Review* a month after his death (which critics have seen as her attempt to atone for her satirical portrait of Rahv in *The Oasis*) or in the eulogy Elizabeth Hardwick gave at his funeral and then published in the *New York Review of Books.* See "Philip Rahv, Critic, Dead at 64; English Professor at Brandeis," *New York Times* (December 24, 1973), 16; Mary McCarthy, "Philip Rahv, 1908–1973," *New York Times Book Review* (February 17, 1974), 1; Elizabeth Hardwick, "Philip Rahv (1908–1973)," *New York Review of Books* (January 24, 1974), https://www.nybooks.com/articles/1974/01/24/philip-rahv-19081973/. But even in assessments of Rahv that came later and that had the explicit goal of offering more judicious and less hagiographic portraits of him by dealing with unpleasant aspects of his personality and behavior, Birstein goes unmentioned, and no one mentions sexual misconduct. For example, William Barrett's *The Truants: Adventures among the Intellectuals* (Garden City, NY: Anchor/Doubleday, 1982) is a book-length memoir that focuses on Barrett's relationships with Rahv and Delmore Schwartz, and it is motivated explicitly by Barrett's feeling that in McCarthy's *New York Times Book Review* remembrance of Rahv, "the rough edges of Rahv's personality were bathed in a rather rosy light" (4). While Barrett designates Rahv as *the* New York Intellectual par excellence (69) and recounts their working relationship (Barrett was an editor at *Partisan Review*) and friendship over several decades, he also notes that Rahv was "a complex, often self-contradictory and secretive character" (74) and that he did "outrageous" things (72), and at times "frightened, irritated, and depressed" Barrett (74). He does not mention Birstein or, among the many flaws of Rahv's he describes, anything we might retrospectively characterize as sexual misconduct. Another example is a short, vivid memoir of Rahv, first published in 1976: Mark Krupnick, "Philip Rahv: 'He Never Learned to Swim,'" in *Jewish Writing and the Deep Places of the Imagination* (Madison: University of Wisconsin Press, 2005), 157–77. Krupnick calls Rahv "one of the most distinguished critics of his generation" (159) and offers an intimate portrait of him around the year 1970, while also surveying his earlier years. Krupnick notes that Rahv "appears in fiction only as a caricature," referring to McCarthy's *The Oasis* (170) (and not mentioning *Dickie's List*). In a 2003 afterword to that memoir, Krupnick notes that when he sent the piece to editors in New York, including Ted Solotaroff at *New American Review* as well as the editors of the *New York Review of Books* in 1975 or 1976, they told him that "instead of [his] cavils, [he] should have been expressing gratitude for Rahv's help and [his] memoir should have been an unambivalent tribute" (173), suggesting that the piece, in 1976, was seen as too critical. Krupnick, in 2003, returned to reconsider Rahv's life and legacy and concludes that his own earlier memoir was, "if anything, too respectful" (173) of Rahv; in that later addendum, he goes into detail about his disappointment that Rahv did so little to help him when he was going up for tenure at Boston University and explores several other troubling aspects of Rahv's behavior. Still, even here, Krupnick does not mention anything about Birstein or sexual misconduct.

75. Josie (Johanna Davis) to Ann Birstein, August 14 [1973?], box 22, ABP. Quoted with the permission of Nick Davis.

76. Haydn et al., "Women on Women," 612.

77. See caption in the *Jewish Floridian* (April 8, 1960), B1; "Dramatic Interpretation," *Rostrum* (National Forensic League) 37 (1962): 17; "Drama: Silver Knight Winners," *Miami Herald* (October 29, 2008), https://www.miamiherald.com/site-services/miami-herald-events/silver-knight/article1930282.html.

78. "'Convention Girls' Has Topped $4 Million Mark," *Box Office* (August 28, 1978), 15.

79. Alex Ben Block, "'Convention Girls' . . . How a B-Movie Is Born," *Detroit News* (June 27, 1978), 7-B; Nan Robertson, "Self-Professed Worrier Whose Writing Shocks," *New York Times* (June 14, 1984), C18; Marian Christy, "Petite Author Packs a Powerful Punch," *Boston Globe* (August 12, 1984), A13.

80. Dwight Garner, "Even Bookworms Like to Bed-Hop," *New York Times* (June 16, 2017), C19.

81. T. Gertler, *Elbowing the Seducer* (New York: Random House, 1984), 87. Subsequent citations of the novel appear parenthetically in the text.

—

82. Robertson, "Self-Professed Worrier"; Michele Slung, "Book Report," *Book World* (May 27, 1984), 19; Christy, "Petite Author."

83. Paula Span, "If T. Is for Truth," *Washington Post* (September 2, 1984), B1.

84. "Small-Town Ohio, Pym Pen Pals," *Boston Globe* (June 23, 1985), A12.

85. Jane O'Reilly, "Literary and Other Submissions," *New York Times Book Review* (June 24, 1984), BR34.

86. Barbara Koenig Quart, review of T. Gertler, *Elbowing the Seducer, Ms.* (July 1984), 33.

87. Carolyn Clay, "Bed, Book, and Scandal," *New York* (May 28, 1984), 89–90.

88. Span, "If T. Is for Truth."

89. Pat Miller, in a 1993 journal article about the novel, calls it a "purported *roman à clef*" and declares that "whether readers can identify Howard and Newman, as one reviewer claims they might, is finally irrelevant to the central issue of the novel." Miller, "When Men Are Men and Women Are Men, Too: On Gender, Art, and Reading T. Gertler's 'Elbowing the Seducer,'" *CEA Critic* (Fall 1993): 27.

90. Slung, "Book Report."

91. Mimi Kramer, "What I Know about Gordon Lish . . . So Far," *Spy* (October 1986), 38–39.

92. "Lish Ash-Canned, with Perfect Civility," *New York* (December 12, 1994), 14.

93. One unusual and recent example of an essay in which Ritchie's being based on Lish is accepted as a fact—though, nonetheless, its author does not seem concerned about the potential that the novel might be revealing some misconduct on Lish's part—is Snowden Wright, "The Fictional Gordon Lish," *Passages North* (February 18, 2014), https://www.passagesnorth.com/passagesnorthcom/2014/02/writers-on-writing-73-snowden-wright.

94. On Lish's later conduct with young women writers and students, see Carla Blumenkranz, "Seduce the Whole World: Gordon Lish's Workshop," in Chad Harbach, ed., *MFA vs. NYC* (New York: n+1/Faber and Faber, 2014), 209–22. Consider also Ottessa Moshfegh, "Jailbait," *Granta* 144 (August 2018), https://granta.com/jailbait/, which is published as nonfiction and describes Moshfegh's relationship with a writing teacher who might be modeled on Gordon Lish, though she gives that figure the name of "Rupert Dicks" in the essay. In an interview, Moshfegh mentions "the pressure of having to dazzle in that Gordon Lish way," suggesting at the very least that Lish was an influence of one kind or another for her. Benjamin Nugent, interview of Ottessa Moshfegh, *BOMB* (September 18, 2018), https://bombmagazine.org/articles/ottessa-moshfegh-1/.

95. Cook's biography of Alfred Kazin mentions Birstein's story "Love in the Dunes" as her "most aggressive statement to date that she had her own resources [and] was not to be taken for granted" but never mentions *Dickie's List* or Birstein's account in her memoir of how Kazin read the manuscript for "Love in the Dunes" without permission and then how Rahv groped her when she met with him about it (*Alfred Kazin,* 205). In general, Cook somewhat downplays Birstein's accusations of physical abuse, regarding "the violence, anger, and pain" of the relationship as mutual, as "punishing and destructive for both of them" (260),

—

and including "occasional bouts of physical violence on both sides" (327). One reason critics and scholars—even the ones writing for the famously sassy *Spy* and *New York* and even feminist academics—may have avoided mentioning Lish's name when discussing *Elbowing the Seducer* is that Lish once described himself (perhaps jokingly) as having "a litigious personality" and did in fact sue *Harper's* for publishing excerpts, without permission, from a letter he sent to his creative-writing students, and so they may have been afraid of being sued for libel. See "Gordon Lish Interviews Gordon Lish," *Genesis West* 3 (Winter 1965): 9. On the *Harper's* case, see Bruce Weber, "Public Words, Publishing Questions," *New York Times* (September 22, 1992), B1; and *Lish v. Harper's Magazine Foundation*, 807 F. Supp. 1090 (S.D.N.Y. 1993).

96. Silverman, *Time of Their Lives*, 462.

97. For the claim that Sontag was the "true author" of Rieff's book, see Benjamin Moser, "Regarding the Pen of Others," *Harper's* (September 2019), 16–18; and Allison Flood, "Susan Sontag Was True Author of Ex-Husband's Book, Biography Claims," *Guardian* (May 13, 2019), https://www.theguardian.com/books/2019/may/13/susan-sontag-her-life-benjamin-moser-freud-the-mind-of-the-moralist-philip-rieff. For a critical response to Moser's claim, see Janet Malcolm, "Susan Sontag and the Unholy Practice of Biography," *New Yorker* (September 16, 2019), https://www.newyorker.com/magazine/2019/09/23/susan-sontag-and-the-unholy-practice-of-biography.

98. Joyce Johnson, who worked as an assistant to the editor in chief of William Morrow in the 1950s, has been reported to be working on a novel about that time. See Allison Geller, "'Minor Characters' Author Joyce Johnson Remembers Life Among, and Apart From, the Beat Generation," *A Women's Thing* (blog) (January 12, 2018), https://awomensthing.org/blog/joyce-johnson-women-in-publishing/. See also Marian Thurm's "Out to Lunch," *Narrative* (Winter 2019), https://www.narrativemagazine.com/issues/winter-2019/fiction/out-lunch-marian-thurm, a short story about a woman hired as an assistant, in 1976, "at one of those glossy magazines."

99. Clare Virginia Eby, *Until Choice Do Us Part: Marriage Reform in the Progressive Era* (Chicago: University of Chicago Press, 2014).

100. An example of such a project—which may or may not ultimately contribute to the way such men as Les Moonves and Donald Trump are remembered and talked about—is Jean Carroll's *What Do We Need Men For? A Modest Proposal* (New York: St. Martin's, 2019).

101. When a new wave of rejection of sexual misconduct swept through a variety of industries, under the banner of #MeToo, in 2017, a number of prestigious publishers were among the men removed from their positions, including Lorin Stein, editor at the *Paris Review* and at Farrar, Straus & Giroux. See Alexandra Alter and Sydney Ember, "Paris Review Editor Resigns amid Inquiry into His Conduct with Women," *New York Times* (December 6, 2017), https://www.nytimes.com/2017/12/06/books/lorin-stein-resigns-the-paris-review.html. For the high rates of sexual assault and harassment reported by women in contemporary publishing generally, see Rachel Deahl, John Maher, and Jim Milliot, "The Women of Publishing Say #MeToo," *Publishers' Weekly* (October 20, 2017), https://www

—

.publishersweekly.com/pw/by-topic/industry-news/publisher-news/article/75175-sexual
-harassment-is-a-problem-in-publishing.html.

CHAPTER 4. PARENTS AND CHILDREN

Epigraph: Ann Kazin to Elizabeth Ames, January 30, 1959, Yaddo Records, Manuscripts and Archives Division, New York Public Library, Astor, Lenox, and Tilden Foundations.

1. Alan Mintz, *"Banished from Their Father's Table": Loss of Faith and Hebrew Autobiography* (Bloomington: Indiana University Press, 1989), 3.

2. Abraham Cahan, *The Education of Abraham Cahan,* trans. Leon Stein, Abraham P. Conan, and Lynn Davison (Philadelphia: Jewish Publication Society, 1969), 150–51.

3. Anzia Yezierska, *Bread Givers: A Novel: A Struggle between a Father of the Old World and a Daughter of the New* (Garden City, NY: Doubleday, Page, 1925); Bernard Cohen, *Sociocultural Changes in American Jewish Life as Reflected in Selected Jewish Literature* (Rutherford, NJ: Fairleigh Dickinson University Press, 1972), 75.

4. D. J. R. Bruckner, "A Candid Talk with Saul Bellow," *New York Times Magazine* (April 15, 1984), 52; James Atlas, *Bellow: A Biography* (New York: Random House, 2000), 12.

5. Norman Podhoretz, *Making It* (New York: Random House, 1967), 7, 14, 27.

6. An example of the latter would seem to be Philip Roth's father; Roth noted that while he "had given [his fictional character] Nathan Zuckerman a father who could not stand his writer son's depiction of Jewish characters . . . fate had given [him] a fiercely loyal and devoted father who had never found a thing in [his] books to criticize." That said, there is no evidence that Roth's parents had any particular connections to help him as he set out on his literary career or any special insight into his work. Roth, *Patrimony* (New York: Simon & Schuster, 1991), 188.

7. See also Colm Tóibín's moving essay, in which he considers his mother's and uncle's literary aspirations and those of the fathers of V. S. Naipaul and Jorge Luis Borges: "Writers and Their Families," *Guardian* (February 17, 2012), https://www.theguardian.com/books/2012/feb/17/colm-toibin-how-i-killed-my-mother.

8. On Ozick's relation to her uncle, the somewhat obscure American Hebrew poet Abraham Regelson, see Ozick, "Nobility Eclipsed," *New Republic* (June 7, 2012), https://newrepublic.com/article/103913/sanctuary-wilderness-cynthia-ozick.

9. One notable exception was Allen Ginsberg, whose father was a published poet.

10. Al Silverman, *The Time of Their Lives: The Golden Age of Great American Book Publishers, Their Editors and Authors* (New York: St. Martin's, 2008), 343.

11. Leonore Fleischer, "A Letter from New York," *Washington Post Book World* (August 19, 1979), 15.

12. In a major sociological study of people who inherited wealth, the authors note that "the often debilitating degree of guilt that is felt and expressed by many inheritors is rooted in the fact that they did not earn the freedom and power of wealth through their own creativity or effort. . . . No matter what they accomplish, many inherited can never be sure to what extent their achievements result from their personal skills and talents rather than what

—

was given to them." Paul G. Schervish and Andrew Herman, *Empowerment and Beneficence: Strategies of Living and Giving among the Wealthy: Final Report of the Study on Wealth and Philanthropy* (Boston: Social Welfare Research Institute, Boston College, 1988), 51. See also Ann Perry, *The Wise Inheritor* (New York: Random House, 2003), 98–112; and for a more recent sociological study, Rachel Sherman, *Uneasy Street: The Anxieties of Affluence* (Princeton, NJ: Princeton University Press, 2017), which notes the perceived "illegitimacy of inheriting" (72) as a factor in how contemporary New Yorkers who inherit large fortunes behave and understand themselves. On nepotism in contemporary Hollywood, where an "assumption of unearned success" bedevils children of successful parents who "follow in the family business," see Tatiana Siegel, "You Always Fight That Nepotism Label," *Hollywood Reporter* 423:39 (December 18, 2017): 116–19. The reasons inheritors feel such intense guilt is surely that, as Jens Beckert argues, "the institution of inheritance. . . . contradicts the meritocratic self-conception of modern societies" and is "the central institution of social privilege in modern societies that is based not on effort, but on birth." Beckert, *Inherited Wealth,* trans. Thomas Dunlap (Princeton, NJ: Princeton University Press, 2007), 13, 14. Or, as Émile Durkheim phrased it, "It is obvious that inheritance, by creating inequalities amongst men from birth, that are unrelated to merit or services, invalidates the whole contractual system at its very roots." Durkheim, *Professional Ethics and Civic Morals,* trans. Cornelia Brookfield (Glencoe, IL: Free Press, 1958), 213.

13. On these relationships and companies, see Silverman, *Time of Their Lives,* 214–43, 341–76.

14. Robert Conley, "3 Book Executives Forming Own Firm," *New York Times* (March 15, 1959), A1.

15. Hiram Haydn, *Words and Faces: An Intimate Chronicle of Book and Magazine Publishing* (New York: Harcourt Brace Jovanovich, 1975), 112, 119.

16. Haydn, 122, 123.

17. Louis Sheaffer, "The Reminiscences of Simon Michael Bessie," Oral History Research Office, Columbia University, 1976, 4. All subsequent quotations from Bessie refer to this oral history and appear parenthetically in the text.

18. Atheneum, at its beginning, contracted with Allen Lane to distribute Penguin Books in the U.S., which gave the founders a catalog to sell in their first year, as they began to develop books of their own, but that arrangement with Penguin ended relatively quickly.

19. A comparison case from the same period was the adaptation into French of Elie Wiesel's 1954 Yiddish memoir *Un di velt hot geshvign* into the 1958 French memoir *La nuit* (which was translated into English in 1960), under the influence of the Catholic Nobel Laureate Francois Mauriac; Naomi Seidman has considered the degree to which this process involved a "cultural translation of Jewish into Catholic idioms." Seidman, *Faithful Renderings: Jewish-Christian Difference and the Politics of Translation* (Chicago: University of Chicago Press, 2006), 229–30.

20. André Schwarz-Bart, *The Last of the Just,* trans. Stephen Becker (New York: Overlook, 2000), 4.

21. These books, all published by Atheneum, were Jacob Klein-Haparash, *He Who Flees* *the Lion* (1963), Ilse Aichinger, *Herod's Children* (1964), George Steiner, *Anno Domini* (1964), Elie Wiesel, *The Town beyond the Wall* (1964), Frederic Morton, *The Rothschilds: A Family Portrait* (1961), and Meyer Wolf Weisgal and Joel Carmichael, eds., *Chaim Weizmann: A Biography by Many Hands* (1963).

22. According to the best bibliography of Hebrew literature translated to English, in the unpublished Hebrew-language dissertation of Yuval Amit, while plenty of Hebrew literature had been published in translation in the U.S. before 1960, virtually all of it was published by Jewish houses like Bloch and Schocken or smaller committees or organizations. With only a couple of exceptions — the publication of Ari Ibn-Zahav's *Jessica, My Daughter* (1948) and *David and Bathsheba* (1951) by the commercial house Crown and the republication of Shlomo J. Kahn's anthology *A Whole Loaf: Stories from Israel* (1957) and the publication of Moshe Shamir's *The King of Flesh and Blood* (1958) by the small but prestigious Vanguard Press — nonsectarian U.S. publishing houses had not published any Hebrew literature in translation, and Knopf would not do so until 1972, when it published Amos Oz's *My Michael*. See Yuval Amit, "Yitsu shel tarbut yisraelit: Pe'ulatam shel mosadot rishmiyim betirgum sifrut me-'Ivrit le-Anglit" (PhD diss., Tel Aviv University, 2008). At the same time, Omri Asscher has shown that by the mid-1950s, critics writing in national U.S. publications were emphasizing their interest in translations of Israeli literature, so Atheneum's willingness to get into this market may have been a response to a sense of a market opportunity. See Asscher, *Reading Israel, Reading America: The Politics of Translation between Jews* (Stanford, CA: Stanford University Press, 2020), 40–41. Kaniuk has recalled in his somewhat fictionalized memoir of that period that he was introduced to Atheneum by Timothy Seldes, an editor at Doubleday, who suggested that while he could not publish Kaniuk, the manuscript was "just what [Atheneum was] looking for." Haydn was the editor who read the novel first, and Kaniuk recalls drinking a toast with Bessie to celebrate the deal and picking up the proofs from him on the same day his daughter was born. Kaniuk, *Life on Sandpaper* (Champaign, IL: Dalkey Archive, 2003), 402.

23. Samuel Yellen, *The Wedding Band* (New York: Atheneum, 1961), 3. Subsequent citations of the novel appear parenthetically in the text. It is particularly noteworthy that Yellen published his previous book, a collection of short stories, with Knopf in 1957 — so he followed Pat Knopf to Atheneum, so to speak. Unfortunately, because of the COVID-19 pandemic, it has been impossible for me to consult Yellen's files in the Knopf archives at the Ransom Humanities Center during the final stages of research and writing for this book. I presume that file contains a discussion by Knopf editors of *The Wedding Band*, and it might indicate why Yellen published the novel with Atheneum.

24. See Yellen, 30–31. Alexandra recounts her father's mistake, during her childhood, of congratulating his wife on their twelfth wedding anniversary in February, "whereas [Alexandra] was going to be twelve years old the coming August" (30).

25. On Atheneum's poetry program in general, see William Targ, *Indecent Pleasures: The Life and Colorful Times of William Targ* (New York: Macmillan, 1975), 180–81.

26. Donald Finkel, "Note in Lieu of a Suicide," in *Simeon* (New York: Atheneum, 1964), 42, quoted with permission from the Estate of Donald Finkel.

—

27. For biographical details about Milton Millhauser, see "Milton Millhauser," in *Gale Literature: Contemporary Authors* (Farmington Hills, MI: Gale, 2002), http://link.gale.com /apps/doc/H1000068911/BIC?u=mlin_m_wellcol&sid=bookmark-BIC&xid=f46dc8b2.

28. J. D. O'Hara, "Novels: Nabokovian, Plangent," *Washington Post* (September 24, 1972), BW8.

29. Steven Millhauser, *Edwin Mullhouse: The Life and Death of an American Writer 1943– 1954 by Jeffrey Cartwright* (New York: Knopf, 1972), viii. Subsequent citations of the novel appear parenthetically in the text.

30. See Jonathan Freedman, *The Temple of Culture: Assimilation and Anti-Semitism in Literary Anglo-America* (New York: Oxford University Press, 2000). Millhauser was born on August 3, 1943, while Edwin was born on August 1, 1943. Both have one sister. Millhauser's paternal grandparents were German Jews, and his maternal grandparents were Russians, like Edwin's. Also like Edwin's, Millhauser's mother and pediatrician both spoke Yiddish, while his father did not. Edwin's father relocates his family to central Connecticut "after a long instructorship in English at the City College of New York" (3), while Millhauser's father, Milton Millhauser, served as an instructor in English at CCNY from 1931 to 1946 and then took a position as an assistant professor of English at the University of Bridgeport, Connecticut, beginning in 1947. Milton Millhauser received his PhD from Columbia University with a dissertation on Robert Chambers, and while Dr. Mullhouse specializes in the literature and thought of the nineteenth century, Milton Millhauser published articles on figures including Walter Pater, Charles Dickens, Herman Melville, and Alfred Lord Tennyson, as well as a book-length study of Chambers. Like the punning Dr. Mullhouse, Dr. Millhauser also displayed a playful sense of humor, which he demonstrated in comic poems, satires, and ironic short stories on the subject of academic life that he published in the *AAUP Bulletin*.

31. For a more extensive study of the novel and its reception, see Josh Lambert, "Identity Recruitment and the 'American Writer': Steven Millhauser, Edwin Mullhouse, and Biographical Criticism," *Contemporary Literature* 54:1 (Spring 2013): 23–48.

32. Mrs. Mullhouse and the family physician speak a Yinglish patter, but not Dr. Mullhouse: the only time he slips into Yinglish is during a clever extemporaneous rendering of the story of Chicken Little into exaggerated accents, in which the Jewish ("Pebble, schmebble, the sky is falling and you're talking pebbles") is just another one of a stock set of Hollywood regional speech conventions, including Mexican, western, and southern, over which he displays flexible mastery of performance.

33. On Hansen's Law, see Eugene I. Bender and George Kagiwada, "Hansen's Law of 'Third-Generation Return' and the Study of American Religio-Ethnic Groups," *Phylon* 29:4 (1968): 360–70.

34. Though Milton's competence as a Hebraist has been the subject of some debate, he knew at least enough to paraphrase and translate psalms from Hebrew to English and Greek. See Gordon Campbell and Thomas N. Corns, *John Milton: Life, Work, and Thought* (Oxford: Oxford University Press, 2008), 86.

35. "Milton Millhauser."

36. Steven Millhauser, email to the author, October 25, 2009.

—

37. Steven Millhauser, "A Voice in the Night," *New Yorker* (December 2, 2012), https://www.newyorker.com/magazine/2012/12/10/a-voice-in-the-night.

38. Millhauser.

39. Erik Wensberg to Jason Epstein, November 18, 1960, Random House Records, Columbia University Rare Book and Manuscript Library, New York (hereafter RHR).

40. Philip Nobile, *Intellectual Skywriting: Literary Politics and the "New York Review of Books"* (New York: Charterhouse, 1974), 91. The review in question, of a volume titled *The Dyer's Hand,* is Jason Epstein, "Auden's Essays," *Partisan Review* 30:2 (Summer 1963): 281–85. Epstein fondly remembers "W. H. Auden in torn overcoat and carpet slippers delivering the manuscript of *The Dyer's Hand,*" in the first chapter of *Book Business: Publishing Past, Present, and Future* (New York: Norton, 2000), 5. Nobile also discusses David Rogers's claim that Epstein unethically drew on the manuscript of a book, written by Rogers, that Epstein edited for Random House for Epstein's own articles about school bureaucracy in New York (*Intellectual Skywriting,* 91–92).

41. Jason Epstein, *The Great Conspiracy Trial: An Essay on Law, Liberty and the Constitution* (New York: Random House, 1970). Though the book is, primarily, about the trial of activists including Abbie Hoffman and Bobby Seale after the 1968 Chicago Democratic National Convention, Epstein offers a history of conspiracy law. He explains that during the twentieth century, U.S. conspiracy law was expanded with antitrust provisions that "made it a crime for businessmen to combine in restraint of trade." In such cases, Epstein explains, a prosecution does not have to show that "the illegal combination actually produced harmful effects," as "the illegality of such a combination in the restraint of trade derives from the greater strength of the combination to damage its competitors and gain its harmful objective" (88). While Epstein criticizes the way that these principles have been applied in conspiracy indictments for other kinds of crimes, outside the realm of antitrust law (such as in the cases of "Ethel and Julius Rosenberg, who were convicted not for having stolen atomic secrets, but for having conspired to do so" [90]), he does not criticize such laws when they remain restricted to the area of antitrust and the unethical conspiracy of people in business to strengthen their positions through mutually beneficial actions with other companies, at the expense of their competitors. In considering the administration of Mayor Richard J. Daley in Chicago, which had pushed for the conviction of the activists, Epstein excoriates it for nepotistic practices—Daley doled out positions of influence to allies and their children, while members of Daley's family, including his son, benefited from collusive relationships—and characterizes Daley's forces not as a "political machine" but rather "a rich, proud, and powerful family" (198).

42. "Jason Epstein *et al.* Speak," *New York Times* (April 16, 1972), SM38.

43. Charles Neider to Jason Epstein, April 18, 1974, RHR; John O'Neill to Jason Epstein, July 2, 1969, and Barbara Epstein to John O'Neill, July 9, 1969, New York Review of Books Records, Manuscripts and Archives Division, New York Public Library, Astor, Lenox, and Tilden Foundations (hereafter NYRBR); Jason Epstein to Charles Neider, April 23, 1974, RHR.

44. Barbara Epstein to John Gross, July 19, 1974, and John Gross to Barbara Epstein, July 25, 1974, NYRBR.

—

45. Jason Epstein to Robert E. Ginna, October 26, 1978, RHR. The copy of this letter in Jason's papers bears a handwritten note, "Not sending, 10/30/78, as per Jason," which suggests that Jason possibly reconsidered the wisdom of sending such a letter (though this leaves open the possibility that he conveyed the same information to Ginna by telephone or in person).

46. Jacob Epstein, handwritten note on copy of *Wild Oats* sent to Gore Vidal, AC95. V6675.Zz979e, Houghton Library, Harvard University, Cambridge, MA.

47. Robert Emmett Ginna Jr. to Lillian Hellman, December 6, 1978, RHR; quoted with permission of Robert Emmett Ginna Jr.

48. Jacob Epstein, *Wild Oats* (Boston: Little, Brown, 1979), dust jacket. Subsequent citations of the novel appear parenthetically in the text.

49. Richard Dyer, "Peter Pan, Class of '78," *Boston Globe* (June 24, 1979), 92; Anne Tyler, "Two Novels: Growing Up," *New York Times Book Review* (June 17, 1979), 14, 38; Josh Rubins, review of Jacob Epstein, *Wild Oats, Saturday Review* (June 23, 1979), 43–44; review of Jacob Epstein, *Wild Oats, Critic* 38 (1979): 8; review of Jacob Epstein, *Wild Oats, Choice* (October 1979), 1017; review of Jacob Epstein, *Wild Oats, Time* (July 2, 1979), 82.

50. Dyer, "Peter Pan, Class of '78," 92.

51. Josh Rubins, review of Jacob Epstein, *Wild Oats, Saturday Review* (June 23, 1979), 43–44; Martin Amis, "A Tale of Two Novels," *Observer* (October 19, 1980), 26.

52. Amis, "Tale of Two Novels."

53. Edward Deitch, "Literary Theft or Honest Error?," *Boston Globe* (November 23, 1980), B1, B8.

54. Charles Lamb, "*New York Review of Books*," interview with Barbara Epstein, *Book TV*, C-SPAN 2 (October 3, 1998), https://www.c-span.org/video/?112694-1/new-york-review -books&start=1100; Sam Tanenhaus, "Sam Tanenhaus on Martin Amis, Electro-Shock Novelist," *Newsweek* (June 25, 2012), https://www.newsweek.com/sam-tanenhaus-martin -amis-electro-shock-novelist-65135.

55. Dyer, "Peter Pan, Class of '78"; Thomas Mallon, *Stolen Words: Forays into the Origins and Ravages of Plagiarism* (New York: Penguin, 1989), 135.

56. Jacob Epstein, untitled speech, n.d. [1996?], folder labeled "Jacob Epstein 1996," NYRBR.

57. Amis, "Tale of Two Novels"; Mallon, *Stolen Words,* 135.

58. One teenager, quoted in a 1970 government report, sums up the taken-for-granted quality of this dynamic: "I don't think any of my friends really think about it, as such. It is just commonly accepted that everyone hates her parents." Elizabeth Herzog, Cecelia E. Sudia, Barbara Rosengard, and Jane Harwood, *Teenagers Discuss the Generation Gap* (Washington, DC: U.S. Children's Bureau, 1970), 3. The "generation gap" was widely discussed in the late 1960s and 1970s; see, e.g., Margaret Mead, "The Generation Gap," *Science* 164:3876 (April 11, 1969): 135; and especially Edgar Z. Friedenberg, "The Generation Gap," *Annals of the American Academy of Political and Social Science* 382 (1969): 32–42, which discusses the link between changes in laws and conventions governing inheritance and the relations between children and their parents.

—

59. On these developments, see Lila Corwin Berman's *The American Jewish Philanthropic Complex: The History of a Multibillion Dollar Institution* (Princeton, NJ: Princeton University Press, 2020).

60. On the history of estate tax in the U.S., see Jens Beckert, *Inherited Wealth*, trans. Thomas Dunlap (Princeton, NJ: Princeton University Press, 2004), especially 69–80 and 171–208. Beckert divides the modern history of U.S. estate taxes into two periods, with the first, "between 1890 and 1935," being the time that "the estate tax was introduced"—with figures like Theodore Roosevelt and Andrew Carnegie arguing on its behalf, on the basis of U.S. discourses of equal opportunity—and the second period, "from the late 1960s to today," being characterized by "the estate tax com[ing] under increasing political pressure" (171) as part of "the second 'great transformation' of the economic system in the twentieth century" (194).

61. On Adam Wilson's relationship with his father, see Jacob Silverman, "Adam Wilson, Author of 'Flatscreen,' Talks about Sex, Drugs, and Misery, but in a Funny Way," *Politico* (March 2, 2012), https://www.politico.com/states/new-york/city-hall/story/2012/03/adam-wilson-author-of-flatscreen-talks-about-sex-drugs-and-misery-but-in-a-funny-way-067223.

62. See Margaret A. Salinger, *Dream Catcher: A Memoir* (New York: Washington Square / Simon & Schuster, 2000); and Gregory Bellow, *Saul Bellow's Heart: A Son's Memoir* (New York: Bloomsbury, 2013). An example of a literary scholar who comes to mind is my graduate school advisor and mentor, Jonathan Freedman, who taught at Yale and the University of Michigan and whose father, Ralph Freedman, was a German-Jewish immigrant to the U.S. who received a PhD in comparative literature from Yale in 1954 and then taught at the University of Iowa and Princeton.

63. Alfred Kazin's son, Michael, is an American historian who publishes trade books and who has written, "Ever since [he] began composing little editorials for [his] middle-school newspaper, people have asked, 'What is it like being the son of a famous father?'" and who was featured in a photo in the *New York Times Magazine* during his first year of college, with a caption of "Famous-Name Freshmen," as "son of critic Alfred Kazin." See "Confronting a Father's Legacy," *Chronicle of Higher Education* 54:17 (December 21, 2007): B10–11; and Steven Kellman, "A Freshman Paper on Harvard Freshmen," *New York Times Magazine* (December 11, 1966), 81. Daniel Bell's son, David, is a historian of early-modern France, currently at Princeton, whose books have been published by academic and trade presses. Richard Hofstadter's son, Dan, served as a professor at Bennington College and writes trade nonfiction on various subjects in art and cultural history. Lionel Trilling's son, James, is an art historian, and Irving Howe's son, Nicholas, was a scholar of Old English literature who taught at Rutgers, the University of Oklahoma, Ohio State, and Berkeley. Norman Podhoretz's son, John, worked as a speechwriter for Presidents Reagan and George H. W. Bush and as a journalist, before taking the role as editor of *Commentary*, previously held by his father, in 2009. Saul Bellow's son Adam worked as an editor in trade publishing; see the discussion of his book *In Praise of Nepotism* later in this chapter.

64. One such list can be found in Adam Bellow, *In Praise of Nepotism: A Natural History* (New York: Doubleday, 2003), 493.

—

65. See Jan O. Jonsson, David B. Grusky, Matthew Di Carlo, and Reinhard Pollak, "It's a Decent Bet That Our Children Will Be Professors Too," in David Grusky, ed., *The Inequality Reader: Contemporary and Foundational Readings in Race, Class, and Gender* (New York: Routledge, 2011), 499–516. These authors explain that "parents accumulate much occupation-specific capital, identify with their occupation, and accordingly 'bring home' their occupation in ways, both direct and indirect, that then make it salient to their children and lead them to invest in it. It follows that children develop a taste for occupational reproduction, are trained by their parents in occupation-specific skills, have access to occupational networks that facilitate occupational reproduction, and use those skills and networks to acquire more occupation-specific training outside the home" (514).

66. See Raymond Williams, "The Social History of English Writers," in *The Long Revolution* (New York: Columbia University Press, 1961), 230–45; and Richard Altick, "The Sociology of Authorship: The Social Origins, Education, and Occupations of 1,100 British Writers, 1800–1935" (1962), in *Writers, Readers, and Occasions: Selected Essays on Victorian Literature and Life* (Columbus: Ohio State University Press, 1989), 95–109. In *Marxism and Class Theory: A Bourgeois Critique* (London: Tavistock, 1979), Frank Parkin observes "how relatively few of the children of successful footballers, boxers, baseball and tennis stars, or the celebrities of the stage and screen have succeeded in reproducing their parents' elevated status," offering as an explanation for this phenomenon that "the skills called for in these pursuits are of a kind that must be acquired and cultivated by the individual in the actual course of performance, and which are thus not easily transferred from parent to child. That is, there seems to be no equivalent to cultural capital that can be socially transmitted to the children of those gifted in the performing arts that could give them a head start in the fiercely competitive world of professional sport and show business" (55–56). My sense is that Parkin's original observation is only half right, at best — Hollywood and theater family dynasties have been common — and that the examples of many literary children of literary parents given here (and available, among non-Jews, in earlier periods) suggest that there is indeed "cultural capital that can be socially transmitted to the children . . . that could give them a head start" in the literary field.

67. See Harold Bloom's classic *The Anxiety of Influence: A Theory of Poetry* (Oxford: Oxford University Press, 1973), where parent-child relations serve as the allegorical model for relations among poets and poetry, for example: "What is the Primal Scene, for a poet *as poet?* It is his Poetic Father's coitus with the Muse" (36–37).

68. Jaclyn Trop, "A Conversation with Francesca Segal," Jewish Book Council (July 10, 2012), https://www.jewishbookcouncil.org/pb-daily/a-conversation-with-francesca-segal.

69. Jeff Vasishta, "Francesca Segal's Modern Families," *Interview* (May 14, 2017), https://www.interviewmagazine.com/culture/francesca-segal.

70. Francesca Segal, "In My Father's Footsteps," *Granta* 104 (2008): 223, 224.

71. Francesca Segal, *The Innocents* (New York: HarperCollins, 2012), front flap. Subsequent citations of the novel appear parenthetically in the text.

72. Werner Sollors, *Beyond Ethnicity: Consent and Descent in American Culture* (New York: Oxford University Press, 1986), especially 155–66, quotation on 159–60.

—

73. Munson's mother, Naomi Munson (née Decter), was Midge Decter's daughter from her first marriage and Norman Podhoretz's stepdaughter; Munson has been regularly described as Podhoretz's grandson in the press (see later in this chapter).

74. See, e.g., Jeet Heer, "Affirmative Action, Meritocracy, Nepotism and the Podhoretz Clan," *sans everything* (blog) (October 19, 2007), https://sanseverything.wordpress.com /2007/10/19/affirmative-action-meritocracy-nepotism-and-the-podhoretz-clan/; Patricia Cohen, "New *Commentary* Editor Denies Neo-Nepotism," *New York Times* (October 24, 2007), E1.

75. Sam Munson, "A Triumph of Style," *Policy Review* (December 1, 2002), https:// www.hoover.org/research/triumph-style. The Hoover Institution hosted Norman and John Podhoretz for conversations many times and reviewed their work; see also Mark Gerson, "Norman's Conquest," *Policy Review* (September 1, 1995), https://www.hoover.org /research/normans-conquest. On the ideology of the Hoover Institution, see Victor David Hanson, "100 Years of the Hoover Institution," *National Review* (July 30, 2019), https:// www.nationalreview.com/2019/07/hoover-institution-100-year-anniversary-conservative -stronghold/, where it is referred to as "a conservative atoll in a progressive sea."

76. Sam Munson, "Slices of Life," *Commentary* (June 2003), 67–69.

77. See, all by Sam Munson, "The Book Club," *Commentary* (September 2003), 72–74; "Born in the U.S.A.," *Commentary* (November 2003), 68–72; "Abroad at Home," *Commentary* (March 2004), 68–70; "Tales Tall & Small," *Commentary* (December 2004), 75–78; "In the Aftermath," *Commentary* (May 2005), 80–85; "The Poet's Poet's Poet," *Commentary* (May 2006), 82–84; "His Gulag," *Commentary* (April 2007), 76–79; "The Artist as Critic," *Commentary* (July 2008), 76–78; "From Hungary: The Curious Case of Sándor Márai," *Commentary* (November 2009), 66–69; "Mitchell's Lama," *Commentary* (November 2010), 62–64; "Graying the Line," *Commentary* (February 2011), 67–68; and "The Free Reputation," *Commentary* (June 2011), 61–62.

78. Sam Munson, "About Us," *Commentary* (December 26, 2006), https://www .commentarymagazine.com/culture-civilization/about-us/; Munson, "Help Wanted: Graphic Designer," *Commentary* (September 18, 2008), https://www.commentarymagazine.com /culture-civilization/help-wanted-graphic-designer/.

79. Leon Neyfakh, "Sam Munson, Grandson of Norman Podhoretz, Taking Debut Novel to Market," *New York Observer* (January 16, 2009), https://observer.com/2009/01 /sam-munson-grandson-of-norman-podhoretz-taking-debut-novel-to-market/. See also Ruth E. Kott, "Literary Agents: Three Young-Alumni Authors Have Gotten Big-Time Book Deals, Thanks to Agent Stephen Barbara," *University of Chicago Magazine* (November–December 2009), http://magazine.uchicago.edu/0912/arts_sciences/agents.shtml.

80. D. G. Myers, "*The November Criminals* by Sam Munson," *Commentary* (June 2010), https://www.commentarymagazine.com/articles/the-november-criminals-by-sam -munson/.

81. In a blog post, Munson dismissed questions about literary influence: "Who can say, after all, what the decisive moments in his own biography are? Who knows his own influences?" Jason Chambers, "When We Fell in Love — Sam Munson," *3G1B: Three Guys One*

Book (blog) (April 19, 2010), https://threeguysonebook.com/when-we-fell-in-love-sam
-munson/. On "legacy admissions" as one of the "mechanisms" used by the "Protestant
Establishment . . . to perpetuate its prominence," along with "inheritance," see James D.
Davidson, Ralph E. Pyle, and David V. Reyes, "Persistence and Change in the Protestant
Establishment, 1930–1992," *Social Forces* 74:1 (1995): 157–75, quotations on 160.

82. Sam Munson, *The November Criminals* (New York: Doubleday, 2010), 22.

83. On Steven Munson and Naomi Munson, see Thomas L. Jeffers, *Norman Podhoretz:
A Biography* (New York: Cambridge University Press, 2010), 158–59, 207, 263. Steven
Munson seems to have contributed to *Commentary* starting in 1998 (eighteen years after
marrying Naomi) and to have continued doing so until 2008, i.e., writing for the publication
for several years while his son was a contributor and editor there — and writing almost exclusively about art.

84. Munson, *November Criminals*, 2.

85. Kate Wolf, review of Sam Munson, *The November Criminals*, *Bookforum* (April–May
2010), https://www.bookforum.com/print/1701/-5369.

86. Norman Podhoretz, "My Negro Problem — and Ours," *Commentary* 35:2 (February
1963), 93–101. Subsequent citations of the essay appear parenthetically in the text.

87. For one example where Addison's thoughts reflect a common neoconservative talking
point, often articulated by his grandfather, see his reaction to a classmate's speech "about the
problems of young black men," which he sees as revealing the truth that affirmative action
and Black History Month, while "created and preserved as lip service to the highest progressive principles" are "dedicated in actuality to the perpetuation of hatred." Munson, *November
Criminals*, 236. Compare this to Podhoretz's description of affirmative action as "implicitly
racist" in *Breaking Ranks: A Political Memoir* (New York: Harper & Row, 1979), 302.

88. Joseph Salvatore, "Uncommon App," *New York Times Book Review* (June 6, 2010),
37; Michael Lindren, "Book Review: Sam Munson's *The November Criminals*," *Washington
Post* (May 26, 2010), https://www.washingtonpost.com/wp-dyn/content/article/2010
/05/25/AR2010052504912.html.

89. It is worth noting, given Munson's extended family and his consistent lack of trans-
parency about any help he might have received from them, that Munson looks a little ridiculous, or at least self-serving, when he makes fun of a book blogger, Maud Newton, for
noting a potential conflict of interest, asking, "Isn't it incumbent upon a critic not to allow
his social duties to impede his professional ones?" Sam Munson, "A Farewell to Blogs," *New
Partisan* (July 20, 2004), https://web.archive.org/web/20060328152928/http:/www
.newpartisan.com/display/ShowJournalEntry?moduleId=4763&entryId=33569.

90. The film itself exhibits the degree to which things changed from one generation to
the next; while Arthur Miller says that his brother "became loaded with the responsibility
for the family business," while he "escaped, thank God" — suggesting that his career as a writer
required him to get away from his family — and remarks that among animals, "the most
dangerous person or animal to the young male is his father," Rebecca Miller recalls a close
and connected relationship in which her father, Arthur Miller, would "confide" in her and "talk

to [her] about his worries about being able to write": "It was as if I was part of him." *Arthur Miller: Writer,* dir. Rebecca Miller (HBO Documentary Films, 2017).

91. Jonathan Rosen, *The Talmud and the Internet: A Journey between Worlds* (New York: Farrar, Straus & Giroux, 2000), 26; and Rosen, "What Jewish Book Changed Your Life?," *JBooks.com,* accessed December 1, 2020, http://www.jbooks.com/nfjc/index/IP_What _Jewish_Book.htm. A note at the end of *A Family Passover* explains that its "writing . . . was a true 'family affair,' a group effort by . . . Norma Rosen . . . [and] her two children, Anne, a freshman at Yale, and Jonathan, a junior at New Rochelle High School." Oddly, or perhaps in a surprising autofictional gesture in a book for young children, *A Family Passover* presents a fictional protagonist named Anna (not Anne), a ten-year-old who takes the reader through the preparations for a Passover seder and whose older brother is named Robert (like Norma's husband and Jonathan and Anne's father, who is for no discernible reason listed in the authors' note: "The husband and father of the family is Robert S. Rosen, a professor at the City University of New York"). See Anne Rosen, Jonathan Rosen, and Norma Rosen, *A Family Passover* (Philadelphia: Jewish Publication Society of America, 1980), 59.

92. Barbara Presley Noble, "One Daughter's Rebellion or Her Mother's Imprint?," *New York Times* (November 10, 1993), C1; Katie Roiphe, "Sharing Her Secrets," *New York Times* (March 24, 2011), ST1.

93. Sam Apple, email to the author, May 14, 2019.

94. Yael Goldstein Love, email to the author, July 12, 2019.

95. Miriam Cohen, "Mothers, Daughters, and the World: Talking with Yael Goldstein," *Zeek* (June 2007), http://www.zeek.net/706review1/. Interestingly, and similarly to Mill-hauser's case, this reading of Goldstein Love's novel suggests that one means by which the author distinguishes herself from her mother is by rejecting her treatment of Jewishness; *Overture* does not have much explicit Jewishness, and the journalist wondered, "Might this un-Jewish novel be a very Jewish rebellion against a mother who raised her children Orthodox without believing in it, and yet whose own body of work is primarily Jewish?"

96. A. Bellow, *In Praise of Nepotism,* 23.

97. A. Bellow, 14, 15.

98. A. Bellow, 14.

99. A. Bellow, 10.

100. Jens Beckert, "Are We Still Modern? Inheritance Law and the Broken Promise of the Enlightenment," in John Cunliffe and Guido Erreygers, eds., *Inherited Wealth, Justice and Equality* (London: Routledge, 2013), 79.

101. Joanne B. Ciulla, in *Business Ethics Quarterly* 15:1 (2005): 153–60, concludes that "while Bellow intends to praise nepotism, his careful research and reporting actually sounds the alarm against it" (160); Charles J. Whalen, in the *Journal of Economic Issues* 40:1 (2006): 219–21, notes that when Bellow attempts to dispense "with the problematic side of the current trend" toward more nepotism, "neither part of [his] hand waving is convincing" (220); Robert G. Jones, reviewing the book in *Personnel Psychology* 57:2 (2004): 550–53, remarks that Bellow's book "might better have been titled in terms of apology rather than praise" (553).

—

102. A. Bellow, *In Praise of Nepotism,* 471–72.

103. See Phillipa K. Chong, *Inside the Critics' Circle: Book Reviewing in Uncertain Times* (Princeton, NJ: Princeton University Press, 2020), 8.

CONCLUSION

1. David Carr and David D. Kirkpatrick, "The Gatekeeper for Literature Is Changing at *New Yorker,*" *New York Times* (October 21, 2002), C1. On Remnick, Treisman, and Jewish writers in the *New Yorker,* see Josh Lambert, "Since 2000," in Hana Wirth-Nesher, ed., *The Cambridge History of Jewish American Literature* (New York: Cambridge University Press, 2015), 622–41.

2. See particularly Don Share, *Squandermania* (Norfolk, UK: Salt, 2007).

3. In most cases, I make the claim that these editors are Jewish, part Jewish, or of Jewish ancestry on the basis of having spoken to them in person about it, casually; Wolff, Chasman, and Zimmerman were gracious guest speakers at a writing residency I directed at the Yiddish Book Center, and Nemens was a participant in that program. For a personal essay about Krotov's "first job in publishing," in which he "got off easy" because he was "similar enough on paper [to his boss, Peter Mayer] – white, male, Jewish, a Columbia alum, quick enough with a retort," see Mark Krotov, "Peter Stories: On Peter Mayer, 1936–2018," *n+1* (May 18, 2018), https://nplusonemag.com/online-only/online-only/peter-stories/.

4. For the most part, I cannot point to published sources in which these editors self-identify as Jewish, and I include them here on the basis of public records (marriage records, obituaries, census records, and so on) and in the knowledge that they may have converted to another religion or rejected Jewishness but on the assumption that it is still fair to say that they are of Jewish ancestry even if that is the case. Cases in which the Jewishness of these editors has been discussed in published sources include Temple referring to himself as "an avowed agnostic (of the Jewish persuasion)" in "The First Annual Three-Borough Subway Party," in Jacquelin Cangro, ed., *The Subway Chronicles: Scenes from Life in New York* (New York: Plume, 2006), 89; and Glusman writing about his father's experiences as a Jewish doctor during World War II, in his book *Conduct under Fire: Four American Doctors and Their Fight for Life as Prisoners of the Japanese, 1941–1945* (New York: Viking, 2005). Nosowsky's father is Emmanuel "Manny" Nosowsky, a retired urologist and admired crossword-puzzle creator, whose own "father was a chazzan [prayer leader] back in the 1930s at San Francisco's Congregation Beth Sholom." Dan Pine, "My Word!," *j., the Jewish News of California* (August 25, 2006), https://www.jweekly.com/2006/08/25/my-word/.

5. In a memoir, Paul notes, "Like many other morbid kids with Jewish ancestry, I was drawn to Holocaust reading from the moment I entered adolescence." Pamela Paul, *My Life with Bob: Flawed Heroine Keeps Book of Books, Plot Ensues* (New York: Henry Holt, 2017), 65. Katy Waldman describes herself as "a casually Jewish woman," in "((((The Jewish Cowbell)))): Unpacking a Gross New Meme from the Alt-Right," *Slate* (June 2, 2016), https://slate.com/human-interest/2016/06/the-jewish-cowbell-the-meaning-of-those-double-parentheses-beloved-by-trump-supporters.html. In addition to Winkelman's role at *Kirkus,* he is also

—

"the secretary of The Elie Wiesel Foundation for Humanity and the secretary of the National Jewish Democratic Council." See "Our Team," *Kirkus*, accessed December 1, 2020, https://www.kirkusreviews.com/about/team/.

6. The independent children's publisher Lee & Low Books conducted Diversity Baseline Surveys in 2015 and 2019. See Lee & Low Books, "The Diversity Baseline Survey," accessed December 1, 2020, https://www.leeandlow.com/about-us/the-diversity-baseline-survey. In the authors' analysis of the results of the first survey, they noted that they "received more than 50 write-in comments for this question [about race] from people who did not feel that any of the options offered adequately represented them. Some identified as Jewish or European." Lee & Low Books, "Where Is the Diversity in Publishing? The 2015 Diversity Baseline Survey Results" *The Open Book Blog* (January 26, 2016), https://blog.leeandlow.com/2016/01/26/where-is-the-diversity-in-publishing-the-2015-diversity-baseline-survey-results/. In order to more effectively compare the two surveys, the creators of the survey say, "We stuck with the racial breakdowns we offered in the first survey . . . with a few adjustments" for the 2019 survey. See Lee & Low Books, "Where Is the Diversity in Publishing? The 2019 Diversity Baseline Survey Results," *The Open Book Blog* (January 28, 2020), https://blog.leeandlow.com/2020/01/28/2019diversitybaselinesurvey/.

7. At the time of writing, it is distressingly easy to find websites and social media accounts promoting anti-Semitic conspiracy theories, including the myth of Jewish media control. One relevant recent evolution of such claims is the popularization of the phrase "Khazarian mafia" to describe the supposedly nefarious activities of Ashkenazi Jews.

8. Calvin Reid, with reporting by Tania Padgett, "Houses with No Doors," *Publishers' Weekly* (May 23, 1994), https://www.publishersweekly.com/pw/by-topic/industry-news/publisher-news/article/69645-houses-with-no-doors.html; Doreen Carvajal, "An Emerging Prominence for Blacks in Publishing," *New York Times* (June 24, 1996), D1, D6.

9. In *The Price of Whiteness: Jews, Race, and American Identity* (Princeton, NJ: Princeton University Press, 2006), 102–8, Eric Goldstein details how concerns about immigration restriction led Jews in the early twentieth-century U.S. to oppose the inclusion of questions on the census about race – and how this was part of efforts to assert Jews' whiteness.

10. Reid, "Houses with No Doors"; Carvajal, "Emerging Prominence."

11. Antonio Aiello, "Equity in Publishing: What Should Editors Be Doing?," PEN America (October 24, 2015), https://pen.org/equity-in-publishing-what-should-editors-be-doing/.

12. On Mehta as an "exception" to the relative dearth of South Asian Americans in U.S. publishing, see Rajini Srikanth, *The World Next Door: South Asian American Literature and the Idea of America* (Philadelphia: Temple University Press, 2004), 128.

13. Ignoring early surveys by the Association of American Publishers and by the Equal Employment Opportunity Commission, the authors of the Diversity Baseline Survey (DBS) claimed, "Before the DBS, people suspected publishing had a diversity problem, but without hard numbers, the extent of that problem was anyone's guess." See Lee & Low Books, "Diversity Baseline Survey."

14. Christine Pride, "5 Things I Want to Tell My White Friends," *A Cup of Jo* (June 23, 2020), https://cupofjo.com/2020/06/a-letter-to-my-white-friends/. Another prominent

———

African American book editor, Chris Jackson, has remarked that diversity in publishing just "doesn't exist." Jackson, "'Diversity in Publishing' Doesn't Exist—but Here's How It Can," *LitHub* (October 10, 2017), https://lithub.com/diversity-in-publishing-doesnt-exist-but-heres-how-it-can/.

15. See Reid, "Houses with No Doors"; and Maris Kreizman, "Want to Fix the Racial Disparity in Book Advances? Pay Assistants More," *Los Angeles Times* (June 17, 2020), https://www.latimes.com/entertainment-arts/books/story/2020-06-17/racial-disparity-book-advances-pay-assistants-more.

16. Rosabeth Moss Kanter, *Men and Women of the Corporation* (New York: Basic Books, 1977), 207.

17. Kanter, 207. Other scholars have countered Kanter's claim that "it was rarity and scarcity, rather than femaleness *per se*, that shaped the environment for women." See, for example, Lynn Zimmer, "Tokenism and Women in the Workplace: The Limits of Gender-Neutral Theory," *Social Problems* 35:1 (1988): 64–77. It is not my subject here, but it seems quite plausible that Kanter's upbringing in a Jewish family may have informed her ideas, in *Men and Women of the Corporation*, about minorities and majorities.

18. Olof Åslund, Lena Hensvik, and Oskar Nordström Skans, "Seeking Similarity: How Immigrants and Natives Manage in the Labor Market," *Journal of Labor Economics* 32:3 (2014): 407; William R. Kerr and Martin Mandorff, "Social Networks, Ethnicity, and Entrepreneurship" (Working Paper no. 16-042, Harvard Business School, Cambridge, MA, June 14, 2016), 2.

19. Kerr and Mandorff, "Social Networks," 1–2.

20. The classic account of prejudice as driving specialization is Gary S. Becker, *The Economics of Discrimination* (Chicago: University of Chicago Press, 1957).

21. Clayton Childress refers to this, as mentioned in the introduction, as "the twinned problems of oversupply and uncertainty over quality." See Childress, *Under the Cover: The Creation, Production, and Reception of a Novel* (Princeton, NJ: Princeton University Press, 2017), 169.

22. See Kerr and Mandorff, "Social Networks," tables 1a and 1b.

23. "Brown nepotism" was coined, sort of, by Sherman Alexie in a letter he released in 2015 weighing in on the case of a white writer who had assumed a Chinese pseudonym and ended up being selected, by Alexie, for *The Best American Poetry*. "Sherman Alexie Speaks Out on The Best American Poetry 2015," *The Best American Poetry Blog* (September 7, 2015), https://blog.bestamericanpoetry.com/the_best_american_poetry/2015/09/like-most-every-poet-i-have-viewed-the-publication-of-each-years-best-american-poetry-with-happiness-i-love-that-poem-je-1.html. For a cogent critique of the concept of "brown nepotism," see the comments of Alexander Chee in Aiello, "Equity in Publishing." Audre Lorde once complained about a "black literary mafia"; see Claudia Tate, "Audre Lorde," in *Black Women Writers at Work* (New York: Continuum, 1983), 100–116.

A recent controversy at the National Book Critics Circle (NBCC) illustrates the contemporary fear of BIPOC overrepresentation. In June 2020, during the wave of protests following the murder of George Floyd by the Minneapolis police, several members of the board of the NBCC resigned. Some of these former board members were unwilling to continue to serve alongside one of their fellows, a former president of the organization named Carlin Romano. According to press accounts, Romano had rejected a statement drafted by a board committee, led by a Ugandan American poet, Hope Wabuke, that emphasized that the organization had been complicit in "stifl[ing] black voices" and "operating with the full benefits of white supremacy and institutional racism." Romano responded to the statement with clichés, including, by way of conclusion, the familiar meritocratic fantasy that his colleagues could just reward "the best books, period, regardless of author ethnicity." The statement drafted by Wabuke's committee lamented that the NBCC's board "is 75% white," and Romano felt that was nothing to apologize for, asking, "What should the breakdown of the Board be in a country in which 13.4% of the population is African American?" Whereas the statement noted with dismay that the publishing business is "84% white," with "just 5% of publishing staff [being] black," Romano wondered, "What should African American representation in book publishing be given these realities," that is, of a population that is 13.4 percent African American? Not leaving the question open, Romano went on to suggest two possibilities that by implication, according to his view, might seem ridiculous or worrisome: "Twenty-five percent? Fifty percent?" The email leaves the implications of that question vague but could be read as suggesting that it would be a problem, or ridiculous, if African Americans ended up overrepresented on the board of the NBCC or in the U.S. publishing industry overall. On the controversy, see John Maher, "NBCC Board Gutted as Fallout over Leaked Emails, Race Issues Widens," *Publishers' Weekly* (June 15, 2020), https://www.publishers weekly.com/pw/by-topic/industry-news/publisher-news/article/83592-fallout-continues -at-nbcc.html. Quotations from Romano's email taken from screenshots of that email posted to Twitter by Hope Wabuke, @HopeWabuke, "This is the email I wake up to . . . ," Twitter (June 11, 2020), https://twitter.com/HopeWabuke/status/1271076878745505794. See also Members of an NBCC Working Committee, "The National Book Critics Circle's Anti-Racism Pledge" (June 11, 2020), https://www.bookcritics.org/2020/06/11/6792/.

24. Every study of the history of U.S. publishing I can think of mentions this belief. See, for example, Laura J. Miller, *Reluctant Capitalists: Bookselling and the Culture of Consumption* (Chicago: University of Chicago Press, 2006), which notes, "Throughout the twentieth and into the twenty-first century, there has been a consistent belief in the distinctiveness of the book" (19); Miller cites one bookseller's belief that "books are essential to democracy" (82), along with many booksellers' beliefs that books are "carriers of ideas and embodiments of culture" and not just "any other consumer good" (84). See also Lewis A. Coser, Charles Kadushin, and Walter W. Powell, *Books: The Culture and Commerce of Publishing* (New York: Basic Books, 1982), 374. While it would be hard to argue that the position of books in U.S. culture has not changed in the twenty-first century, polling suggests that people in the U.S. read books regularly, visit libraries more than any other cultural institutions, and purchase hundreds of millions of new books every year. See, e.g., Andrew Perrin, "Book Reading 2016," Pew Research Center (September 1, 2016), https://www.pewresearch.org/internet /2016/09/01/book-reading-2016/; Brigit Katz, "Americans Went to the Library More Often than the Movies in 2019," *Smithsonian Magazine* (January 30, 2020), https://www

.smithsonianmag.com/smart-news/americans-went-library-more-often-movies-2019
-180974091/; Jim Milliot, "A Surprisingly Strong Year of Book Sales Continues," *Publishers'*
Weekly (October 9, 2020), https://www.publishersweekly.com/pw/by-topic/industry-news
/bookselling/article/84593-a-surprisingly-strong-year-of-book-sales-continues.html.

25. A useful model for how attention to the role of Jews in the publishing industry can
inform studies of Anglo-American literary modernism is Cristanne Miller's "Tongues 'Loosened
in the Melting Pot': The Poets of *Others* and the Lower East Side," *modernism/modernity* 14:3
(2007): 455–76. Miller attends to the ways "Jews in New York directly influenced the
publication of modernist literature through their predominant ownership of presses willing
to publish innovative poetry and fiction" and how that contributed to "associations between
modernist poetry and Jewish immigration in New York" for a group of poets associated with
the little magazine *Others* (457). The conclusion of Lise Jaillant's *Modernism, Middlebrow,*
and the Literary Canon (London: Pickering & Chatto, 2014) furnishes an example of how a
scholar has recognized the role of American Jewish publishers and editors in defining the
boundaries of the literary canon—specifically, in this case, how the Jewishness of the publisher Bennett Cerf and the editor Saxe Commins can be understood to have influenced their
handling of Ezra Pound's work in the 1940s (145–49). Loren Glass's *Countercultural Colo-*
phon: Grove Press, the "Evergreen Review," and the Incorporation of the Avant Garde (Stanford,
CA: Stanford University Press, 2013) attends with sensitivity to the fact that while Barney
Rosset, the publisher of Grove Press, "didn't see himself as Jewish *or* Catholic" (though his
father was Jewish and his mother was Catholic), "Rosset was perceived by many as Jewish,
and most of the key players at Grove were New York Jews," including "Fred Jordan, Rosset's
right-hand man throughout the 1960s [who] was a Holocaust survivor" (14), as well as a
handful of other men who "came from traditions of left-wing Jewish activism and cultural
entrepreneurship" (15). Glass's work suggests the degree to which one particularly crucial
institutional patron of U.S. postmodernism should be considered in relation to the positioning and opportunities of Jews in 1960s U.S. culture.

26. I am speculating here, admittedly—but there may be a pattern worth investigating
in the interest of American Jews in translating and publishing Japanese literature, from Isaac
Goldberg and Harry Schnittkind's edition of Goldberg's translation of Kenjiro Tokutomi's
The Heart of Nami-San (Hototogisu) (Boston: Stratford, 1918) through Harold Strauss's
enthusiastic support of Japanese translations at Knopf in the 1950s—see Strauss's pamphlet
On the Delights of Japanese Novels (New York: Knopf, 1957)—to the roles of translators Alfred
Birnbaum and Jay Rubin in popularizing the work of Haruki Murakami (on which, see David
Karashima, *Who We're Reading When We're Reading Murakami* [New York: Soft Skull,
2020]). Similarly, one might explore the motivations of various American Jews who have
been influential in the translation into English and popularization of Brazilian literature,
again starting with Goldberg in the 1910s (see Frederick C. H. Garcia, "Critic Turned Author: Isaac Goldberg," *Luso-Brazilian Review* 9:1 [1972]: 21–27), passing through Knopf
at midcentury (see Carlos Cortez Minchillo, "Risky Books, Rejected Authors: Alfred Knopf
and the Screening of Brazilian Literature," *Novos Estudos CEBRAP* 37:3 [2018]: 489–504)

to contemporary translators and critics including Benjamin Moser and Idra Novey who have helped to generate renewed interest in the works of Clarice Lispector in the U.S. (see David Shook, interview with Magdalena Edwards, *Los Angeles Review of Books* [November 23, 2018], https://lareviewofbooks.org/article/the-real-clarice-a-conversation-with-magdalena -edwards/).

By contrast, in Horace H. Underwood's "Korean Literature in English: A Critical Biography," *Transactions of the Royal Asiatic Society, Korea Branch* 51 (1976): 65–115, I see no example of a publishing house founded or led by Jews having published important works of Korean literature in translation before the second half of the twentieth century. And in the extensive bibliography in Salih Altoma's *Modern Arabic Literature in Translation: A Companion* (London: Saqi Books, 2005), 61–90, it seems noteworthy that mainstream U.S. presses published no Arabic literature in English translation (with a couple of exceptions, most prominently Knopf's phenomenal success publishing the work of Kahlil Gibran but also the 1952 edition of Mikha'il Nu'aymah's *The Memoirs of a Vagrant Soul* published by the Philosophical Library, a press founded in New York in 1941 by a Romanian-Jewish immigrant, Dagobert D. Runes). Until recently, it seems to have been Three Continents Press, founded in 1973 by the scholar and former diplomat Donald E. Herdeck, that has done the most to support the publication of Arabic literature in translation in the U.S., in contrast to what looks like significant disinterest of editors at larger publishing houses. On Herdeck, see Matt Schudel, "Donald E. Herdeck Dies," *Washington Post* (April 24, 2005), https://www.washing tonpost.com/archive/local/2005/04/24/donald-e-herdeck-dies/d37d7cdc-e134-4c8c -8725-f0d74455e847/.

27. In *Black Writers, White Publishers: Marketplace Politics in Twentieth Century African American Literature* (Jackson: University Press of Mississippi, 2006), John K. Young acknowledges that "reduc[ing] the field to oppressive white editors and publishers and ultimately powerless black authors would be both simplistic and inaccurate" (7), and drawing on the research of George Hutchinson, he goes on to note that "most of the Jewish publishers interested in New Negro works — such as Alfred and Blanche Knopf, Ben Huebsch, and Horace Liveright — were themselves marginalized by the mainstream Protestant New York firms and, therefore, turned to minority literature as a way to establish new and independent backlists" (7–8). The case studies that follow in Young's book do not take up questions about when or why Jewish publishers and editors in later decades committed themselves to publishing African American literature, but it is clear that other literary historical moments and cases would benefit from thoughtfulness on the question of Jewish editors' positioning in U.S. culture. For one example, in a fascinating study, *Street Players: Black Pulp Fiction and the Making of a Literary Underground* (Chicago: University of Chicago Press, 2018), Kinohi Nishikawa notes as a biographical detail that Bentley Morriss, a founder of the sleaze-turned-Black-pulp publisher Holloway House, had served as "president of the local B'nai B'rith lodge" (20). Elsewhere Nishikawa refers to Morriss and his cofounder simply as "white men" (4) and does not address the question, explored by Jay Gertzman and others, of why American Jews, like Morriss, were so prominent in publishing what Nishikawa calls "sleaze." On

—

that question, see Gertzman, *Bookleggers and Smuthounds: The Trade in Erotica, 1920–1940* (Philadelphia: University of Pennsylvania Press, 2001); and Josh Lambert, *Unclean Lips: Obscenity, Jews, and American Culture* (New York: New York University Press, 2014).

28. On Dreiser and Cather, see Donald Pizer, *American Naturalism and the Jews: Garland, Norris, Wharton, and Cather* (Urbana: University of Illinois Press, 2008). Pizer suggests that Dreiser's 1926 quarrel with his publisher, Horace Liveright, "activated" Dreiser's "core of underlying belief" in a "Shylock stereotype" (36). However, when Pizer discusses Cather, he relegates to a footnote the fact that "in later years, Cather was friends with the Jewish publishers Blanche and Alfred Knopf" (75n11). For a thoughtful study of Wright's representations of Jews in *Native Son,* which devotes only a single footnote to his extensive personal and editorial relationships with Jews, see Josep M. Armengol, "Blacks as 'America's Jews'? Revisiting Black–Jewish Relations in Richard Wright's *Native Son,*" *Critique: Studies in Contemporary Fiction* 58:5 (2017): 558–74. For an excellent study of Plath's use of Holocaust and Jewish metaphors in her poetry, which does not explore Plath's relationships with Jewish people — such as the critic Alfred Kazin, who was her teacher at Smith College — during her life, see James E. Young, "The Holocaust Confessions of Sylvia Plath," in *Writing and Rewriting the Holocaust: Narrative and the Consequences of Interpretation* (Bloomington: Indiana University Press, 1988), 117–33.

29. On Pynchon's *Bleeding Edge* (2013) as his "most Jewish" novel, see Gary Lippman, "Pynchonicity," *Paris Review* (September 5, 2013), https://www.theparisreview.org/blog/2013/09/05/pynchonicity/; Joshua Ferris, *To Rise Again at a Decent Hour* (New York: Little, Brown, 2014); Nell Zink, *Private Novelist* (New York: Ecco, 2016); Zink, *Nicotine* (New York: Ecco, 2016); Gish Jen, *Mona in the Promised Land* (New York: Knopf, 1996); on Alexie, see Nancy J. Peterson, "'If I Were Jewish, How Would I Mourn the Dead?': Holocaust and Genocide in the Work of Sherman Alexie," *MELUS* 35:3 (2010): 63–84; Zadie Smith, *The Autograph Man* (New York: Random House, 2002).

30. Rebecca Carroll, "A Reckoning Long Overdue," *Los Angeles Times* (July 30, 2020), https://www.https://www.latimes.com/entertainment-arts/books/story/2020-07-30/dana-candey-and-lisa-lucas-new-publishers-in-conversation; Poetry Foundation, "Announcement of Changes to *Poetry* Magazine" (June 26, 2020), https://www.poetryfoundation.org/foundation/press/153883/announcement-of-changes-to-poetry-magazine.

INDEX

251

INDEX

253

INDEX